THE
CUSTODY
HANDBOOK

Persia Woolley

SUMMIT BOOKS
NEW YORK

Copyright © 1979 by Persia Woolley

All rights reserved
including the right of reproduction
in whole or in part in any form
Published by *Summit Books*
A Simon & Schuster Division of Gulf & Western Corporation
Simon & Schuster Building
1230 Avenue of the Americas
New York, New York 10020
SUMMIT BOOKS and colophon are trademarks of Simon & Schuster

Designed by Stanley S. Drate

Manufactured in the United States of America

1 2 3 4 5 6 7 8 9 10
1 2 3 4 5 6 7 8 9 10 Pbk.

Library of Congress Cataloging in Publication Data

Woolley, Persia, date.
The custody handbook.

Bibliography: p.
Includes index.
1. Custody of children—United States.
2. Divorce—United States. 3. Children of
divorced parents—United States. 4. Single
parents—United States. I. Title
HQ777.5.W66   301.42′84   79-10862

ISBN 0-671-40032-0
ISBN 0-671-44841-2 Pbk.

Dedicated to all the divorced parents
who so freely shared their feelings,
ideas, and experiences
in order to help others facing the same problems.

Contents

Introduction

There are few times more perilous, or decisions more crucial, than those encountered when a couple with children decide to end their marriage. The simple question "What will happen to the youngsters?" carries with it a thousand unspoken concerns: whom will they live with; where will that be; how will they adjust; what will their new life-style include; when will they get to be with which parent; and how deeply hurt or badly scarred will they become as a result of our decision?

These are all valid questions, and of vital importance to the well-being of both the children and the parents. Yet little effort has been made to encourage divorcing families to seriously consider each of these questions, to answer them according to the needs of the individual members of the family, and to seek their own solutions to the problems. Consequently, the vast majority of divorcing couples assume that the children will go live with the mother, while the father supports them financially and visits occasionally; every other weekend and one night during the weeks between visits is the customary arrangement. Unfortunately, this traditional division of responsibility for the offspring after divorce not only fails to take into consideration the psychological and emotional needs of either the parents *or* the children; it also creates further difficulties of its own.

I became particularly aware of these problems during the year after my first book, *Creative Survival for Single Mothers,* was published, when I was asked to lead numerous discussion groups, classes, workshops and conferences on single parenting. As a result I talked with and listened to many hundreds of divorced parents. Having been a single mother myself for thirteen years, I was more than familiar with the problems such women encountered. But for the first time I began to hear about the difficulties experienced by divorced fathers. These men were just beginning to put their pain and confusion into words, and starting to make the rest of the world aware of their situation. Like most ex-wives I had been too close to the problem (and too involved in my own reactions) to be willing or able to understand my ex if he tried to express his thoughts, doubts, fears and hopes about his relationship with our kids. But I could and did listen to what other men had to say on the subject, and I became convinced that if their story was told in such a way that their ex-partners could gain a better understanding of what was happening, some of the friction and misunderstanding after divorce might be lessened.

It was during these discussion times that the corrosive nature of our present custody system began to be obvious. The single mother's problems generally stem from carrying the full weight and responsibility of raising the children alone, while the divorced father becomes alienated, bitter and depressed because of too little meaningful contact with the youngsters. In this sense the difficulties reported by divorced couples are actually opposite sides of the same coin, but instead of being self-correcting, the situation generates more discord, causes further tensions, and adds additional hostilities to the already strained relationship between the adults. And, needless to say, it is the children who suffer the most as a result of this kind of parental stress.

As I began researching this subject, two things came to light:

not only is our present custody practice detrimental to most families, there are an increasing number of divorced parents who have devised their own custody arrangements in order to avoid the most common hazards of the traditional method. These people have been willing to work together in order to meet the continuing needs of their youngsters and to provide them with the security of two loving, supportive, and concerned parents. In other words, they have found ways to share their youngsters although they, as adults, are no longer marital partners.

This phenomenon is not simply a local California trend; I have had contact with sharing parents from all parts of the country, including the South and Midwest, as well as the East and West Coasts. Shared custody is happening all over the nation, and is much more common than most people realize. There seems to be more of it in the cities and suburbs than in the country, but this may be because of the larger divorced population in metropolitan areas. Although I had to rely on personal introductions and word-of-mouth referrals in order to find such families, I soon discovered I had far more contacts than it was possible to pursue.

For the purpose of this book, the term ''sharing'' means any form of custody *or visitation* arrangement which allows both parents to have lots of normal, day-by-day interaction with the offspring and provides that each adult participates in both the responsibilities and the rewards of child raising. Sharing in one way or another can be incorporated into almost any form of child custody; it's a matter of attitude and appreciation of the child's needs rather than a question of legal documents and court orders. Basically it's as much a question of philosophy as it is of logistics, and in that sense is very much up to the parents involved.

In interviewing professionals on the subject of divorce and child custody, I found that many of them are as baffled about how to handle these matters as their clients are. Almost all agreed that those arrangements which *the family members themselves* developed were far and away the best, but no one knew exactly how to go about helping such couples find specific answers for their individual circumstances. And then one particularly thoughtful and concerned attorney said, ''Give us a book that the parents themselves can use to work out their own solutions. We don't know what to recommend, we can't play God for them, and most of us don't want to; we just tell them what's legally acceptable. If there were a truly helpful handbook on the subject, I'd tell every divorce client with children to get that book, read it, do their homework, and then come back so we can discuss what *they* want to do.''

It was with that directive in mind that I began to weave together the various subjects of divorced parents, child-custody practices, and the ways and means to help you establish what is best for your own family. I have included a great deal of information about alternatives to the traditional custody arrangement because so many people have found they work so well. Indeed, the enthusiasm of divorced parents who use some form of shared custody often rekindled my sometimes flagging energy, and continually renewed my faith in parental love and concern for the children after divorce. One of the most fascinating aspects of shared custody is the diversity of arrangements people come up with, so don't hesitate to pick and choose from several methods, or invent an entirely new solution of your own. Keep in mind that each family is unique, and you are the best judges of what you all are willing and able to try.

The word "coparenting" can be applied to any adults who share their youngsters, but I do differentiate between the *single* parent and the *divorced* one; "single" mother or father denotes one who is presently acting as the main parent, while "divorced" mother or father refers specifically to a noncustodial parent.

Because California has been a pioneer in changing the legal statutes involved in divorce and child custody, it has been referred to frequently. There are a number of other equally progressive areas, however, and it should be noted that some of the best programs for helping families in transition have been developed in Michigan, Minnesota, and Wisconsin and also in Georgia, Oregon, and Florida. There is a good deal of concern in the legal and psychological professions about the effect of the adversary system where child-custody conflicts are concerned, and some recent professional articles and reports have called for support of coparenting systems in the courts. In that regard the times are definitely changing and, let's hope, improving.

There are a number of people who have helped make this work possible, and I'd like to express my appreciation for their encouragement, enthusiasm, and understanding. In the field of psychology, Dr. Melvin Roman and Dr. Alice Abarbanel have been particularly generous with their time and information. Dr. Art Bodin and Jay Muccelli provided both direction and resources, and Dr. Barry Grunland and Kay van der Veur added immeasurably to my confidence in compiling the exercises included in this book. Among the attorneys I've worked with, Larry Stotter, George Duke, and Jerome Fishkin have been invaluable in their assistance, and I am much in debt to both Professor Robert Mnookin and Professor Ann Diamond for their ideas, responses, and questions. And I'd especially like to thank Conrad Rushing for giving me the impetus to go back to work when I thought I'd reached a dead end.

Last, but certainly most importantly, I am grateful to my new husband, Dr. Edward Garwin, and his children, without whose patience, support, and encouragement I could never have begun this project, much less completed it.

1
Prelude: What It's All About

A Look at Divorce and Child Custody

"Once upon a time . . ." marriage was considered a lifelong commitment, a partnership in bliss (or boredom, depending on how you interpreted living "happily ever after"), and even if nothing much was said about children and such, it was assumed that the protagonists would bear offspring, pay their taxes regularly, and generally conform to the social expectations of creating a nice, stable family. That was what the majority of the populace did, after all.

So common was this idea during the last century that those people who were not married and raising children were either pitied or scorned—unless they were world-famous adventurers or self-proclaimed artists; in which case they were obviously eccentric and probably suspect to begin with. Most people married and settled down with the firm conviction that that was what life was all about, and the person who was left without a spouse, usually through death or desertion, was considered to be the living embodiment of a tragic fate. The "poor but honest widder-woman" or the "*unfortunate* Mr. Jones" who was raising his children by himself may have elicited respect and admiration of a sort, but no one intentionally emulated them.

Times have changed, however, and our concept of marriage has been reassessed. Many people no longer see it as a lifelong contract, or an absolute necessity: a personal preference in most cases, yes; an economic and social requirement, no. The divorce rate in the United States has doubled since 1950; in 1976 more than one million marriages ended in dissolution (and frequently disillusion as well, at least for a time), and divorce no longer carries the social stigma of inadequacy and failure that it once did. All but three states have now adopted some form of "no-fault divorce" in order to take the adversary, blame-and-defend aspect out of ending a marriage, and it is now possible for two people to decide to terminate a domestic relationship without being forced into the roles of victim and villain.[1]

Divorce Trauma

Although divorce has become part of our everyday life in this society, that doesn't keep it from being a traumatic situation. Regardless of the motives behind getting married to begin with, the very fact of having once set up a partnership connotes hopes and expectations of some sort on the part of the participants, and the act of dissolving that contract in itself says that those expectations won't be met. Nothing is more painful than the sharp edges of a broken dream; and it doesn't matter whether the investment made was emotional, financial, social, or physical: a hope for the future has been abandoned. For some couples this takes the form of slow disintegration, a kind of grinding pressure which gradually exhausts the capacity to believe that the relationship will ever get better. For others it is a volatile and eruptive process full of anger and hurt and bitterness, in which one or both partners voice their disappointment in terms of broadside accusations, righteous countercharges, and the absolute conviction that the other person is out to make their lives as miserable as possible. The majority, however, fall somewhere between the Noël Coward drawing room and the last act of a Wagnerian opera, combining both civility and chaos in various degrees. Yet even the most outwardly calm and rational decision between past partners to simply walk away with no hard feelings is touched with some sorrow and sense of loss, and usually sadness and acrimony lie just beneath the surface.

The rawness of these feelings begins to mellow after a while, and many couples eventually achieve an equilibrium of dissent whereby each accepts the fact that the partnership didn't work, and now it's time to go on living under a new (and separate) arrangement. This takes place fairly quickly for some, while with others it's a matter of years before they can feel comfortable about each other. And of course, there are those who never do accomplish such a balance; these are the people who are convinced they are justified in pouncing at every opportunity to prove their exes are arch villains and deadly enemies. It takes a lot of time and energy to maintain this position, however, and much of life can go by unappreciated when you are busy nourishing a grudge.

That some or all of these emotions are part of the initial reaction to the ending of a marriage is to be expected. For the couple who have no children, or whose youngsters have already grown to adulthood and left the nest, the crisis of divorce involves mainly their individual emotional responses and the division of property. But for the family that includes children, arrangements have to be made as to where the offspring go; who is responsible for their daily care and safety; how their needs are met, bills paid, and raising accomplished. It becomes necessary, therefore, to reach some sort of agreement as to who does what for the youngsters once the nuclear, two-parent family is no longer viable.

Ironically, questions concerning the who, when, and how of future child rearing don't usually come up until the parents have discovered they can't seem to agree on anything, and the difficulty of working out a rational, positive solution to the problem is directly proportional to the anguish involved in the separation. The greater the emotional chaos between the parents, the less likely they are to find some form of accord on the subject. It is rather like falling head over heels down a pitch-black rabbit hole where you are twisted and turned and buffeted about in the dark, and then called on to stand upright and point, with unerring accuracy, to the invisible North Star! The whole world has turned topsy-turvy, and the pressures to find a firm direction can be so great that it is easy to panic and make a blind stab, regardless of how dizzy and confused you are. And once you have taken a stand, it too often becomes a locked-in position. There is a tendency to cling to that attitude in the frantic hope that here, at least, is something solid and stable around which the rest of your spinning universe will begin to reassemble itself.

This is particularly true where the question of child custody is concerned. Caught in the middle of your own emotional upheavals, you're forced to make decisions that will affect the entire future of your children as well as yourself. Too often the arrangements settled on in this fashion are the result of crisis decisions, snap judgments, and overreaction to the other parent. Frequently they are based on traditional practices rather than specific evaluation of the needs of the family concerned, and almost always they are made unilaterally: "I'll keep the children and you get out!" or "The children and I are leaving, and you can go to hell!" Occasionally they are the result of coercion: "If you don't let Johnny come with me, I won't give you a penny of support for any of the kids!" And sometimes they involve threats such as "I'll never let you keep the kids; we'll fight you all the way in court, and my attorney says we stand a good chance of winning!"

A legal battle over child custody, with attorneys, depositions, name-calling, court testimony, and astronomical legal fees is one of the most harrowing and debilitating experiences any family can go through. As each parent becomes polarized against the other, they believe themselves absolutely justified in the havoc they are bringing about because their fear, frustration, vindictiveness, and "righteous" rage can all be cloaked in the rationale of "looking out for the children's welfare." Many courts now try to head off knock-down, drag-out brawls of this sort, recognizing that they are almost always the result of two emotionally embattled adults' indulging in a deadly game of one-upmanship and attempting to destroy each other even at the cost of their children's security, stability, and future happiness. Thus the courts will refer the opposing partners to various forms of counseling, conciliation service, and arbitration in order to bring some perspective into their lives. This can be quite beneficial, unless the couple are so bent on mutual destruction that they no longer care what toll their children must pay.

Fortunately, the majority of child-custody arrangements are settled between the parties out of court, with only 10 percent of such cases having to be decided by a judge.[2] In one way or another the parents reach some kind of agreement, the question of who has custody of the youngsters is "uncontested," and the judge is asked simply to formalize the settlement and make it legal. In such situations the terrible ordeal of a court battle is avoided, and each parent accepts, however grudgingly, the responsibility of living by the agreement.

Yet whether the question of custody is resolved by the parents themselves or settled by the courts, in almost all cases it results in an arrangement that denies the children access to one of their parents on a normal basis. Because we have tended to assume that the distribution of responsibility for raising youngsters after the parents have separated must be an either/or thing, sole custody is given to one parent with the other being provided with the right to visit, but not actually participate in the raising of the progeny. A visit every other weekend, during some holidays, and occasionally over the summer vacation is the typical arrangement sanctioned by the court and accepted by most parents. It may not be the optimum solution, but it has been standard practice for years, and for many parents it is the only arrangement they have heard of.

That there are problems involved in this sort of situation goes almost without saying. As things currently stand, divorce means the loss of contact between child and father; in 85 to 90 percent of all divorces that involve children, custody is awarded to the mother. Although there is no overt condemnation of either parent, the psychological and emotional impact of such arrangements too often has an obviously punitive effect on all concerned. Single mothers are saddled with the full responsibility of raising the children alone. Usually they work to support themselves (and to some extent the children as well), run a household big enough for the whole family, attend to their education or career advancement if possible, and, most difficult of all, try to find some time for an adult private life of their own. Divorced fathers, on the other hand, are devalued and depersonalized. Continually reminded of the failure of their marriage by the loss of their children, angry at the idea of supporting people with whom they have so little contact, and frequently lonely and depressed, they too often become emotionally withdrawn and alienated from their youngsters. And the offspring, instead of being happy and secure with each parent, find themselves feeling confused, guilty, and defensive about loving either of them.

In a none-too-subtle way, these problems have been considered the punishment for not having succeeded in making the marriage work. Hence when a father grumbles about the emptiness of his relationship with the kids, his infuriated ex is likely to reply that he should have thought of the consequences before the marriage fell apart, instead of complaining about it afterward, when it is too late. And the woman who is inundated with too many decisions, commitments, and conflicting demands on her time and energy is usually asked what else she expected when she opted for living without a partner.

To some degree this is a natural reaction on the part of bickering parents, but on a much deeper level it reflects a basic cultural attitude about divorce. Ever since Martin Luther sanctioned the right of a man to put aside his wife if she "were taken in adultery," the idea of wrongdoing, sinfulness, and misbehavior has been made part and parcel of dissolving a marriage; punishment and the loss of rights (financial, emotional, or both) have been seen as the natural result of a divorce, and considered the price one paid for no longer being married.

Recognition of the fact that a marriage may end simply because the two adults are no longer compatible has led to "no-fault divorce" and a major reevaluation of our concepts of marriage, family life, the right to divorce and the legal ramifications thereof. Yet our custody practices continue to be administered on the same basis as before, and the fact that the youngsters involved are unduly deprived of a balanced childhood is almost entirely overlooked. To punish the children because of their parents' decision to end an unsatisfactory relationship is not only unfair to the youngsters and unhealthy for society, it is also *unnecessary*. It's time to take a closer look at our approach to child raising once the parents are no longer partners, and examine ways of improving the situation; in other words, we need to explore the possibility of "no-fault custody."

Parent–Child Bonds

The primary purpose of divorce is to disengage a pair of dissenting adults and provide them with an opportunity to lick their wounds and go on to create separate futures, apart. It is designed to free them from the social and moral obligations of wedlock, and to formally recognize this change in status. There is nothing, either in law or in human nature, which decrees that divorcing parents shall cease to love their offspring, or must break the parent–child bond that has developed. (In those situations in which a parent wants to disassociate from the entire family, the action usually takes the form of desertion, and any divorce that follows is a *result* of such broken ties, not the cause of them.)

Both parents and children have a heavy psychological and emotional investment in the bonds between them—a fact that becomes apparent even at an early age. Recent studies with infants indicate that, given the opportunity for close contact, very young babies recognize and respond to mother *and* father more or less equally.[3] Certainly the idea that small children relate better to the mother than to the father appears to be a reflection of our cultural practices rather than any innate preference on the part of the youngsters. Granted, there is usually a difference in the content of these bonds, but that is no more remarkable than the fact that the same parent will have very different relationships with his or her different offspring.

Yet our present system of child custody completely overlooks the fact that the children have already established complex and vital bonds with *each* parent. This tendency to ignore the importance of the bond between the child and the "noncustodial" parent is an all but barbaric practice. Anyone who has spent a period of his or her own childhood separated from a parent will remember hours of fantasizing about that missing adult: what it will be like when we're all together again; if only they were here now, they'd understand my feelings; or, that parent would never be as unfair as this parent is being. The roots of the relationship go deep, and will tug and pull at the child's heartstrings regardless of whatever "facts" are involved. There is no separation that is irrefutable in the eyes of a child, and even death is not without a possibility for bargaining in most young minds.

When a child and parent are parted by choice, and that not of the youngster's doing, there is a continued longing which can characterize much of that child's life, even as an adult. Anaïs Nin explored this problem in several of her short stories, and touched on the influence her absent father had over her life in *The Diary of Anaïs Nin*. Even when children have never known their natural parents, as in the case of some adoptions, they think about them, and it has often been noted that youngsters who have suffered severe physical abuse at the hands of their parents will still opt to return to them if given the opportunity. Surely a need as deep as this should be taken into account when there are two competent and willing parents who are seeking to divorce each other, but not their children!

In Theory

In most cases, each parent continues to love the children and wants to work out a custodial arrangement that allows him or her and the progeny the reassurance of continued contact with each other. What would be more natural, then, than to arrange child custody in such a way that the youngsters are allowed to maintain as normal contact as possible with each parent? As long as the children are not subjected to all sorts of negatives and hostilities between the two adults, they would be free to respond in a natural, loving, and trusting manner to both, individually. A child's stability and confidence come not from being in only one environment all his life, after all, but rather in feeling accepted, understood, and appreciated by the people he is with at the time. If the adult members of the family accept the child's right to interact with each of them, and acknowledge it as a useful, productive, and essential part of the youngster's life, the child will have the opportunity to explore these benefits for himself and react accordingly.

Children are remarkably clear in identifying something by experience rather than by concept, and the actual fact of being able to continue ongoing relationships with separated parents is of greater validity and import to them than all the best-meaning words in the world. Indeed, the process of assuring our offspring that both parents still love and cherish them, and then promptly denying them access to one of those parents, is ludicrous, as every child in that position will tell you: "But if Daddy really loved me, why did he go away?" Sadly enough, the overview of life that the child in the typical custody arrangement encounters is one in which the parents' personal hostilities are of greater importance than is the love of their offspring. The words may say "I love you and don't want to leave you," but the actions prove that the unresolved anger between the adults takes precedence.

On the other hand, the youngster who experiences not only verbal reassurances of the continuing care and concern of both parents, but also the actual fact of being free to love each of them independently is much less likely to find the separation debilitating. Research by Wallerstein and Kelly in California and Hetherington, Cox, and Cox in Virginia indicates over and over again that the children who were able to continue to have close contact with *each* parent suffered far less as a result of the divorce.[4] And certainly if one is to consider what is best for the child, the idea of avoiding the terrors of abandonment and desertion which parental divorce so frequently brings on must be one of the primary considerations.

Logically, therefore, the children of divorce should be entitled to the benefits of two loving and supportive homes, each considered equally valid, though different from one another. All children share their parents' genes and are accorded by society the birthright of their parents' social backgrounds, attitudes, philosophies, and advantages, as well as the right to the comfort and security of being accepted and nourished by both adults. There is no reason why, just because the parents decide to live separately, the offspring should be denied these legacies, and there is every reason to believe that they will be hurt by being deprived of them.

In Actuality

Our present custody practice is based not so much on the actual needs of the children as on two classic sexist traditions: Mother knows best (at least about raising children), and Father is an aggressive, competitive businessman who is incapable of being a tender, nurturing parent. These notions were basic tenets during the last century, when roles were rigidly defined and almost as stiffly adhered to. Thus women accepted motherhood as a built-in destiny, preconditioned by their gender, and men defined their function in the family as "bringing home the bacon" and making sure Junior did his chores. Fathers represented the authority and discipline required by the outside world, while mothers provided nourishment for the individual psyches of the family and made sure that dinner was on the table on time. (A wife was often referred to as "my better half"—a euphemism that carries a connotation of superiority, though in actual fact women were given little power over their own destinies. The phrase also implies that husbands, being made of cruder and less sensitive stuff, were incapable of supplying the emotional and psychological support women were called upon to provide.)

The outdated notions that a woman is automatically the better parent to raise a child, since she is the one who bore it, and that men are not, by nature, equipped to nourish and care for young ones still hold sway in the divorce courts today. It is not uncommon for judges, after *finding both parents to be equally fit,* to remand the children over to the mother's care simply on the basis of "customary practice." That the courts are notoriously slow to change is understandable, in part; they are set up in such a way that decisions are arrived at by looking back to past cases in order to find a precedent to follow. This makes for a firm and solid legal system, but in areas of family relations it can become woefully out of date. There are changes being made in family law throughout the country that will alleviate this situation, and they are discussed in a later chapter; suffice it to say that in the overall view, most courts perpetuate the idea that child custody should be awarded to one parent only, and that parent is almost always the mother.

Changes in Attitude

Social conventions (and our present custody practices are simply social conventions) are developed to meet the needs of the culture under a specific condition. They are not absolutes carved in stone, but rather the result of efforts to find the best solutions to fundamental problems common to many people. Ultimately the change in social mores must come about in the attitudes of the people involved. This is beginning to happen where child custody is concerned, as more and more people are looking for alternative methods of handling the care and raising of youngsters after divorce. I've spent two years talking with divorced parents who have successfully devised ways to provide their youngsters with two parental homes through many different arrangements and for many different reasons. Occasionally this sharing of responsibilities is provided for in the court order; the parents are granted *joint legal and physical custody*. More often, it is worked out between the two adults, although one of them has been specified as the "custodial" parent while the other has broad rights of visitation. In either case the result is the same: the children have a chance to grow up knowing each parent individually in the normal course of everyday interaction.

Some people work it out on an alternating-week basis, while others find larger blocks of time more satisfactory; some maintain their two households near enough so that the children can move back and forth on whatever schedule feels comfortable for everyone at the time, while others live many miles apart and take turns parenting on a summer/winter system. There are as many different and unique ways of meeting the children's needs as there are couples who are trying, and many more people have opted for some form of shared custody than I had realized when I began this project. How well these different solutions work depends largely on the people involved. The best arrangement for one family may not work for another, and what is practical and desirable at one phase of a child's life may not be suitable later on. Yet all of them have one thing in common: the desire to raise healthy, confident youngsters whose relationship with their parents is based solely on personal interaction and experience, untainted by the conflicts so often created by the either/or system we currently use.

How did these parents arrive at an agreement to share custody? Certainly not without a lot of soul-searching! In some cases there was such animosity and anger beforehand that each was preparing for a pitched battle in the courts. In other situations it was a conclusion already reached by the time the parents agreed to separate, as neither was willing to deny the youngsters access to the other. A few of the couples consented to try a shared arrangement as a result of counseling and the recommendation of professionals; and many, as I did, stumbled into it only after years of sole custody. All of them had some reservations about it to begin with, and most have felt the condemnation of traditionalists who accuse them of treating their children like footballs, or using them as guinea pigs in a sociological experiment. In most instances, the end results have proved to be far more positive than negative for all concerned, and the reaction of the children to such arrangements can pretty well be summed up by one articulate 11-year-old who looked at me solemnly as she said, "Thank goodness my parents love me enough to let me love both of them!"

That is not to say that shared custody is the only valid means of raising youngsters once the nuclear family has divided. In some cases the sole-custody arrangement is preferred by both parents, whether it is the father or the mother who assumes the full load of child care. And occasionally, particularly among teen-agers or children who have polarized against one of their parents before the separation, shared custody is not acceptable to the offspring. Each family needs to work out its own solution to the problem. It is important, however, to explore the options that are available so that you can make an informed choice, rather than just accepting the traditional arrangement because you aren't aware anything else is possible. Why grasp at a straw when there are a whole raft of hay bales available?

Yes, But . . .

Where does one begin, if custody is the question and the two parents are at loggerheads about everything from the division of the pots and pans to who gets the cuckoo clock? Helping you find the ways and means to arrive at a reasonable solution to your custody problems is what this book is all about. Recognizing both the pressures and the pitfalls of our present system will help, and understanding the process of divorce and its consequent whirl-pool of emotions should provide you with a better opportunity to work toward both a constructive divorce and a more positive aftermath. Once you have had a chance to explore the possible alternatives where custody is concerned, there is a step-by-step chapter to help you determine what are the most important factors to consider in your own case, and suggestions on how to cope with friends, relatives, attorneys, and the courts themselves. Nor is the information limited in usefulness to those couples who are just now contemplating divorce. The material covered is just as valid if you have been divorced for some time, but currently are having doubts, questions, squabbles, or impending battles about the care and control of your offspring.

All the attorneys and every marriage counselor I've talked with has stressed that the biggest problem between divorced or divorcing parents is the lack of communication. With all the tensions, worry, and hurt that go along with the ending of a marriage, it is easy for fear and frustration to evolve into distrust on both sides. Pretty soon neither person can hear what the other is saying, much less understand what is meant.

This book is set up specifically to be used as a communication tool if you so desire. Since it presents both men's and women's sides of the custody question, it will deal with a number of the common things that tend to be misunderstood between exes. I suggest that you read it with a large yellow marker pen in hand, and underline each and every sentence that reflects how you feel about things. That may be just every once in a while, or whole paragraphs at a time; the quantity isn't as important as the honesty is.

Remember, this applies only to your *own* feelings, fears, apprehensions, and hopes, *not what you think* your partner feels or thinks or does. The next step is to give the book to your partner, with the suggestion that he or she do the same, using a different light-colored marker. After your ex has finished the book and given it back, you'll each have a better idea of how the other feels, as well as a clearer understanding of your options and a basis for beginning to discuss the subject.

The books that are recommended as Suggested Reading cover a wide range of subjects, from how to have better fights (obviously a handy thing for exes to know) to ways of coping with your offspring more effectively. The period following the end of a marriage is well known to be a time of pain and sadness, and often brings with it upheavals and reorganization of one's entire life structure. For many it becomes an opportunity for personal growth and development unlike anything they have encountered before. Since most of our social attitudes, self-images, and expectations were formulated when we were quite young, the chance to reassess them in the light of mature experience can be not only extremely exciting, but also a highly rewarding process. The reevaluation of philosophies and priorities, the discovery of new self-definitions and goals, and the development of new relationships between ourselves and our children are all potentially very positive. A number of the books listed in Suggested Reading relate to these broader horizons, and are included because many other divorced or divorcing people have found them to be helpful. The rest, of course, deal specifically with divorce or child raising, and as such should be directly useful.

The same holds true for the exercises at the ends of different chapters. They are offered simply as a means of helping you to clarify your own feelings and thoughts, and are not to be considered as "tests"; there is no right or wrong about how you answer them, and if you wish to share them with your ex at a later time, by all means do so.

It is not the aim of this book to bring couples back together again by trying to scare them out of divorce with horror tales about raising children separately. Parents who "stay together for the sake of the children" but continue to fight and bicker between themselves only add the children's resentment to their problems and certainly do their offspring no favors!

Neither can I promise that the reading of this book will heal all wounds and turn your ex into the most reasonable creature this side of yourself. What I hope it will do is give you both enough information and understanding of your situation so that you can comfortably reach a solution that takes into account the needs of the whole family. There are certain advantages to the single-parent family that are beneficial to both the parent and the children, and they bear keeping in mind regardless of what specific form of custody you agree upon.

It is not my intent to present a sociological report on the custody practices of this country, although statistics and quotations are referenced in the Notes section at the back of the book. Other things that might be useful, such as addresses of specific organizations, examples of custody-contract paragraphs, and a bibliography of professional works on children and divorce are included in the Appendices. For the most part, however, I have simply gathered information from families who have been willing to discuss their custody solutions, and these are offered as ideas for you to consider. Each family's needs and capacities are different, and you may conclude that the traditional arrangement of sole custody to either father or mother is most suitable for yours, or you may devise a totally new approach no one else has tried before. The important thing is to find a solution that feels right for both you and the children, and only you can know how much and in what ways you are willing and able to make it work.

2
Social
Pressures

What's Behind Our Present Practices

The basic cultural concepts such as honor, patriotism, family structure and function, masculinity, and femininity are developed by a society over a long period of time. They are the ways and means of doing things, the representation of "the way things are . . . or *ought* to be"; and whereas at first they evolve in an attempt to stabilize the society, they gradually become the backbone of convention, slide into the position of tradition, and are eventually rejected when the culture no longer finds them applicable.

Such attitudes and assumptions come to us through our parents and peers when we're young, and are further colored and confirmed by the kind of community we live in when we reach adulthood. We each have a full network of such beliefs, ranging all the way from overall cultural philosophy to the intensely personal expectations we develop as a result of our own experiences. Of course, a number of these social assumptions and expectations are involved in both marriage and divorce. In and of themselves they don't necessarily cause problems, but when they come into play during a divorce, they can snap a mind shut faster than the proverbial bear trap!

Unfortunately, the confusion, pain, and misery of ending a marriage often make us cling to whatever traditional solutions and past stability we can find. We look to the established conventions for answers as to how to cope, forgetting that most of these traditions were formed when divorce itself was a rarity. Thus we are influenced, whether we realize it or not, by social attitudes and pressures which have not changed much over the last seventy years. Many of them are no longer applicable, and the whole lot should be reevaluated and updated in the light of our own cultural changes.

One of the most basic of these assumptions is the belief that there must be an either/or choice when it comes to who will raise the children after the adults have separated. This creates a polarization between the two parents, and automatically casts them as competitors vying for control of the youngsters. And, as is always the case when there is an either/or attitude, there are both a "winner" and a "loser" as a result of the system. The fact that the children become "losers" no matter which parent wins, as a result of having lost contact with the other parent, is generally overlooked.

There are several intertwining attitudes behind this sole-custody tradition; that parents who can't agree to stay married won't be able to agree on raising their offspring afterward, that children will feel insecure and unloved if they don't have one authoritative home, and that Mama invariably knows best when it comes to being a nurturing parent are just a few of them. Underlying all else, however, is the antiquated belief that children are the possessions of their parents, part of the goods to be disposed of in a divorce along with the pots and pans and the division of chickens and cows.

Children as Possessions

Until the middle of the last century, children were indeed considered chattels in the eyes of the law. In Victorian England, for instance, a man was perfectly within his rights to indenture his offspring (sell them into the service of someone else) and keep the money therefrom for himself. This was accepted as his right and due, since he bore the full responsibility of supporting his youngsters, and like his house, land, and wife, they were his to control and dispose of as he saw fit. Nowadays we deplore such an attitude (even when our little darlings drive us up the wall) and wonder how this inhumane practice could have persisted for so long a time. Yet oddly enough, there is still a strong vestige of that concept reflected in the language used for child-custody cases by the court.

For instance, we have custody "contests" in which the "winning" parent is "awarded" control of the children, for all the world as though they were prizes in a TV game show. Although these terms are not consciously intended to negate the human status of the youngsters, or downgrade the noncustodial ("losing") parent, their use unconsciously perpetuates an attitude that does just that. The subliminal idea communicated is that the children are to be wrested from an opponent in some sort of battle, and carted off by the victor as the spoils of war. Any child who has been through the grueling experience of being the center of a custody dispute will tell you that it made him feel debased, torn, abused, cornered, unrecognized, and violated. Terrified at the notion of having to make a choice between their parents, yet wanting to be heard and understood, children in this situation discover that everyone claims to know what's best for them regardless of their own feelings. It's no wonder that they end up carrying the greatest and longest burden of pain from such a contest.

Even when there are no battles and the question of custody is "uncontested," the children are usually given over to the custodial parent not because that is the best choice for the whole family, but because of the various social pressures brought to bear on both men and women.

Women as Nurturers

For instance, there is an automatic assumption that the divorcing mother will keep the children with her, whether she wants them or not. In most cases the woman never even questions the situation, but simply accepts it as a foregone conclusion. For some, motherhood is the only occupation they have known, and these women cling to the presence of their offspring as an actor clings to an Actors Equity card! Having defined themselves in terms of their relationships with other people ("wife of So-and-so, mother of Such-and-such"), they are understandably frightened at the idea of being identified simply as Sarah Brown or Marcia Smith. Often they can't imagine what they would do with themselves if they didn't have children to take care of, and usually refuse to consider the fact that those very same youngsters are going to grow up and leave home anyhow, one day in the future. Motherhood gives them the acceptance of society in general, respect in the eyes of like-minded friends and relatives, and a certain amount of authority over the comings and goings of young lives. Why on earth should they be willing to give it all up, even temporarily? As one very proper woman quite graphically explained: "When I went into that courtroom, I knew I was going to be stripped of half my title and rights in society; I was no longer to be considered a wife. If you think I'm going to give up the other fifty percent by allowing him to have the kids, even on an equally sharing basis, you're crazy. That's the same as complete castration!"

Not every mother is that dependent on her maternity, of course, but for those who do rely on it as the most important facet of their lives, it can take on an addictive power not unlike that of some drugs. Without it these mothers feel they are nothing, even though the full weight of sole custodial responsibility for a brood of youngsters can be exhausting, debilitating, and enervating. They are so frightened by the prospect of not having that crutch that they compulsively limit their own lives to the constant care and feeding of the very responsibility that keeps them from developing other areas of endeavor. (Having been in that place myself, I know how easy it is to rationalize your own inertia in terms of having to meet the needs of the children!) Nor is this attitude limited to divorcées. Many a married woman in the past has devoted so much time and energy to her children that her own personal needs and interests were overlooked, and when the kids left the nest and moved out on their own, she found herself lost and confused and somehow useless. Obviously, submerging yourself *completely* in your motherhood is a dangerous practice to follow, as more and more women are coming to realize.

A number of other women recognize that there are new horizons and broader opportunities opening up to them now, yet they fear that if they agree to share the children in order to direct their time and energy toward other things, they will be branded as "unfit." This is a cultural assumption that directly reflects the attitude of the courts since the turn of the century. Because a father had to prove that his ex-wife had an immoral influence on the children, had deserted them, or was incapable of providing them with adequate care if he hoped to be given the right to raise them himself, there grew up a general assumption that divorced women who had children but weren't raising them must have been found "unfit" by a judge. As a result, the social pressure for a woman to maintain her role as parent and guardian has more than once created unnecessary pain in a family where all the members would have benefited from sharing.

In one specific case, a woman called me about coming to a workshop I was conducting on being a single parent. When I asked her what her situation was, she suddenly became very tentative and withdrawn, and in the ensuing conversation it gradually came out that her 13-year-old son had gone to live with his father after spending four years with her, and she was deeply upset about it.

"How is it working out for him?" I asked. "Fine, just fine" was the response. He and his father were getting on famously, and her own relationship with the father had relaxed and improved to such a degree that they were going in on a joint birthday present for their son. She herself had just finished getting her B.A. in Business Administration when the boy left her, and during the ensuing six months she had found, and now settled into, a new and exciting job. Not only that, she was beginning to socialize in a way never possible in her life before, and felt very happy about the way things were going in general.

Why, then, I wondered, had she seemed so hesitant and unhappy when we first began talking? "I'm scared!" she answered. Scared of what people must think because she didn't have her son with her; scared that she must be an unnatural or uncaring woman because she was enjoying her life doing something besides being a mother; scared because of all the social pressures that implied she had done an inhuman thing in recognizing the boy's need and desire to be with his father. "I didn't let him go willingly," she hastened to assure me. "I only consented because if I hadn't, there would have been a custody battle. But even so, I feel so guilty. I let my child go live with someone else!" (The fact that that "someone else" was also a blood parent to the boy provided no solace for her.) So strong was her awareness of the taboo against mothers' "giving up" their children that she concluded the conversation with the statement "What kind of woman could do a thing like this?"—even though her own experience indicated that it was resulting in positives for all concerned!

Most mothers are neither so totally dependent on their children that they must protect their "right" to custody above all else nor so pressured by society that they are afraid to accept what is actually proving to be a very plausible solution to the problem at hand. Usually they have not even heard of shared custody, never questioned whether one or more of the offspring would be happier and better off with the father, and certainly haven't thought in terms of having a choice in the matter. Women simply accept the assumption that they will keep the youngsters, as though it were as inevitable as snow in the Arctic Circle. "I'm their mother; what else am I going to do?" was the incredulous remark of a woman deeply puzzled by the very idea of looking at other possibilities.

Men as Providers

Thus many women hang on to their children more from lack of options or fear of censure than because they honestly feel the father would be a *bad* influence. And in fact, until quite recently there really weren't many other possibilities. Twenty years ago the divorced father expected to be cut off from his kids. He might feel hurt, sad, lonely, deserted, rejected, or angry, but he didn't feel guilty about his children as long as he continued to pay the child support. Providing financially for his youngsters was his basic function, and whether he liked it or not, he usually accepted it as fulfilling his obligation as a father.[1]

The notion of a man being caring, tender, emotionally responsive, nurturing, gentle, and intuitively aware of the spiritual and emotional needs of his children (all of which is expected of a woman the moment she gives birth to the infant) has not been exactly encouraged by our culture. Judges, social workers, attorneys, and the public at large usually don't consider fathers to be adequate single parents precisely because they *are fathers*. In many cases, if a father asks for custody in court it is expected that he prove he is able to hire a full-time housekeeper, or has a close relative who qualifies as a substitute ''mother'' for the children. Naturally, it makes sense to be sure that young children will be well cared for while the parent is at work; yet I know of no case in which a working mother was denied custody because she couldn't afford to hire a housekeeper! Certainly the single mother's need for physical and psychological help and relief in coping with the full responsibility of family and career is just as great as the single father's, yet she is expected to be able to cope, while he is told he cannot. The obvious message is that women are the only creatures equipped to raise children, and that fathers are so incapable of handling the situation that pseudo mothers must be provided for the single father's children. Yet, as many social scientists are pointing out, that's only another cultural assumption, not a fact of nature (or nurture).

The Male Mystique

Our cultural heroes have tended to be the strong, silent type: the cowboy/sheriff who tamed the hostile environment, the lone-wolf cynic, or the robber baron who enjoyed proclaiming that he was a self-made man. It was the Bogarts, the Waynes, the McQueens who provided us with images of masculinity: tough, aggressive, quick to take the initiative and press their own advantage. Patterned on our romanticized notion of the self-reliant frontiersman, this pasteboard example has led many of our men into straitjacketed behavior where emotions are largely suppressed and physical or financial performance takes the place of human interaction. By contrast to women, who are encouraged to be soft, pliant, warm, trusting, vulnerable, and not very adventurous, men are expected to see themselves as hard, cool, strong, shrewd, impregnable, and willing to risk anything, as long as it doesn't involve feelings.

Everything from nursery rhymes to school sports reinforces this concept of "maleness" and "femaleness" in our impressionable years. Little girls may be made of sugar and spice and everything nice, keep diaries, and share secrets at slumber parties, but boys are assumed to be rowdy roughnecks who mustn't cry for fear of being called a sissy, and who concentrate on playing Cops and Robbers, King of the Mountain, and other territorially aggressive games. While pompon girls romp about in front of the grandstand, organizing and providing the moral support for the team, it is the boys who are actively involved in achieving the victory. Regardless of how many cut lips, swollen eyes, and broken bones the young contender comes up with, he's considered a hero as long as he can pretend the pain, fear, and tension of the game don't "get to him" emotionally. Since he can't turn off the importance of achieving in this society, too often the young man's only real choice has been to turn off his feelings and direct his energies into areas that aren't likely to call for subtleties of perception on the emotional level. It's no real wonder, then, that when a divorcing father expresses his desire to assume the more gentle, emotional nuturing roles of parenting, he's likely to run into all sorts of social pressures standing in his way, not the least of which is the attitude of the courts themselves.

Bias Against Fathers

When it comes to the question of child custody, the courts have been notoriously biased against men. It is obvious, blatant, and generally recognized by attorneys and judges alike, and it goes on continually. As James Levine says in *Who Will Raise the Children?:*

> With every instance of divorce in which custody of children is an issue, a man realizes—perhaps for the first time in his life—that he

can be denied something other than the ladies room because of his sex.[2]

Child custody is the one area in which men, by virtue of being male, are at an automatic disadvantage in the eyes of the law, and many fathers who have encountered this prejudice have real horror stories to tell. Although most states have reworded their custody guidelines to eliminate the presumption that children should always go to the mother if both parents are considered "fit," both judges and attorneys have been slow to put this kind of equality into effect. Even when the mother's care has proved to be negligent, as in one case I know of where the child had to be hospitalized for malnutrition, the judges continue to remand the children to the mother on the basis of "tradition." Books such as *The Disposable Parent* and *Who Will Raise the Children?* document heartbreaking situations, and any group of divorced fathers, such as Equal Rights for Fathers or Fathers for Equal Justice, will provide you with more current examples. There are many reasons for the persistence of this legal attitude, some of which will be covered in Chapter 14. Suffice it to say that men are so conditioned to believe they can't get custody of their children, they frequently are afraid to ask.

Until recently, most attorneys counseled fathers against seeking child custody. Knowing that the judicial bias was generally against a man's taking over the parental task, lawyers tried to discourage their clients from even thinking about it. As James P. Rorris stated in an article for the *1971 Minnesota Practice Manual, Family Law* section:

> Except in very rare cases, the father should not have the custody of the minor children of the parties. . . . A lawyer who encourages his client to file for custody, unless it is one of the classic exceptions, has difficulty collecting his fees, has a most unreasonable client, has taken the time of the court and welfare agencies involved, and has put a burden on his legal brethren.[3]

Parent by Default

If a divorced or divorcing father does pursue his chances of raising his children himself, he is confronted with the most vicious social attitude of all: the only way he can hope to gain custody is by default. If he is willing and able to destroy his wife's reputation in court, if he will try to prove her to be "unfit," he may be given the children simply because *she is being denied them*. For many fathers, the name-calling, mud-slinging siege that custody battles so often turn into is too high a price to pay for what should be a natural right. A number of fathers have expressed their feelings quite openly: "I don't want to have to ruin her just to be able to be with our kids more often. She's a fine mother . . . not much good as a wife where I was concerned, maybe, but that doesn't keep her from being a good parent. I can't face the idea of trying to destroy her in court when I know she's not a bad person. I just want a little equality and justice for myself, not a lot of pain and misery for her."

Yet pain and misery are what custody battles are all about. One horrified father explained how the hiring of a detective, keeping notes of every conversation and contact, and dragging out any scrap of possibly damning behavior, no matter how trivial, made him feel rotten himself. He was in a continual state of righteous rage, spite, and vindictiveness, and the whole thing became a terrible, corrosive ordeal. Later, sitting in court and hearing the testimony of his own detective as to his ex's alleged indiscretion with her attorney, he was moved to tears. "I didn't want to hurt her . . . it was all so *public,* somehow. I ended up feeling sorry for her, of all things. It all sounded tawdry and cheap, and I was so embarrassed for her, I couldn't even look at her." (Perhaps part of that embarrassment was for his own part in this unsuccessful attempt to ruin her reputation; the judge still ruled in her favor, and the case has yet to be resolved.)

Fortunately, it is not *always* necessary for parents to so thoroughly castigate their exes in order to get custody. When Dr. Lee Salk, a noted child psychologist, won custody of his two young children in a New York court in 1975, the case was reported in papers all over the country. Neither parent had tried to besmirch the capabilities, character, or reputation of the other; each contended that they were both fit, but that he or she was just a little fitter. And because of the nonaccusatory attitudes taken, it is considered a landmark case. The result was still an either/or situation, but at least the character assassination of the parents was not part of it.

Although there are precious few statistics available about contested custody decisions, and virtually none on how custody agreements are reached out of court, the unofficial estimates one hears from judges, commissioners, and attorneys indicate that the vast majority (between 80 and 90 percent) of the contested cases involve two perfectly fit parents, each of whom is capable of raising the children. And while in occasional situations there is a clear-cut case of instability, neglect, or abuse on the part of one parent, the average custody case involves two fully competent adults so caught up in the traditional system that they haven't been able to see beyond the win/lose situation they're in. So the question comes up: if, as in most cases, both parents are fit, and if the either/or solution creates a losing situation for the children, why don't more parents look for ways to share child raising after divorce?

Children as Weapons of Power

There seem to be several personal factors involved in the usual determination to insist on sole custody, over and above the general social pressures already outlined. Unfortunately, these have more to do with the continuance of the relationship between the divorcing adults than they do with the welfare of the children. And while they are easy to spot if you're outside the situation looking in, it's not always so easy to see what's happening when you're caught in the middle of it yourself.

There are some parents who refuse to recognize that the win/lose, either/or situation works a hardship on the children, or else they see and understand it, but don't care. Often these people (either consciously or subconsciously) have decided to keep control of the children in order to spite their exes. I have seen this happen where both men and women are concerned: the woman who feels she's been rejected in favor of another will sometimes cling to the children both to reassure herself that she is still loved by someone, and to remind their father that he has to pay a high price to get rid of her. Or the man whose ego is severely battered by his wife's decision to go out on her own may decide that he'll show her who's boss after all by trying to turn the children against her. These tactics are shabby and hurtful to the children, and usually backfire in that the youngsters simply begin to discount all the hostile and unpleasant things they perceive coming from the custodial parent. When a parent becomes so full of bitterness, spite, and corrosive revenge, such attitudes will not only prove to be poisonous to the adult, but also sooner or later drive the children away. Ironically, it's the parent who tries to subvert and manipulate the children's feelings about the other who most often loses the love and respect of the kids by the time they are grown.

If the children are little, they may actually accept all the vilification and negatives such a parent spews forth, in which case it may take a number of years and lots of pain before the youngsters grow mature enough to start questioning for themselves. On the other hand, if the children are coming into puberty, chances are they will very soon recognize the warpage of reality on the part of their daily parent, and begin to counteract it in their own minds. In either case they are burdened with needless guilt, resentment, conflicting loyalties, and the realization that at least one of their parents is neurotic, unfair, and so selfish that he or she can't or won't consider the children's feelings at all.

Negating the Past

In many other cases the adults' efforts to deny each other contact with the youngsters come not from a desire to maintain power over each other, but from a belief that the only way to be free of the marriage itself is to eliminate the other parent from the child's life too. Frequently these people expect divorce to wipe out the past, undo all previous problems, and provide a completely clean slate on which to begin anew. It's easy to think that all the difficulties, self-doubts, and hurt feelings that developed over the years of marriage were brought about mainly by your ex, and once that person is banished from your life you'll be able to move on to the bigger and better future you deserve. No more snide remarks; no more innuendos, tearful scenes, violent arguments, or the stifling of your own loving and caring nature. The divorce provides an opportunity to admit that the union was a mistake, the particular partner poorly chosen (or at least didn't live up to premarital expectations), or the two of you have simply grown apart in the natural course of events. Therefore you may conclude it's best to make a clean sweep of it, and by so doing, get rid of all the garbage from the past.

It's not uncommon for parents who view divorce in this light to think they can make the divorce a success only by putting an end to all contact with the past. So they attempt to cut all ties (including those of the children), in order to move away from the anguish that's gone before. That they create a win/lose, either/or situation may be seen as unfortunate, but, after all, that's the way things are.

Except that that's *not* the way things are! When you have children, there is absolutely no way you're going to be able to blot out the past. They are the continuing, living, present results of your marriage, and they carry the remains of it into their own futures as well. You are just as much bound to your ex as you are to your offspring (though certainly in a different fashion), and any attempt to sever the tie between them and their other parent will more than likely put a tremendous strain on your own child/parent relationship. There is no way to eliminate that other adult from your youngster's thoughts; the bond is all but indestructible. You can twist it, fray it, drive it underground, yes . . . but erase it completely, *never*. And even if the noncustodial parent is banished forever from the family, you as well as the children will be affected by that parent's absence. A moody, sulky youngster depressed and frightened by the loss of a parent is bound to be harder to get along with than a child who loves and knows he or she is loved in return by both parents. And whether or not the child is willing or able to express the feelings that are rampaging around inside, those angers and hurts and bewilderments won't just disappear because the parents get a piece of paper saying they don't have to live with each other any longer. To add to all that turmoil by trying to further alienate parent and child is not only cruel and abusive to the youngster: it will probably backfire on both you and the child in the years to come.

I met one young woman who told of her parents' very bitter divorce when she was 6 years old. The father simply disappeared; it was forbidden to mention his name in front of the mother, and his identity as a human being was carefully wiped out. Eventually, when the girl turned 18, she contacted an aunt who gave her the current address of her missing sire. So one morning a rather bedraggled bachelor was in the midst of shaving when there came a knock on his door. Still half lathered, he stumbled to the entrance and, opening it, found himself confronted with a very comely, full-grown stranger who announced, "Hello, Dad . . . I'm your daughter." It was not a comfortable encounter, bringing up thousands of sad memories of abandonment and loss for each, but for the girl who had hitchhiked across the continent to find the parent she had lost so long ago, it was something she had had to do; the need for contact and verification of her heredity had grown stronger, not weaker, during those twelve years of silence.

Expectations of Divorce

In the course of interviewing divorced parents, I found an interesting and unexpected phenomenon: the more disappointed the parent is about what his or her life as a divorced person turns out to be, the angrier he or she gets at the ex. This is particularly noticeable if things seem to be going well for the opposing partner. And it doesn't seem to matter who initiated the divorce: the man who "wanted out at any price" and then feels trapped financially and the woman who thought she would become the belle of the ball and instead finds herself playing the wallflower are both likely to berate their exes with the bitterest of recriminations once the reality of their situation hits home.

Frequently this is related to what has been called the "myth of romantic divorce." As the dissolution of marriage becomes more common, some people, bored by the complacency of their marriages, begin to think that getting a divorce will solve what are actually internal problems of their own. Not only do they look (with possible justification) at the aggravations of the marriage they have; they also begin to fantasize about how much better it would be if they were single again, and/or free to choose another mate. But instead of preparing to cope with the realities attendant to being divorced parents, they embroider elaborate dreams about future freedom and the new potentials that await them once the present domestic situation is done away with. These people dance down a primrose path of self-deception, so beguiled by their own assumptions and expectations for the future that they feel cheated and angry when the garden turns out to be full of weeds and thorns as well as roses. As the disappointment and resentment build up, such a person turns a castigating eye on his or her ex-partner and puts as much blame on the other as possible.

And all of this is reflected in how that parent relates to his or her children. Anger, frustration, cynicism, and bitterness may not be consciously directed at the youngsters, but it's bound to affect them. And if it's heaped abusively on the other parent, that will affect the children too. So it's a good idea to have as clear an understanding as possible not only of why you're ending the marriage, but what you expect from your singleness, and how you think your life will be once you become a single parent. If you are supposing that being a single mother will automatically lead to your playing the role of the Gay Divorcée, or that the alluring life of a Bachelor About Town will magically blot out the pain and sadness of being separated from your children, you are in for a terrible shock.

This is not to say that most divorces should not happen, but rather that it is important to have a realistic understanding of what your new status will entail. Naturally, just as each marriage is individual to the couple who create it, so each divorce is unique to the person going through it. Different feelings, attitudes, and reactions will show up at different times, depending largely upon both the people and circumstances involved. The exercises at the end of this chapter are designed to allow you to explore some of the concepts you have about divorce in general, and your singleness in particular. The more you can acknowledge your hopes, fears, and worries, the better prepared you will be to handle them when the time comes. (And if you are already divorced, even if it's been some time since the actual separation, try the exercises anyhow; you may be able to see what areas you still wish to develop or improve upon.)

TWO YEARS FROM NOW . . .

Sit down for a few minutes and think about what you want to be doing in two years' time. Let your mind explore all the most interesting and positive things you can think of, regardless of what your situation is presently. This may involve career, children, remarriage, education, travel, creative projects, a long-planned vacation—whatever feels happiest to you.

How can you move from your present position to that of your fantasy? How much depends on other people, and how much can you create for yourself? Where do the children fit into it? Your ex? How would this projected future be changed if you let your ex have custody of the children? If you took sole custody yourself? If you agreed to share the children on a part-time basis?

SELF-EXPLORATION

Complete the sentence "I am nothing if not _____."

What would it feel like to be "nothing"?
How does this belief dictate what you do with your time and energy?
When did you begin to define yourself in this way?
Are you following what your parents taught? Rebelling against them? Pressured by social assumptions and your peer group?
Do you expect others to be this way too? Why?
How does it limit you as a person? As a parent? As a spouse?
How does it affect your divorce or custody attitude?

DIVORCE EXPECTATIONS

Just as different people view the ending of a marriage differently, so too they have different ideas about what their divorce will entail. Below is a list; using these terms and any others that you can think of, arrange them in descending order of magnitude. Feel free to leave out whatever simply doesn't apply.

I SEE THE DIVORCE AS . . . .

Putting an end to hostilities
A chance to get even
Wiping the slate clean
An unpleasant necessity
Creating a family scandal
Being fair and equal, without name-calling
Opening new doors for renewed dating
Leading to a better relationship between us
Being an opportunity for new growth

Punishing my ex for past behavior
A tragedy I didn't ask for
Leading to remarriage
Good riddance to a bad situation
A sign of failure and defeat

EXPECTATIONS OF SINGLEHOOD

Everyone envisions his or her life following divorce as including some of the following things. Rearrange the lists for yourself, with the most important expectations, desires or fears at the top, the least important at the bottom; and by all means add anything else that you can think of.

I WANT MY NEW LIFE TO INCLUDE:

More social contacts
Further education
Time for personal growth
Peace and quiet
A better relationship with
  my ex
Children
More excitement

Travel
Career opportunities
Romance
A chance to be me
Remarriage
Freedom
Good relationships with the kids

I AM AFRAID MY NEW LIFE WILL INCLUDE:

Loneliness
Fear
Fights with my ex
Guilt
Social rejection
Depression

Financial insecurity
Difficulties with the kids
Frustration
Sorrow
Loss of the children
Failure

When you're finished making your lists, take a look at how much you can do to achieve the positives and alleviate or cancel out the negatives. Perhaps you will want to discuss these things with your ex, but don't feel you have to; this is just to help you get your own feelings organized.

What are you feeling at this very moment? Rage____ Fear____ Hope____ Challenge____ Rejection____ Relief____ Sadness____ All of the above____ None of the above____ Who knows?____

3
I Didn't Order This

Traditional Custody from the Woman's Viewpoint

Few people realize beforehand what being a divorced parent involves. It is not, after all, something that one looks forward to with great anticipation and excitement, hardly able to wait for its accomplishment. Women aren't encouraged to dream about it during childhood and adolescence, nor do men assume it will be part of the inevitable pattern of their lives. Friends don't give showers or send cards of congratulation, and whatever the expectations are about it, it invariably turns out to be both better and worse than imagined.

Most of us have little or no preparation for being divorced parents, having been raised with the traditional assumption that the nuclear family (that is, mother-father-and-children) is the basic life-style of all mankind. At best we think of the single-parent family as a sort of TV situation comedy, and at worst it connotes a morass of guilts and resentments, tattered psyches, and vestiges of the old "broken home" concept which assumes that every child with divorced parents is going to turn out to be a juvenile delinquent. Few courses in Family Living at the high school (or even college) level deal with the concept of "life after divorce," and we tend to take the ostrichlike attitude that if we don't learn about it beforehand, it won't happen later. There seems to be a conviction that recognizing the single-parent family as a viable way of life will undermine everyone's commitment to marriage. This is exactly analogous to the philosophy which says if you don't teach children about birth control, they won't have sex. And certainly the statistics for both single-parent homes and unwed mothers put that kind of thinking to shame!

Transition

For the typical divorcing mother who retains sole custody of the children, the first six months to a year are so full of decisions, rearrangements, and regrouping of energies, she doesn't have time to assess what effect the traditional child-custody arrangement has on her family. During this time her main concern lies in keeping the show running while she confronts such problems as whether or not to move, how to fix the water heater, who will handle what bills, and how to cope with all the emotions and miseries of her personal reaction to the ending of the marriage. Eventually she'll get around to seeing it as a general testing of her own independence and competence, but in the beginning she's likely to feel that she's just barely hanging on by her fingernails.

She is usually worried about the effect of the separation on the offspring, and probably recognizes that no matter how relieved she may be to be out of a bad marriage, the children undoubtedly have their own conflicted feelings about it all. If they are old enough to be in school, she will tend to watch their grades closely to see if they show signs of depression, inattentiveness, or unusual behavior in the classroom. If she is the practical sort, she may meet with the children's teachers or counselors in order to explain to them what the children are coping with at home. (This is an excellent idea, and most teachers appreciate it, as it gives them an opportunity to take into consideration the personal stresses the youngster may be trying to handle but is unable to discuss. That is not to say the teacher will single the child out for special attention; but by being aware of what is happening, the teacher will be better able to evaluate and understand the youngster's reactions in class. If you feel apprehensive about having other people know about the divorce, it may help to realize that in some suburban schools the majority of students in a class are children with divorced parents!)

If she hasn't worked before, this may be the time for the single mother to consider that possibility, particularly once she finds out that her budget refuses to stretch as far as she had expected. She may or may not take to socializing, and if she was involved in a relationship with someone else at the time of the divorce, chances are it will change simply because her own status has changed. If she wanted the marriage to continue, and therefore feels rejected and abandoned by her husband, she will probably need extra time to lick her wounds and gain some sort of perspective on what her new life entails. The violent emotional storms and wild fits of weeping or nightmares or nausea which she may have experienced at the beginning of the separation will gradually run their course, and she will eventually accept, as most of us have at one time or another, that people rarely die of broken hearts.

In any event, no matter how she is handling her own individual adjustment to the situation, there is so much happening, both within her and around her, that the single mother in transition isn't likely to really settle into the single-parent role comfortably until all the smoke has cleared and she's had enough experience to discover she can handle it. The Navy wife who is used to having her husband gone for months at a time on tours of duty will be much more familiar with the practical aspects of running a home without a male partner than will the "little woman" who has been encouraged to be a dependent and nonassertive housewife throughout her marriage. But both will have to deal with the emotional traumas inherent in ending one chapter and beginning another.

During all this time there will probably be occasional and unavoidable contact with your ex. Everyone's nerves are still likely to be raw from the decision to end the marriage, and your relationship will reflect the attitudes and moods brought on by the divorce itself: sullen, grim, politely formal, raucously hostile, poisonously caustic, or even coolly friendly. Some couples, finding the separation to be much more difficult than they had anticipated, become even more bitter and vindictive toward each other, while others, experiencing a relief from tensions, begin to establish a guarded but humane truce. Regardless of how you choose to handle your relationship, the fact that you are both parents to the same offspring means you will have to be in contact to some degree.

Staggering under an immense load of responsibilities, trying to juggle children, home, career, budget, and some sort of personal life for herself, the newly single mother may be quick to become resentful and angry about anything that threatens to upset her precarious balance. It isn't uncommon for her to express a rigid and righteously unbending attitude toward her ex; if she carries any sense of guilt or doubt about having ended the marriage herself, she may well jump at any chance to point out how poorly her past spouse is now behaving. And if the divorce was not her idea and she's feeling hurt and disoriented, anything he does may add to her sense of betrayal and vulnerability. In either case, the result is often a hostile, defensive woman who is desperately trying to put as much distance and formality between herself and her ex as possible.

Many women going through this transition become adamant about little details such as phone calls to the children, or the exact times and circumstances of the father's visit with the kids. Frequently they insist that each visit adhere to the court order right down to the minute, and the slightest deviation may bring out the irate mother-bear aspect of their personalities. Generally this is a defense tactic employed to keep her world from coming completely unglued; by nailing down every and any loose edge, she feels more confident that her ex won't knock over her house of cards. Falling back on the absolute letter of the court orders, she demands that he conform to every jot and tittle therein. That her understanding of what was ordered may differ from what her ex heard, and both may be at variance to what the judge himself meant, is a moot point, as the woman in this condition is rarely willing or able to discuss the problems involved directly with her ex.

Sometimes the relationship between the parents is kept so formal and aloof that neither one has any idea of what the other is experiencing. When this happens, the resentments can build up unnoticed and then suddenly explode without any warning. More than one single mother has ended up screaming about some minor thing which she would normally have handled much more calmly.

I know a young woman who burst into a fit of tearful rage over the fact that the father brought the children back from a weekend in the country with dirty clothes. Refusing to recognize that he had no way of washing the items his offspring were wearing, she could only sob that it was typical of his thoughtlessness and lack of consideration to leave all the dirty work for her after she had taken great pains to present him with spic-and-span kids the day before. Her own psychological fatigue brought all her past hurts to the surface, and they erupted in a noisy tirade in front of the children—which naturally upset and angered their father. Perhaps if he had recognized that she was driven to the ragged edge of her resources, not specifically by his actions but by the whole situation, he might have found a better way of handling the scene. As it was, her attack only made him less likely to appreciate her problems, and more inclined to defend and protect himself from her. Thus his own pain and hostility were called into play, and the entire sequence added one more layer of spite and revenge and fear and distrust between them. This is the kind of painful twisting of misunderstood motives, messages, and actions which accumulate during the early stages of a divorce and make both people cynical and suspicious about anything the other one does.

Gradually, of course, everything settles down a bit. The parents generally work out some means of interaction and communication which doesn't trigger violent scenes, and the children adapt to the visitation process as kids have adapted to things ever since we first stood on our hind legs. How difficult that adjustment is depends on the parents involved, and the degree of maturity they are each willing to bring to the situation. Among the majority of people I've interviewed, those who have been divorced longest seemed to be the most amiable (provided they were still in contact through the kids). Those who tended to carry complaints and grudges past the transitional period of a year or so were usually so neurotically entangled with each other that they had never achieved an actual divorce, regardless of what the legal documents said. For the most part, however, both parents had reached an equilibrium of dissent, and had set about building new and separate adult futures which nonetheless provided for the very present needs of their mutual youngsters.

It is at this point, when most of the initial fireworks have sputtered out and there is some semblance of reliable stability in the relationships between the family members, that the long-term complaints and disadvantages of any custody arrangement come to the surface. These are the deep-rooted problems, the comments that reflect concern about the overall way of life, not just the passing abrasions between particular personalities. I have heard them from young women with preschoolers, older mothers whose children are almost grown, career women and those who have opted to stay at home. They are the same concerns voiced by the welfare recipient and the financially comfortable, and neither race nor religion nor education seems to have much bearing on them. Sometimes the words come out as indictments, sometimes whines. Occasionally they will be whispered without hope, or presented as flat statements of fact, but they always connect with a place of pain and disappointment, either for the mother herself or for the children.

Unfortunately, instead of blaming the custody system which creates many of these difficulties, the single mother tends to blame her ex. She sees the problems as being the result of his behavior, and finds justification in pointing out how his actions, or lack of them, are contributing to the discomfort of "her" family. Obviously, if he would change his attitude, things would be better for all concerned. Whether she takes the position of a martyred matriarch who is grieving for her deprived children or that of an infuriated and castrating tigress, she lays the woes of the world on her ex's doorstep and sees his inability to do anything about them as another example of the failure between them.

"Why Doesn't He Devote More Time and Interest to the Children, Both for Their Sakes and for Mine? The Boys Particularly Need a Father Figure."

This is the classic comment from single mothers, and one of the first expressed in discussion groups. It is invariably brought up by the women who have been divorced for more than a year, and seems to stem from a vague, if only sometimes grudgingly admitted, recognition that the children need their father. It also makes an oblique plea for an occasional small vacation from motherhood for herself, something that most mothers feel the need of, but are afraid to acknowledge openly.

There are a number of factors that contribute to this complaint, and they range from the casual awareness that it's awkward being without a male parent (what do you do for Father-Daughter Banquets, for instance, or Dad's Day at the local ball park?) to the all-out worry about the effect of the father's absence on the children in general. Therefore it's worth looking at the components of this problem simply to gain some concept of the scope involved.

No matter what your family structure was before the separation, there are bound to be areas of skill, knowledge, or simply time-sharing companionship which your ex contributed to the children, and which you notice the lack of now. It may have been the capability of building or repairing toys, trains, or bikes; the removal of splinters (and fears); the telling of stories or reading of the funny papers; the organizing of fishing weekends; or making homework understandable. Whatever his talents were, they aren't there on a regular basis anymore, and you'll probably find yourself caught in the classic double bind that almost all single mothers experience: "Why the blazes isn't he here when the children need him? If he so much as sneezes in our direction I'll drive him off with a shotgun!"

These conflicting feelings, which include but are not limited to vexation, frustration, justification, indignation, and perpetuation of all of the above, frequently bring on all kinds of mental twitches. These are the sort of psychological tic that surfaces when you realize you're in a double bind which is both ludicrously funny and bruisingly serious. For instance, if your forte is Political Science and his is Math, you're likely to experience one of these twitches if your progeny comes home with a less than acceptable grade in Algebra. Feeling on the one hand that the children should have the benefit of the sort of help their father could give them, and resenting that they don't have it, you also have to admit that if he took to showing up to help them with their homework every couple of days you would consider it a complete and unwarranted invasion of your own space and privacy, and not be willing to tolerate it. You can't expect the homework to pile up between visits, but you break out in hives at the idea of more frequent contact, and instead of doing anything really constructive about the problem, you sit and twitch, running the gamut from a sort of ticklish jerk to the onset of a full-scale epileptic seizure. It's the basis of grand tragedy and comic opera at one and the same time, and if you can see the humor in it and in yourself, it will help a lot where your sanity is concerned.

Sometimes single mothers try to take the place of two parents in their offspring's lives. Recognizing that somehow the adults have cheated the children out of the natural interaction with two parents, she may try to supply twice as much of her company, on the theory that quantity will obscure the difference in quality. This is particularly noticeable in the mother who is raising a son alone. It is assumed that daughters, living with the same-gender parent, will automatically have parental support and encouragement in their activities, but boys, lacking a daily father, will miss the chance to share recreational pursuits with a caring adult. Thus many single mothers become involved in Boy Scouts, go out to every Little League game, and learn to fish, ski, or talk intelligently about CBs in an effort to give their sons support in such areas. Some may already be actively involved in these pastimes, while others make a point of taking them up in order to have things to share with their sons. This is all very fine (provided it doesn't embarrass the boy), but if you think that by so doing you can be a "dad" to your child, you're woefully mistaken!

You may be a more than adequate mother—a real jewel, as a matter of fact; but there is no way under heaven that you can be a father. And the children know it, feel it, and often resent it. This is particularly true of the pubescent boy, who may be inwardly very angry and hurt that he doesn't have closer contact with his absent father, and outwardly takes it out on the too-present mother. That's not to say that such boys don't love their mothers: only that those mothers can't fill the youngsters' needs for a father.

Single mothers consistently worry about whether or not their sons have an adequate male role model. Sometimes this is the result of realizing the boy's own needs and desires for a father, but more often it stems from anxiety about the young man's sexual orientation. There is a great deal of fear in our society that our sons will grow up to be homosexual, and almost every single mother I've talked with who had male children has expressed concern about this possibility. The more pronounced the mother's dependency on stereotype role definitions (all little girls grow up to be mommies, and all little boys must become he-men), the more likely she is to feel real consternation at the notion that her children might not learn how to follow those rigidly prescribed roles. The idea seems to be that if there is an oversupply of female authority in his life, the boy-child will tend toward homosexuality, either because he himself wishes to be a woman, or because he needs to attract the love of a man to replace that of his missing father. One can counter this dictum with an equally valid and often-voiced admonition against putting boys in an all-male environment, where the continual contact with the same sex for all social, emotional, and physical companionship could encourage too much social, emotional, and physical intimacy. Both arguments are considered sound as far as the psychological dynamics are concerned, as each has been a recognized factor in the backgrounds of various homosexual people. But it should be noted that the parental fear and anxiety on this subject appears to be far greater than the actual statistics would seem to warrant, since the estimated number of homophiles is considerably lower than the estimated percentage of boys raised without fathers.[1]

How reasonable these fears are depends largely on the individuals involved, and the sense of love and approval and acceptance the child receives from both sexes. The dynamics of any adult love relationship, be it homosexual or heterosexual in nature, are much too beautifully complex to be summed up in a single broad statement about a person's childhood, however. So if this worry has been nagging at the back of your mind of late, remember that almost all single mothers have the same doubts and qualms, and that encouraging consistent, supportive contact between the boy and his father will at the very least help to alleviate your own anxiety on the subject.

By the same token, daughters are just as much in need of adult male companionship as sons are. Although the obvious need for an adult model of the same gender is met when a girl lives with her mother, the effect of father-absence on daughters can be quite traumatic. Without the natural contact and give-and-take between herself and a trusted older male relative, the girl may become shy, reticent, or even fearful of men. I've never heard a mother worry that the lack of a loving relationship with her father would necessarily lead her daughter to become a lesbian, though it is just as valid a premise as the one about boys and homosexuality. (Probably the idea that the girl will pattern her behavior after that of her mother creates a sense of complacency where society is concerned, and since the mother has demonstrably been involved in a heterosexual relationship, no more is thought about it.) A recent study indicates that father-absence in the lives of young girls can have a notable and lifelong effect on their self-image as well as their concepts of man–woman relationships.[2] While the study did not address itself to lesbianism, it did indicate a higher degree of seemingly promiscuous behavior on the part of girls whose fathers were absent during the daughters' childhood.

Many mothers comment on specific changes in their daughters' behavior following the separation of the parents. These changes range from bitter anger and resentment toward all men to an almost compulsive need to get attention from any male present. One mother mentioned that her grade-school daughter became an outrageous flirt after the adults divorced. If the mother had a date with a man who picked her up at the family home, the girl would throw herself at him, regardless of whether she'd met him before or not. It was obvious to the mother that the child was seeking acceptance from every man in an effort to fill the void left by the father, as well as subtly competing with the mother for attention as a female. Although it upset the mother to a degree, the problem worked itself out naturally; the girl developed a strongly active social life of her own once she reached her teens, and has not fallen into the sexually promiscuous pattern parents often worry about.

The whole subject of the relationship between daughters and their divorced fathers is much more complex than we have assumed in the past, and certainly deserves further in-depth study. In the meantime, Biller and Meredith's *Father Power* offers a number of guidelines which are relevant to the divorced father as well as the married one.

If all of these things sound terribly heavy and depressing, take heart. Most of these worries stem from deep-seated fears, doubts, and guilts that are carried along with our social assumptions, and they are common to almost all single mothers. That doesn't mean they aren't valid concerns, but they are noticeably aggravated by the sole-custody arrangement which cuts off the father's contact with the kids and puts too much responsibility on the mother. Whether her statement concerning her desire to have her ex take more part in the children's lives actually reflects an understanding of their needs, or is simply another way to express her dissatisfaction with him (he can't or won't do anything right!), the fact remains that she has begun to recognize the possibility of her ex's expanded involvement with their offspring.

For some women there is a big gap between "the children need an adult male to relate to" and "they need their father." If she feels that he manipulated, used, or abandoned her, and therefore betrayed the trust between them, she'll certainly fear that he'll do the same thing to the kids. This may be a well-founded concern—as when the father has a severe problem with alcoholism, for instance. Or it may just be a holdover of her own anger. In either case, the more reasonable, cooperative, and trustworthy the father proves to be about visits, mutual decisions, and financial support, the more likely she is to relax enough to accept the idea that he and the children can have a better and more positive relationship than he and she did. It may take a lot of patience and self-discipline on his part to assure her that he won't cause the children the same kind of pain he caused her, but unless she is holding on to a neurotic need to keep the hurt and spite alive between them, she'll begin to see the validity of his increased presence once she's felt the full weight of trying to raise the children alone.

Unfortunately, this realization may not come about until after the woman has so thoroughly entrenched herself in a position of defensive independence that she can't see any way to go back and suggest the two of them work together on the problem. If the father's visits to the children have become irregular, or he's retreated behind a very cool, formal facade, her own resentment may make open communication seem impossible. This is particularly true if he's dating someone seriously, as the mother is likely to feel not only a great deal of apprehension for her children, but also a sense of rejection and depression on a personal level herself. Thus she sits and stews about it, aggrieved that he doesn't participate in the raising of the children more, hurt for her offspring that they aren't getting the kind of attention she thinks they need from their father, and usually unable to find any way to solve the problem.

"If Only the Children Didn't See Him as the Knight in Shining Armor!"

This is the second most common complaint, and it is sometimes accompanied by the gnashing of teeth and rolling of eyes—figuratively, if not literally.

The single mother may or may not be aware of the gigantic load she has assumed in trying to raise the children by herself. For many of us the very concept of mothering involves the meeting of the needs of other, less mature or responsible humans *regardless* of whether we ourselves are tired, depressed, hopeful of doing something with an equally adult companion, or simply starving for some time to be alone. We tend to put our own needs as the lowest priority on the list, and feel decidedly guilty if we haven't filled everyone else's cup before we think about filling our own.

If you have accepted that definition of motherhood, there is little or no doubt as to how you handle the problems that arise: they are there, they affect your children, and it's up to you to cope with them, whether you want to or not. Some women become whiners, martyrs, or sickly complainers, while others take on the Supermom role, playing the executive manager on the domestic front in a manner that would be useful at the White House level itself. Yet regardless of how well (or poorly) she copes with the situation, how cheerfully (or thoughtlessly) she goes about spreading her time and energy out for the care and feeding of others, the single mother knows with a deep, throbbing resentment that the children's father isn't doing any of that sort of thing. Instead, he trots onto the scene like Prince Charming himself, full of enthusiasm and excitement about spending a weekend with his offspring, and then he spirits them off to the beach, lake, local park, or amusement center while she stays home and sorts out their dirty clothes!

The Prince Charming syndrome is particularly hard to deal with if the father lives at some distance and sees the children only once in a while. In the youngsters' eyes he creates an aura of magic and exotic entertainment with movies, picnics, shopping trips, or all-day excursions, and plays the hero to their wide-eyed admiration. By the time he brings them back—tired, probably dirty, and surely stuffed with hot dogs, French-fries, three helpings of chocolate cake, and two Cokes—the children are in a state of stuporous exhaustion, and the mother's fit to be tied. By comparison with him, she's just the daily drudge who makes them keep their elbows off the table and holds their heads when the last Coke decides to come up.

In many cases, this situation is further aggravated by the fact that the single mother doesn't have the time and money necessary to take the children to comparable places herself. With her lower earning capacity and overcommitted timetable, she rarely feels she can afford the luxury of an afternoon on the town with her kids. The idea of taking everyone to a matinee may sound just fine, but if you spend the greater part of the performance thinking about the price of your admission compared with the cost of a new pair of sneakers for your youngest, it just isn't going to be much of a party.

On the other hand, if money is no great or immediate problem in your household, and you conclude that if Dad can take them on a weekend trip, you can too, don't be surprised to find that the whole outing seems to fall short of the glamour and excitement that you associate with *his* time with the offspring. No doubt they will be delighted to take part in an excursion with you, and you can all have a good time. But if you are hoping for the same adulation that you think you have perceived in their attitude toward their sire, forget it! It is more likely that the kids will treat you, if not the event itself, with the same infuriatingly casual acceptance that they show during your everyday, commonplace activities. You are, after all, the everyday parent, the taken-for-granted adult who is always there to put Band-Aids on the toddler's knee, make cookies for the class party, and remind the older ones not to stay out too late on a school night. There is no way they can experience the thrill of anticipation about your arrival that they display about their father's; you, after all, walk through their doors numerous times every day.

Not only are you the common denominator of their daily lives; you're also the audience and receiver of news, stories, accounts of derring-do, and reports of what a great time they had with dear old Dad. Yet no matter how marvelous their activities with you are, they can't report them to you in glowing detail because you were there. It is very possible that when they tell their father about what all they've done with you, the story will take on the dimensions of an Arabian Nights adventure, and you'd be amazed to discover it all happened in Technicolor and 3-D. But you aren't likely to hear the retelling of the tale, so your own critical evaluation of it will leave it in black-and-white fuzziness as compared with the Superscope productions shared with their patriarch.

This is the old problem of the grass seeming to be greener on the other side of the fence, and as long as you're doing a comparative thing, you'll always come out lacking somewhere, somehow. The best you can do is accept the fact that for a while the children will idolize their father, and see him in an unrealistic way. Keep in mind that over a period of time their father's romantic and glorified image will gradually shrink to the human scale you know him on, and that eventually his clay feet will leave muddy footprints across the children's consciousness; but as long as he is a sometimes visitor, the bringer of special occasions and bestower of unusual activities, the divorced mother will feel plain, drab, and dull by comparison where her children are concerned. And she will tend to be both hurt and angry about it, particularly since there seems to be nothing to be done to balance things out.

"I Knock Myself Out Keeping This Family Going, While He's Out There Running Around and Having a Fine Time for Himself!"

This lament, although related to the Prince Charming problem, is different in that it involves specifically adult-oriented resentment, while the other is based on the children's reaction. In the first instance the single mother feels that the youngsters find their father more attractive to be with, while she herself is overworked and undervalued. In this case, however, the children have nothing to do with the complaint, though their constant presence is a basic cause of the problem.

The average divorced man, after a hard day at work, has the option of meeting friends for drinks, taking a date to dinner, going to plays, movies, billiard parlors, or just about anywhere else he can afford, and possibly not even returning home at all that night. There is nothing that says he *has* to spend night after night in the deadly tranquillity of his domicile, and his range of activities seems to be limited only by his imagination and willingness to kick over the traces. At least, that's how it appears to his ex.

For the single mother, the evening starts with her heading directly for the stove once her "working" hours are over. From there she cooks dinner, feeds the flock, cleans up the kitchen, and does whatever housework needs to be attended to, tells the youngsters a bedtime story and tucks them in for the night, and then settles down to mending, gossiping on the phone, reading a book, or watching the tube. Whatever she chooses to do, it does not often include going outside the boundaries of her house and garden unless she is pursuing a night-school course or has allowed herself the privilege of a date (and even then there is the problem of paying a baby-sitter). No wonder she feels trapped and angry as she thinks about her spouse with all that freedom at his disposal!

The hardest thing for a single mother to do is make time for herself. As mentioned earlier, the traditional definition of motherhood requires that she consider everyone else's needs to be of greater importance than her own. This is particularly true in the case of the divorcée who feels guilty about having deprived her children of the natural contact they would have had with their father if the marriage had been maintained. Since she has to carry the full brunt of raising the kids, she can easily end up devoting *all* of her time and energy to their welfare, and denying her own needs in the process.

Nor is the question of what she thinks she should do for the children the only consideration that traps her in the home. Many single mothers, painfully aware of their limited financial situation, cannot justify the expenditure of money just so that they can go someplace by themselves for a while. For some this is simply an excuse to stay within the security of the known routine and not venture out into the world, but for most it is a very real consideration. Even if you can appreciate the tightness of your ex's budget, you're frequently aware that he, at least, is able to spend an evening at the library without worrying over the cost of a baby-sitter. His freedom of schedule and opportunity to function as an adult among other adults may even take on the proportions of all-out irresponsibility in the eyes of the single mother who is caught in a classic double bind. On the one hand she is suffering from cabin fever to the point where she is cross and edgy with the children for no reason, and on the other she feels so guilty about putting her own needs first that she can't bring herself to do it on more than an emergency basis. Even though you may recognize that you'd be a better-balanced adult, and therefore a better parent, if you had a chance to satisfy some of your own personal needs, the traditional concept of mother love and self-lessness, coupled with the confusion of trying to be both parents to your offspring at all times, adds to the assortment of mental twitches you have to contend with. So you become a martyr to the system and continue to look upon the carefree bachelor life of your ex with envy, resentment, and frustration.

"He Tries to Control Me, in Both Big and Little Ways, and I Hate It!"

This statement, the last of the most common complaints, is generally voiced by women who had been married for more than five years, who felt their husbands had dominated and run the marriage, or who had very traditional concepts of the man–woman roles in life. Anyone else who mentioned it as a problem was more surprised than aggrieved, though all disliked the feelings involved.

For some women, the concept of taking over the tiller of the family boat and steering a relatively even course is nothing less than revolutionary. Raised in the tradition that a man looks after his wife and children at all times, they never expected to have to assume the role of independent breadwinner and family manager that they have now been called on to meet. Some feel hurt and betrayed, while others find themselves deeply enraged—not that they have to take responsibility for their own lives now, but that they should have been so totally dependent for so long prior to this! For these women, the most important goal seems to be the ability to say "I did it myself, and I did it my way!" and they wonder how they could have spent so many years believing that their spouses were the only ones qualified to make decisions, carry out plans, and generally run the ship.

"To think," sputtered one mother of four who is in her early 40s, "that I used to knock myself out trying to do things his way because I thought he was the only one who knew what should be done. Sometimes I'd want to try something else, or have a different idea about something, and he'd laugh and tell me not to worry about it, that he'd have everything under control if I'd just be quiet and do what he told me to." This woman, a seemingly efficient, well-organized, and competent mother, epitomizes a number of the suburban divorcées I've listened to. With excellent taste and good manners (as befits the wife of a schoolteacher, a businessman, or a lawyer), she verbally laid out her ex and carved him into bite-sized pieces. Why? Simply because he proved, in the final analysis, to be a very human being, and her chagrin at willingly spending years being subservient to him galled her now. That is not to say that she was bitter about him, marriage, or men in general: only that she felt she had wasted those years walking in his shadow instead of constructing her own umbrella. "Now," she says triumphantly, "I can make my own shade whenever I want to, and can stand in the sunshine if I prefer. And the most important thing I'll look for in any future relationships is the space to be myself. I want to be respected as an equal, and treated like one."

When I first began conducting Single Parent workshops and encountered this attitude repeatedly, I was both surprised and puzzled. Having spent the last fifteen years raising my two children by myself, I hadn't been involved in any form of marriage recently, and I didn't look back on my marriages as having been male-dominated. I couldn't believe that marriage patterns had changed that much in so short a time, or that my own experiences had been that uncommon. Although I had read a fair amount of the early Women's Liberation literature, I was certainly unprepared to hear so many middle-class, middle-of-the-road divorcées complaining of oppression, domination, and the dehumanizing aspects of marital bliss. Yet those sentiments came to the fore over and over again. It became abundantly clear that only a few of the women saw their husbands as intentionally using and manipulating them; for the most part, they were willing to concede that their spouses had been just as much victimized by the system as they had been, and that each had been acting out a role they had accepted back in their childhoods. Yet even though they could see that it was a culturally caused problem, they nonetheless held their exes responsible for continuing it after the divorce.

For most of these women, this new independence and self-reliance was hard won and seems, therefore, something to be guarded and protected fiercely. Many have spent months or even years adjusting to their new roles, redefining the terms of their mothering, going back to school or working hard to develop a career. The need to feel that you have established an individual identity is very important, and when an ex-husband cavalierly mentions that he thinks you should do this or that differently, you're likely to hit all the panic buttons. Here is the old domination back again, and you bristle like an angry porcupine the minute you suspect his attitude suggests that you should realign your own to conform with his.

There are several specific examples of how this kind of control can become a major problem for the divorced mother. Financially, if the single mother has to rely on child support to help pay the family bills (and in most cases she does, at least to some extent) and her ex is late or careless about getting the money to her on time, the tightrope she walks seems always to sway at his behest. And if she also gets alimony (or spousal support, as it is called in some states), she is even more dependent on him. Socially, if she has made plans for the weekend when he is going to have the children, and he calls at the last minute to postpone the entire visit, her personal life must suddenly be rearranged in order to accommodate him. These child-visitation times are frequently the only break a single mother gets when she can be away from the children. At last she has hours, or even days, when she doesn't have to worry about the kids; they are with their father, after all. She can curl up with a good book, go out dancing all night, or visit friends and relatives on her own time schedule, a briefly free agent whom no one can accuse of neglecting her offspring. No wonder most single mothers wish their exes would take the children more regularly.

But if these visits start being cancelled at the last minute, the single mother not only finds the mini-vacation she was counting on has vanished, she also has to soothe the hurt feelings of the children, and cope with double bind No. 376. How do you convey to your offspring that you understand how hurt and disappointed they are without making their father out to be an inconsiderate oaf? If you talk against him, they are bound to rush to his defense, and if you're too calm and casual about it, they may conclude that it's normal for divorced fathers to lose contact with their youngsters. Add to that your own feelings of frustration and anger at having to cancel your plans, and the old fears of control and vulnerability start cropping up again as you go into a full-fledged attack of grand mal.

On the more individual but just as important level, many ex-husbands have a particularly galling way of disparaging their wives' attempts at self-reliance. Let the wife buy a new car and the husband will find four ways in which she was cheated even before he knows how much she paid for it. And if she decides to paint the house, take in a student boarder, or move the family to an apartment, he's likely to have half a dozen reasons handy for not doing any of these things before he's found out whether she's seriously planning to do it or only opening up a discussion on the subject. The fact that he might be right on some of them is likely to be overlooked by the single mother who feels cornered, put down, and bossed about by someone who doesn't have any real understanding of the problems she copes with on a daily level.

Different women react to this in different ways. Many become uncommunicative and icily aloof, refusing to listen to a thing the ex might say, or letting him say it but refusing to respond. Others approach every contact belligerently, daring the ex to find fault with anything, and some even feel they have to outmaneuver and outcontrol him in an ongoing battle. The basic problem remains the same, however. It's very difficult to feel that you've actually assumed the responsibility for your own life if everything from the paying of your bills to the keeping of a date is dependent upon the goodwill and cooperation of someone else.

Custody Threats

There are other, much more diffuse fears and anxieties which show up in any discussion with single mothers. These tend to be general in nature, rather vaguely pervasive, and as one woman put it, "the kind of dread that is always lurking around some corner." They usually come from a sense of vulnerability and the fear of being further hurt by someone you loved and trusted. One such anxiety is the constant threat of a custody battle.

Because of the either/or nature of the usual custody arrangement, there will always be one parent who is denied child custody. Yet our courts recognize that children's needs change as time goes by, parents' circumstances may alter, and what was best at one point may not be best in the future. Hence custody matters are always subject to review if there seems to be an adequate reason for it. Although this makes good sense on one hand, some men use it as a weapon against their exes.

Many an irate father, on leaving the family domicile, has sworn, "Just you wait! I'll never let you keep the kids!" even though his attorney may well have told him there was no way he could get custody at the moment. That kind of declarative attack is more a threat against the mother than it is a statement of honest desire to have the children, and is usually aimed at asserting his power over her as he goes out the door. Unless the subject is brought up again, it's more likely that the outburst was a result of his having no other means of venting his anguish: a kind of miserable cannon shot in the dark.

Unfortunately, however, there are some men (and a number of attorneys) who have absolutely no qualms about trying to keep ex-wives "under control" by seeming to be always ready to yank the children away. This is particularly evident if the wife is asking for an increase in child support; it is not uncommon for the father's attorney to mount a custody battle as an automatic counterattack, regardless of how weak the father's case, or how obvious both the need and his ability to support his children more equitably. This sort of thing leads to mothers with ulcers, fathers with big legal fees, and children who have simply been used as pawns again! It is a shabby and wretched practice, and it is no wonder that the mother who is faced with it ends up believing that her ex is a vicious and selfish monster without any real regard for the children's feelings.

Please note that this is a far cry from the father who is seriously asking for and willing to work out some form of shared custody, which rarely takes the form of an attack and is almost always accomplished by agreement between the adults out of court. The father who honestly wants to help raise the children rarely uses his desire as a threat against his ex, since it is something he is hoping to gain, not just take away from her.

Fears of Displacement

Another negative development that often crops up is the emotional turmoil that can be brought about when a single mother discovers that her ex is seriously dating someone else. Sometimes, of course, this "other woman" has been present in the children's father's life since before the divorce; in which case the single mother is likely to make her the scapegoat for any number of things, many of which are probably undeserved. And sometimes the new woman is exactly that: new to your ex as well as your children. That doesn't necessarily make her any more acceptable, however, and it won't be an unusual reaction if you find yourself coming all unglued at the seams just thinking about the two of them together.

There appear to be several different factors involved in this reaction, and on several different levels. Most immediate is a simple, direct, and devastating jealousy which says, "Why wasn't he willing to show me the same sort of good time he's showing her?" as you slam the door on your thumb. The fact that he may have wanted to, and you wouldn't consider it, has nothing at all to do with your present mood; rational and logical responses have no weight in this situation, and there's little you can do besides turning all your thoughts and energies to something else for a while and giving the jealousy time to go away.

On the day my ex remarried, I went through a fire storm of emotions fit for a two-hour soap opera. Although I myself had been very happily remarried for almost a year at that point, I was so overwhelmed by the self-pitying, lost-child, and angry-woman-scorned syndrome, it was all I could do to keep from blurting out, "You see how he prefers her? Just went off and deserted us . . . two little children and all . . . in favor of that little bouncy chit of a girl!" The reasonable part of my brain, which effected a fair day's work at selling scarves, knew full well it wasn't anything at all like that, and that the lady involved was probably quite nice. But the emotions would have none of it at the time. By the next day all those chaotic responses had blown over, and in the years that followed, the children's stepmother and I got along quite well for the most part. But my initial reaction was anything but hospitable.

Nor did this turn out to be a unique experience on my part. The majority of divorced parents I've talked with, regardless of gender, age, custodial status, or present involvement with someone else, have gone through some sort of emotional upheaval on learning that their exes had remarried or were making plans to. There seems to be no way to block out that past connection, so the best you can do is try to turn your attention elsewhere for a while.

The next layer of fear deals with the question of how this new liaison will affect the children. Here is a demonstrable "change of circumstances" where the courts are concerned, and many a single mother girds herself for a custody battle without even finding out if that's what the new marriage will lead to. Whether or not the new stepmother is willing to accept this almost instant maternity is something the single mother rarely stops to inquire about. You know full well this is the next step in your ex-husband's campaign to do you in, and it may even come as something of a shock to discover that the new wife doesn't want the little dears on a full-time basis after all. Certainly it's worth finding out about; you won't feel comfortable until you are reassured that the children aren't going to be spirited away simply because your ex has now provided a full-time housekeeper.

But what if the children *want* to go and spend extra time with this new family? What if they are as smitten with her as he is, and you're left all alone without anyone's love and support? This is the deepest, and longest-lasting, of the fears that crop up when we feel our position in our children's lives is threatened. No matter how secure you are in loving and feeling loved by your offspring, the idea of their finding another adult more enjoyable can cause a lump of pain and confusion to lodge abruptly in your throat. Even with the best will in the world on your part, the most often repeated reminders that all children need contact with lots of other adults, and the full assurances on the other woman's part that she isn't intent on stealing the affection of your offspring, the irrational emotions of sadness, betrayal, rejection, abandonment, and/or all-out jealousy are still likely to be felt at one time or another. We have given so much of ourselves to our youngsters' welfare, how is it conceivable that they should find someone else as lovable?

Rationally, the answer lies in the fact that no one has a specific, carefully measured allotment of love to give, and just because a child loves you doesn't mean he or she can't also love someone else without stealing from your portion of affection. To demand and expect *all* of your youngster's love is selfish, possessive, and potentially quite neurotic if the attitude is fostered over a long period of time. To experience fleeting qualms, occasional pangs, and periodic sadness is simply part of living, and will happen to anyone who is at all sensitive, aware, and caring. So unless you are in a continuous snit about it, and carry the sorrow and anger with you everywhere you go, perhaps you should just chalk it up to the hazards of being human. Insisting that your ex's new lady never have contact with your kids won't help; it will only make them terribly curious, and cause further bad feelings between you and their father.

No one said it would be easy to raise children (either with or without a partner), and the parent–child relationship is probably the most vulnerable and convoluted one there is. For the typical divorced mother who has sole custody of the children and emotions like a frayed rope, it can still be a great experience. And one of the most important aspects of the situation is the willingness to understand what your own feelings are and why, as well as where your ex is coming from. The exercises below deal with your own attitudes, and the next chapter explores the difficulties most often encountered by divorced fathers.

ROLE-PLAYING
(For Women)

For many women the idea of becoming a mother, or at least playing at being a mother, goes back as far as they can remember. But although this may have been treated as something you assumed would happen, there were undoubtedly other things you thought about being; an artist, a veterinarian, a dentist, doctor or cowgirl, perhaps. Think back to those earliest years, and list the different things you once thought you might become (even if only in imagination).

When did you decide to become a mother? Did you simply assume that being a mother was the other half of being a wife? Or did you intentionally choose motherhood? Why?

What would you like to be now, besides a mother?

What are you now, besides a mother?

What do you want to be after your children are grown and leave home?

What would you do for yourself if you didn't have custody of your children (and didn't feel guilty about not having custody)?

How do you feel about other mothers who don't have their children living with them? Why?

What can your ex provide your children that you cannot?

QUALITIES

Take a piece of paper and make a list of words describing the different qualities customarily associated with women. Arrange the headings on the page as follows:

WOMEN ARE   MOTHERS ARE

Include everything you can think of that is appropriate; for instance, socially active, thoughtful of others, busy, sexy, dull, self-sacrificing, complaining, good-natured, tired, gentle, caring, trapped, dependent, and so on. Don't worry about whether all women or all mothers *are* these things; this is simply an outline of what you think of when you think of the two different terms, either positively or negatively.

Now compare the two lists. Which is the longer? Which has more negatives in it, which more positives? Are there expectations that cancel each other out? If so, draw arrows between them and circle the word you feel takes precedence for you. Which list comes closest to your self-image? Do you see yourself as a mother or a woman first, or are they both the same? Are there any basic ways in which one rules out the other?

PARENT MEMORIES
(For Mothers)

Think back to the nicest time you spent, as a child, with your own mother. Relive that experience: where you were, how you felt, what you liked about it, when it happened, and if you know, why it happened. Write it down, or draw a picture of the feelings. Let yourself re-enjoy that child–parent contact. And when you're all through playing with it, think about when, or how, or if you've been able to give your own child a similar experience.

What was the most enjoyable thing you've done with your children recently? Why was it possible? How did it come about? What was their reaction to it? How can you make comparable things happen in the future?

Remember the best time you spent, as a child, with your own father. Relive that experience: where you were, how you felt, what you liked about it, when it happened, and if you know, why it happened. Write it down, or draw a picture of the feelings if you wish. Let yourself re-enjoy that child–parent contact fully. And when you're all through enjoying it, think about what you are doing to allow your children to have a similar kind of relationship with their own father. Are you preventing him from sharing time, energy, or interests on a pleasant basis? Does your attitude keep him or them from enjoying their time together? Do you really want to deprive them of this kind of memory? What can you do to support his efforts to interact with his children more positively? How would your children answer these questions?

EXAMPLES: MOTHERHOOD

The mere fact that our mothers were mothers didn't necessarily make them good ones, any more than having children necessarily makes *us* good mothers. Yet we can learn from the negatives as well as the positives, and sometimes with much better result, since correcting a negative from your own childhood requires specific thought and attention.

Take a piece of paper and make the following lists under these headings:

POSITIVES

My mother was   *I also am*

NEGATIVES

My mother was   *I also am*

CHANGES TO BRING ABOUT

I wish my mother had been   *I am willing to be*

CHILDHOOD PATTERNS

Fill in the form below. (There is an identical one at the end of Chapter 4 for fathers.) There are no "right" or "wrong" answers, and blood relationship doesn't matter; it may have been an aunt, uncle, cousin, or friend who was most involved in your different encounters, rather than a mother or father.

INTERACTION	MALE	FEMALE
Who played with you most often as a child?		
Who punished you most often?		
Whom did you like best among your peers?		
Whom did you like best among the grown-ups?		
Who made you the happiest?		
If you had siblings, which was your favorite?		
If you didn't have siblings, which would you have most wanted to have?		
Whom were you afraid of?		
Whom did you try to please?		
Whom did you succeed in pleasing most?		
Who disappointed you most often?		
Who comforted you?		
Who was most exciting?		
Whom did you wish to be closest to?		
With whom did you share your closest secrets?		
Whom did you miss most if he or she went away?		
By whom did you want to be trusted?		
Whom did you want to be most like?		

Is there a pattern to your answers? How does it carry over to your adult life? How would your own children answer this exercise?

4
No One Ever Told Me

Traditional Custody from the Man's Viewpoint

Just as there are certain basic problems and concerns unique to the single mother in this society, so are there difficulties and worries that are common to most divorced fathers with traditional custody arrangements. These range all the way from the mundane problems about food shopping and preparation when the children visit to the crucial questions of self-worth and personal identity, and they can be literal killers. They have been generally ignored in this culture, perhaps because most of them are internal rather than external in nature, and our society seems to deny the importance of a man's inner life. Many newly divorced men have a good deal of trouble handling the emotions they encounter, and since they have little education or support for dealing with these crises, they often have no means of sharing their feelings. Considering that divorce is ranked as one of the highest-stress situations that can be encountered, second only to the death of a spouse,[1] it is amazing to me that so little has been done to prepare the man, or make comprehensible to the woman, the sort of chaos divorced fathers typically have to cope with. This, then, is a look at the effects of the divorce and customary custody practices as experienced by noncustodial fathers.

At the time of the divorce, most fathers have some sort of vague notion about becoming bachelors again (or perhaps for the first time, if they married at an early age). They may be losing their family, but society is quick to point out that they are at least gaining their freedom. This culture assumes that a newly single man wants more than to fill his life with luscious young ladies, pick up the trappings of the playboy (sports car, weekend ski trips, handsome apartment, and so on), and generally "make the most" of his new status. Still-married friends may nudge you in the ribs in appreciation of their own flights of fantasy about being "on the loose" again, which they can afford to indulge in from the security of their family-man position. The whole social attitude seems to say there's a big wide world beckoning to you, now that the shackles of the past marriage are being removed, so you can expect to start conquering it at any moment; no more worrying about broken washing machines, storm windows that need to be replaced (if she gets to keep the house, she can keep the problems too!), or which in-laws to visit when. Time to get out and about, to take advantage of your newfound freedom, to live out all those dreams that would never have been possible from the position of husband-and-father-in-the-suburbs.

Except that it doesn't work that way. One of the most common attitudes of this culture is that marriage is an invention of women for women, in order to protect themselves and the children, and that men acquiesce to it out of love and devotion to a specific woman, not because they themselves want to settle down. Recent social studies indicate that marriage is far more hazardous to the woman than it is to the man, however.[2] More wives become sick or depressed or suffer nervous breakdowns than do their unmarried sisters. And among the men, there is a higher incidence of illness, mental breakdowns, and suicide in the unmarried population. It would seem, then, that marriage is actually more beneficial to men than to women, in spite of our cultural assumption to the contrary. Certainly any divorced father will tell you that during his early adjustment to being single again, the loss of the family structure was one of the most cru-cially painful experiences.

In the typical divorce it is the father who agrees to move out, leaving the mother and children together in the family nest. There are any number of reasons for this: the assumptions that the children will continue to live with the mother alone, that a man can function more easily on his own than a woman can, that it would look "odd" if the mother moved out; or just because that's the way it's done. (One woman convinced her husband that he should be the one to move out because the children didn't have any friends whose mothers had left home at the time of a di-vorce!)

When, in the heat of anger, hurt, or exhaustion, the father agrees to leave the family home, he usually hasn't really grasped how difficult that may be. Many is the divorcing father who, faced with an order to leave his house within a specified number of days, suddenly finds every place he looks at to be cold, bleak, dreary, and too expensive. Some men procrastinate until literally the last minute, finding dozens of reasons for not taking any of the apartments they look at. And many others move in with friends (usually other divorced men like themselves), to share quarters with them until they can get their feet under them enough to face finding a separate place of their own. Occasionally there is a sense of relief, particularly if he is the one who is seeking the divorce; but even that is generally mixed with grief, fear, anger, doubt, rejection, self-pity, and recriminations. And more than one divorced father has later told of stifling his sobs in a tear-stained pillow before going to sleep during his first nights of newfound "freedom."

Transition

Unlike the mother who remains with the children, the divorcing father hasn't much of a transition period. He is abruptly thrown into his new role, and usually just as suddenly reacts to it. There are the immediate realizations of the economic pinch, the discom-fiture of fending for himself in strange surroundings, and the grad-ual recognition that he must come to grips with his emotions about the ending of the marriage. All of which leads to noticeable depression, instability, sadness, feelings of inadequacy and point-lessness, and the onset of what can become a very important time of reevaluation and exploration.

Much of this is kindled by the question of how and why the marriage failed. Many men don't stop to look at the emotional dynamics of their marriages until it is too late, and then they are inundated by dozens of conflicting emotions all at once. The basic structure of your lifelong belief system has been called into question, and you begin the painful, but potentially constructive, process of recognizing things you simply took for granted before. I recently heard one fellow, now a very aware and sensitive man, admit that during the last five years of their twenty-year marriage his wife had been trying, unsuccessfully, to tell him that the relationship was in real danger. Only when she declared she was filing for divorce was he really willing to listen to her, and by that time it was too late. "I just assumed she had a headache when-ever she brought the subject up," he said ruefully. "Now I won-der why she put up with it for so long!"

And for many men the idea of failure, quite apart from the reasons or the logic involved, casts a kind of pall over everything. One young man I know always mentioned that he was divorced as soon as he was introduced to someone, as though this were something people must be warned about in advance. The social stigma of divorce may have been lifted to some degree, but the psychological blow to the male ego continues to take its toll.

Oddly enough, many men are much better fathers after di-vorce than they were before. They seem to be more willing to invest the time and interest to really listen to, respond to, and become involved with their youngsters with a new enthusiasm. It would seem that the complacency of their marital attitudes and expectations needs to be challenged before some men are able to see what is actually happening. Or perhaps it requires the deeply painful realization that they have lost the right to daily contact with their youngsters to bring about this change in attitude. In either case, many a father finds out just how much his children mean to him *after* he becomes separated from them, and this awareness of loss generally leads to a cycle of depression. It begins when he moves out, and continues to intensify each time he has contact with the children. Now recognized as a very real psychological problem, called separation trauma, it can be summed up in one sentence:

"I'm So Depressed After Seeing the Children, I Begin to Wonder How I Can Go On!"

This comment, heard in one form or another from almost every divorced father with typical visitation arrangements (visits every other weekend, with an evening during the off week), didn't make much sense to me at first. As a single mother with sole custody, I couldn't see where his problem lay. He got to see the children with what the courts themselves said was "reasonable" frequency; was free to take them overnight on alternate weekends; and was encouraged to have contact with them on a midweek night as well. Often this was more specific attention than he had paid to them during the marriage, although fathers under 30 usually have been more involved parents during the marriage than their counterparts who are now in their 40s, and some have had a long history of nurturing their children that goes back to the time of birth itself. I didn't even begin to understand the emotions involved until one father came to talk to me specifically about his views on custody and stayed to share his experiences as a visiting parent.

The story began with the father driving over to pick up his two young daughters for their weekend visit. On the way he began to feel distinctly uneasy, full of fear and apprehension that the mother would somehow keep him from seeing the children. Although she had never done so, her attitude made it very clear that she considered his rights of visitation pretty low on her list of priorities, and he was continually reminded of that fact. Each time he dreaded her appearance in the doorway, afraid she would announce to the whole world that the girls had a cold, a birthday party to go to, or some other reason for not joining him that weekend.

Getting the youngsters safely into the car and driving away made him both angry and scared; there was a feeling that he was some kind of thief, stealing his own children from their home and skulking away with them, and he had to constantly fight the desire to look over his shoulder to see if she was following them, clenched fist waving in alarm. This, coupled with his frustration at not being able to change the situation, triggered a complexity of emotions that amazed him in their powerfulness.

The visits were enjoyable, yet when he woke on Sunday morning there was a knot in his stomach and he rarely ate the big breakfasts he prepared for the children. All morning long he dreaded taking them back, and by the time he turned onto the block where the family house stood, his palms were sweating and he felt decidedly nauseated. Stopping at the curb, he'd let the children out, kiss them goodby, and watch them run up the walk to a house he himself would always be forbidden to enter (although he had bought it for the family several years before, and continued to pay the mortgage on it). Often the mother, not wanting to have contact with him, would stand behind the door and open it without showing herself, so that he had the impression of some giant maw devouring his offspring, and he would sit there with the tears running down his face until he was composed enough to drive away.

After several months of this, when he found that the situation was getting worse rather than better, he took to letting the children off at the nearest corner, waiting to make sure that they went into the house safely but hoping to avoid the agony of too close contact. The mother took great umbrage at this, seeing it as irresponsibility toward the children and demanding that he return to the old pattern of letting them off at the curb in front of the house. In the face of her anger he found it impossible to explain how he felt about the situation, and fearing the loss of even his every-other-week visits, he went back to the original system.

Finally things got so miserable that he picked up the phone one day and called his ex to say that he simply couldn't take the girls on the coming weekend. This became a pattern, at first only occasionally, then gradually more often—not because he didn't want to have his children with him but because he couldn't face the emotional upheaval each time he had to return them. By the end of the year he was seeing them only once a month, and the mother, highly indignant, concluded that "the bastard doesn't care about them anymore!'' and added that to her list of grievances.

This is a classic example of separation trauma, and while not every divorced father attempts to solve the problem by discontinuing his visits with the children, it appears that most consider it, and a surprising number do so. In one study one third of the men ''who had initially been highly involved, attached, affectionate parents reported that they couldn't endure the pain of seeing their children only intermittently and by two years after the divorce had coped with this stress by seeing their children infrequently although they continued to experience a great sense of loss and depression.'' [3]

Obviously, if the depression and sense of loss continue, not seeing the youngsters is hardly an effective way of handling the problem. Nor is a retreat into alcoholism, illness, or suicide; yet these problems are all more prevalent among divorced fathers than among any other group. In interviewing fathers for this book, I ran across case after case in which some major physical accident or sickness had debilitated the father during the first year after separation. Frequently the accidents happened within the first several months; one father I know, during the week after his wife left the house, stepped off a curb outside his office and broke his leg! And another father, on the first weekend of child visiting, took everyone to the ice-skating rink, where he proceeded to break his own hip. Dr. Melvin Roman's research on the effect of divorce upon fathers shows that between 60 and 70 percent of the men studied underwent a serious illness or accident shortly after separation, and all could attribute it, in one way or another, to their depression and confusion over losing their family. [4]

Insurance companies are well aware of the hazards of divorce, and they boost their premiums accordingly. So much of the emotional and psychological confusion spills over into physical misjudgment and dysfunction, there is a notably higher risk of all kinds of accidents.

Nor does the depression go away after the first year. It isn't uncommon for some men to continue to feel the loss of normal contact with their children for many years, and to brood about it off and on until the youngsters are actually full-grown. And when mixed with the other aspects of living in an either/or child-custody situation, the long-term depression, emptiness, loneliness, and general powerlessness lead a man to conclude that he is, in Dr. Roman's words, "the disposable parent."

"I Hate Being a Disneyland Daddy!"

Next to the almost universal separation trauma, one hears laments about the hollowness of the relationship between divorced fathers and their offspring. Many fathers exhaust themselves, and their children, by dashing about trying to make each visit as memorable as possible. So you splurge on trips to special places, unusual shopping sprees, or a round of frantic activities as though you were never going to see the kids again. And in the long run you end up feeling empty, broke, and further depressed. "I know I don't have to 'buy' the children," one father exclaimed, "but when you're stuck in a studio apartment, without even enough beds to go around, how are you going to entertain them at home? Naturally we go out and do things 'out there.' It fills up the time—but it costs a lot, too. And it's usually a matter of someone else entertaining us, not us entertaining each other. So after I take the kids back to their mother's and I try to think about what we *did* together, I feel like there's a big fat zero!"

This problem of what to do with weekend children is a constant and puzzling dilemma. Trying to fit a week's worth of normal and simple contact into two days certainly doesn't make it, and just about the time that everyone has settled down to the routine at Daddy's house, the children have to go back to Mama's. Since many men rent studios or very small apartments at the time of the separation, the lack of household space often enters the picture. Young children are into everything and demand a lot of physical exercise in safe surroundings, so fathers with preschoolers often seem to spend most of their visits in local parks and playgrounds, provided the weather allows it. School-children invariably discover that the book, tools, games, or whatever that they want to use have been left behind at the custodial parent's house, and so resort to TV watching or general boredom. By the time you're dealing with teen-agers, they can be so completely wrapped up in their own lives and interests, it's all you can do to get them to come visit at all, unless you offer some sort of specific outing. So the divorced father muddles through, often trying to alternate between casual visits and special occasions, yet still feeling that somehow the entire relationship is shallow, empty of meaningful experiences, and exhausting financially and emotionally.

"She at Least Has the Children to Keep Her Company; I'm All Alone."

The loneliness of the divorced father seems doubly difficult to handle when he thinks about the fact that his ex at least has the children to talk to on a regular and ongoing basis. For him life may well have become a dismal round of work hours, TV dinners, time spent in front of the tube, and a restless night tossing in a rented bed. Or, unable to face what one divorced father called "the four square walls of anonymousness" that make up the average bachelor apartment, he may go out simply in order to get out. Without direction, particular thought, or deliberate action, he takes to sitting in the local beer hall, going to grade B movies, or looking for some sort of social activity to take his mind off his misery, regardless of how dreary that activity might be. "Anything—I'd do anything, go anywhere, with anyone, just to avoid going home to that emptiness!" exclaimed one recently divorced fellow, and all the other fathers in the group nodded in recognition of that feeling. This is particularly painful to the father whose ex and children have stayed in the family home.

As far as socializing on any kind of intentional level is concerned, that seems to be a very individual matter with each man, though there are general reactions that can be seen as behavioral patterns.

Many is the divorced father who, hoping that his new liberation will lead to exploration of all the things he was too shy or unknowing to take advantage of before he was married, finds that he is still too shy and unknowing. Plus the fact that now he's twice as frightened of risking rejection. This man may not date at all, or only on the most casual level, and then always with one foot outside the door. As one divorce attorney aptly put it, many newly separated men want sex about as much as a man getting over dysentery wants a big meal! So he nibbles a little here and there, but never seems willing to get involved in any truly intimate relationship.

Other men very readily fall into a pattern of heavy social activity, going to parties, dances, singles bars and trips into bed as often as they can arrange it. Frequently this is a desperate effort to fight off loneliness by attempting to find some sort of self-affirmation through the eyes of new women. These relationships are almost invariably based on the man's need to feel attractive rather than on any true rapport with his partner, and in some cases the concept of quantity is substituted for quality; they may all be one-night stands with partners whose names he's forgotten by morning, but they seem better than nothing at all! Although he may announce to the world that he's looking for a "real and meaningful relationship," such a man is mostly asking for ego strokes and a chance to prove what a sexy, desirable, and exciting male he is. Very little of that has to do with the woman involved, however, and he is usually a long way from working out the essential problems that created his divorced state to begin with. As an occasional boost to the morale, a flurry of dating or a limited affair can be good for both men and women, but shouldn't be used to take the place of the honest growth divorce can bring about.

Regardless of how much or how little social and/or sexual activity you're involved in, the fact remains you can't get away from being a divorced father, a family man without family, a patriarch without clan. And when all is said and done, it boils down to the simple fact that you miss the children. Let a mother be deprived of her offspring, and the world cries out with indignation that the sanctity of motherhood has been sullied; but let the father cry out against the outrage of having his children taken from him, and the world tells him he should go on and make a new life for himself. Angry, frustrated, lonely, and hurt, his depression and bitterness deepen, particularly when he thinks of his ex. There she is, sitting by the fireplace, chatting with the youngsters, watching them play checkers, tucking them in at night, knowing there'll be someone to talk to over the breakfast table. For her, life moves on within the comfort of the family system, while he is shunted off to an apartment where even the furniture belongs to someone else! The only statement of his individual presence is the razor by the basin, and that's pretty cold comfort when he's feeling excluded from all the warm things of the world. No wonder he envies his ex, and thinks about getting custody for himself.

"When I Try to Talk with Her, About Anything, She Cuts Me Off and Just Won't Listen!"

Usually expressed with a combination of injured innocence, total bewilderment, and snappish annoyance, this sentiment is heard over and over again. It is most often voiced by the man over 35, the father who had been married for at least five years, or the fellow who has a very traditional view about the roles of men and women in a family. It connotes confusion, hurt, and a sense of betrayal, whether cloaked in anguish or the tones of a martyr, and it stems from all those cultural assumptions we bought as youngsters ourselves.

For many men, the criterion of their personal success was held to be how well they guided the lives and times of their families. A man may be just a cog in the assembly line professionally, but in his home he was boss. These are the fathers who believe that regardless of all else, it is up to them to find the right solution to each problem, make the right decision for the good of the family, and thereby command the respect and admiration of the wife and children. Adhering to the concept of "noblesse oblige," they struggle to keep the family ranks together, the wolf from the door, and anarchy at bay. On their shoulders falls the burden of looking out for the whole clan; it is their responsibility, no matter what, and the fact that their wife went off and did a foolish thing like getting a divorce doesn't change that duty one bit!

One very dear friend put it this way: "I don't have any choice about whether I look after her or not. She cut me up in little pieces, and it's taken me several years to bind up the wounds, but when I see her doing something foolish, I can't just sit by and let her do it, after all. I mean, I have to at least point out what she should do instead.''

Unfortunately, this somewhat condescending, paternalistic approach to an ex-wife is almost guaranteed to stir up trouble. No matter how well-meant your effort, how careful your choice of words, or how sincere the concept you're trying to express, you meet a brick wall of suspicion, resistance, or hostility. The first few times it happens you figure she's had a bad day (like the wife with the headache), but when it reaches the point where you realize she simply won't let you communicate at all, the bottom drops out of your stomach and it feels as though the whole of your identity has just been stamped "null and void." Not only does she have the children, and probably a fair-sized hunk of your paycheck: she also has the power to simply cut you off. You don't exist, your feelings are superfluous, your ability to shape and control the destiny of your family has been wiped out, and you can't even wish her a happy birthday without getting your head bitten off. In short, you have been divorced.

Most men react to this by simply closing up themselves: if she won't listen to them, they won't have anything to say. Forget that you had planned to help the children pick out her Christmas gift; she can do without. And never mind that you were working out a tax-return arrangement that would be advantageous to her as well; she can go scratch for any further help from you on anything! Your pride, ego, identity, and self-esteem have all been assaulted, and you don't know what else to do besides fight fire with fire.

With any luck (and the willingness to reexamine your own attitudes and assumptions), divorce can indeed lead to tremendous personal growth and development. Many are the men, and women, who discover just how limited their perception of themselves and their relationship with their spouses has been, once they stop defending their past positions and start exploring their potential for present improvement. And this not infrequently leads the divorced father to inner discoveries that he specifically wants to share with his ex as the children's mother. (It doesn't mean he's looking for a reconciliation: only for a cessation of hostilities.) Your appreciation of the children as people, not just responsibilities; your recognition of how much she has contributed to their upbringing and development; your sadness over past hurts inflicted by both parties; and your desire to say, "I don't want to be your enemy" may all be on the tip of your tongue when she's not around. Yet her cold determination to deny any sort of personal contact can freeze you into a strangled and icy silence. I have heard divorced fathers, when talking with other people, all but plead for a chance to reestablish some sort of human rapport with their exes, only to come off sounding like verbal armadillos when actually given the opportunity to communicate with them. All those years of training to be aggressive, competitive businessmen somehow get in the way of this once-most-personal-of-all relationships, and the average divorced father falls back on a guarded, gruff hostility that is in no way going to reassure his ex about his intentions. Thus the battle goes on, with no one winning and everyone full of adrenaline and twitches.

Fear of Propaganda

Divorced fathers, like single mothers, experience a number of general fears and anxieties which may not be specific complaints, yet show up over and over again in their conversations. And the most often expressed of these is concern that the mother with sole custody will turn the youngsters against them.

Many divorced fathers feel that the nature of their relationship with their offspring is dependent upon the whims and fancies of their exes, and they find themselves both helpless and angry about this. Just as some women fear financial and psychological manipulation by past spouses, many a father is constantly afraid that if the children's mother is bitter toward him, she'll teach the children to see him in an unfavorable light. Nor is this necessarily an unfounded fear. I know of one family in which the mother spent the first two years of the separation telling everyone, including the youngsters, how badly her husband had behaved. As her bitterness and disappointment in her own single life grew, she spread a number of stories about him, probably feeling quite justified in doing so, but certainly horrifying her ex. Although their mutual friends, and even her own relatives, soon came to see her as a vindictive, shrewish, warped human being, the children accepted her comments as literal truths. "Much of what she said just wasn't true; she was rewriting history to suit her own needs.

But what could I say in my own defense without sounding as though I was attacking the veracity of this poor brave mother who was struggling along all by herself? I knew she'd thrown me out, but to hear her tell it, I'd deserted both her and the children, and they eventually came to believe it," her ex said.

As time progressed, the children grew more and more conflicted in their feelings about their father, and their reaction was doubly painful for him to observe. "It finally reached a point where I couldn't see that anything positive was being served by my visits. Not only was I coping with all my own feelings, but to see the confusion and hostility in my children broke my heart. I simply had to take a step back from the whole thing emotionally, and try to give us all time to get our balance back. I just kept praying that as they got older, they'd begin to understand that there were certainly two sides to the divorce!"

Ironically, when the mother eventually remarried, the children were shipped off to live with their father, since they couldn't get on with the new stepparent. Because this woman had fairly successfully taught the youngsters their father was an ogre, the adjustment to this new development has been rough for all concerned.

Fortunately, not all women are as selfish or neurotic as that mother was; most try to make an effort to keep the children's regard for their father unsullied and intact. Yet just as the constant reminder of an impending custody battle can hang like a shadow over the single mother, the fear of negative propaganda is a source of continual worry for the divorced father. Whether it is a valid one or not, he feels powerless to do anything about it, and it is this helplessness that threatens him most of all. He has lost his sense of power, control, and authority, all of which are things he's been raised to believe he must exercise within his family.

Money Matters

The one last area in which the divorced father maintains some semblance of power has to do with the child support and alimony he gives to his ex, and he often guards it jealously!

To a large degree a man's accomplishment in this culture is measured in terms of money: how much he can command in the marketplace; how well he invests; and how wisely he manages the family fortunes. Women, on the other hand, are frequently taught that it's impolite to discuss money; that it's really rather tawdry stuff, fit only for spending. The past assumptions have been that a woman's financial worth was determined by her choice of a mate, and she was often reminded that "it's just as easy to love a rich man as a poor one." Since there is still little admission that a girl may be the breadwinner in her future family, she is not usually educated to think in heavily monetary terms; it is assumed her husband will handle all the financial matters.

As a result, many women have no notion of how much emotional weight men put on the subject of money, and very specifically, *their* money. A man's financial assets, the fruits of his labors and the expression of his cleverness, may take on a whole symbolic meaning to him which she is never aware of, and probably wouldn't appreciate if she did understand it. I once observed a woman trying to reassure her ex by telling him that she and the children responded to him as a person, not just a source of money. "You aren't your checkbook!" she cried, appalled at the horrible expression on his face. What she meant as an affirmation of his human worth was, in his eyes, a total negation of his past years' work and personal talent. No wonder they hadn't been able to stay married!

When a divorced father feels totally cut out of the family unit, a disposable parent where the children are concerned, disparaged by his ex, and dehumanized to the point of being nothing but a money machine, his bitterness and resentment often spill over into his attitude about sending money to the family he feels he has so little part in. In this area, at least, he retains a vestige of power, and some fathers use money as both a defensive and offensive weapon whenever possible. Yet because there is so much stress put on this one factor, the single father may lose all perspective on the subject.

It is not uncommon for angry and hurting fathers to claim that their exes are keeping the children just to get "a free ride" with the child-support check each month. Far from realizing the problems those exes are coping with, the father is simply using that as a convenient, if shallow, means of letting off steam. He is as righteous in protecting his symbolic child (money) from the demands of his ex as she is in guarding her sense of motherhood by refusing to relinquish her power over the offspring. And while most such fathers are willing to recognize and agree to the idea that they should contribute to the support of their children, they forget that the check they make payable to their ex is actually necessary for the progeny. All they can see is the threat to their one last stronghold, and they may well develop the nature of a bad-tempered pit bull the moment anything having to do with finances comes up. An honest appraisal of the actual cost of raising the children, plus recognition of the time and energy involved, may be helpful in getting them to see that most child-support orders are certainly not even adequate, much less exorbitant;[5] certainly it should help to allay some of the more unreasonable emotional reactions.

Fear of Replacement

For many divorced fathers, the presence of another man in their ex-wife's life is the largest threat of all. One 30-year-old man, who seemed to have made a fairly good adjustment to being single again after three years or so, told of his reaction to the discovery that "*my* nice little Catholic *wife*, Mary Ellen, was actually going out with other fellows!" Infuriated, frightened, outraged, and unable to do anything about it, he walked around in a storm of violent emotions for more than a week, alternately raging and crying. Fortunately, he was going to a psychologist at the time, and they were able to work together on sorting out just what he felt and what he could honestly do about it. "Part of it was pure jealousy and the feeling of being rejected; I still hadn't found a way to live with the fact that it's all right to love Mary Ellen without being her husband. Somehow I hadn't really gotten divorced, emotionally. And some of it was anger that I wasn't doing as well in my own social life. But the biggest aspect of all was the fear that with the daily presence of another man in their lives, my youngsters would quit looking to me as their daddy."

For the man to whom being a father means primarily being the responsible authority in his offspring's lives, the concept of a close liaison between his children and another male is indeed a heavy threat. Someone else will be there to answer all the little questions, to shape the standards, to share the daily delights and disasters. And not only does that someone else get to be with your kids on a more stable basis: you don't have any say in the matter at all. Your ex can go off and marry him without even introducing him to you, and all you'll ever know about him is what the children relate. You feel cut off, ignored, and replaced, all at once, and unable to change any of it. All of which leads many men to wonder if they should simply step out of the picture and disappear once their exes have remarried.

Some men have expressed fear that if the new stepparent wants to adopt the children, there is nothing the father can do to prevent it. This is not the case, legally. Fathers who allow their children to be adopted by their ex's new partner have to sign papers giving their permission; there is no way that can be done surreptitiously. Nor are all stepfather–real-father relationships negative; I've had the pleasure of meeting a number of men in these positions who have worked out comfortable ways of sharing the children so that the youngsters benefit from all their parents. It may not be the most common situation, but it's certainly possible if you want to do it.

And that brings us back to the subject of what you want for yourselves and your children, now that you've had a chance to look at and understand the major pitfalls involved in the traditional custody arrangement. It is my hope that in recognizing the factors involved where each of you is concerned, you'll be able to look for ways to alleviate some of the worst pressures. It is possible, with an honest attempt at understanding what each is feeling and reacting to, for a divorced couple to work out a system of communication, respect, and even trust where the children are concerned so that the "worst of all possible worlds" won't happen to them. You don't need to be friends (although some divorced parents are), nor do you even have to *like* each other. All you have to do is be willing to consider what your priorities are as a divorcing family, and then set about finding ways to implement them. The purpose of the exercises below is specifically to help you recognize what's happening to you, your ex, and possibly even your children as you cope with these problems. And the next chapter deals with specific ways and techniques for creating your own best solution to how to raise the children after the marriage ends.

ROLE-PLAYING
(For Men)

Most boys, as they are growing up, imagine themselves as being any number of different things: a fireman, pilot, writer, teacher, lawyer, or doctor. And some assume that they will also be fathers. Think back to your childhood and try to remember when you first played at being a daddy. Do you remember what you did in that play? Take care of and feed the children? Act as the disciplinarian? Build a house, pay the bills, go off to "work" and only come home in time for the pretend "mother" to fix dinner? List the different things you thought being a father would involve, even if only in imagination.

When did you decide to become a father? Was it a conscious choice, or did it simply happen? Did you assume that being married also meant being a parent? How much were you involved with the youngsters when they were little? Why?

Why do you want sole or shared custody of your children? How much does anger at your ex have to do with it?

If you became a single parent, how would your life change now? How would it affect your work?

Who would care for the children while you're on your job? Would you hire a housekeeper? Why?

What can you provide your children that your ex cannot?

What can she provide that you cannot?

QUALITIES

Take a piece of paper and make a list of words describing the different qualities customarily associated with men. Arrange the headings on the page as follows:

MEN ARE   FATHERS ARE

Jot down everything you can think of that is applicable; for instance, you might include independent, considerate, busy, sexy, responsible, tired, bossy, gentle, socially active, boring, helpful, adventurous, trapped, aggressive, self-sacrificing, complaining, generous, worried, and so on.

Now compare the two lists. Which one is longer? Which has more negatives in it, which more positives? Are there words you feel cancel each other out? If so, draw arrows between them and circle the one that takes precedence. Which list comes closer to your self-image? Do you see yourself as a man or a father first, or are they both the same? Are there any basic ways in which one rules out the other?

PARENT MEMORIES
(For Fathers)

Remember the nicest time you spent, as a child, with your own father. Relive that experience: where you were, how you felt, what you liked about it, when it happened, and if you know, why it happened. Write it down, or draw a picture of the feelings if you wish. Let yourself re-enjoy that child–parent contact. And when you're all through playing with it, think about when, or how, or if you've been able to give your own child a similar experience.

What was the most enjoyable thing you've done with your children recently? Why was it possible? How did it come about? What was their reaction to it? How can you make such things happen again in the future?

Think about the best time you spent, as a child, with your own mother. Relive that experience: where you were, how you felt, what you liked best about it, when it happened, and if you know, why it happened. Write it down, or draw a picture of the feelings if you wish. Let yourself re-enjoy that child–parent contact fully. And when you're all through playing with it, think about what you are doing to allow your children to have a similar kind of good time with their own mother. Are you preventing her from sharing time, energy or interests on a pleasant basis? Does your attitude keep her or them from enjoying themselves together? Do you really want to deprive them of this kind of memory? What can you do to support her efforts to interact with her children more positively? How would your children answer these questions?

EXAMPLES: FATHERHOOD

Many people assume that we learn how to be parents from our own parents, and to some degree this is true. However, it is just as valid to learn what not to do from negative examples as it is to copy what was done on a positive basis. Sometimes, because negative examples require more thought on our own part and the conscious choice not to repeat those problems, such a background can be more useful than a positive one, since we frequently don't question what makes the positives work.

Take a piece of paper and make a list under each of the following headings:

POSITIVES

My father was   *I also am*

NEGATIVES

My father was   *I also am*

CHANGES TO BRING ABOUT

I wish my father had been   *I am willing to be*

CHILDHOOD PATTERNS

Fill in the form below. There are no "right" or "wrong" answers, and blood relationship doesn't matter; it may have been an aunt, uncle, cousin, or friend who was most involved in your different encounters, rather than a mother or father.

INTERACTION	MALE	FEMALE
Who played with you most often as a child?		
Who punished you most often?		
Whom did you like best among your peers?		
Whom did you like best among the grown-ups?		
Who made you the happiest?		
If you had siblings, which was your favorite?		
If you didn't have siblings, which would you have most wanted to have?		
Whom were you afraid of?		
Whom did you try to please?		
Whom did you succeed in pleasing most?		
Who disappointed you most often?		
Who comforted you?		
Who was most exciting?		
Whom did you wish to be closest to?		
With whom did you share your closest secrets?		
Whom did you miss most if he or she went away?		
By whom did you want to be trusted?		
Whom did you want to be most like?		

Is there a pattern to your answers? How does it carry over to your adult life? How would your own children answer this exercise?

5
Easing the Stresses

Alternatives to Consider

So far we've been dealing with the problems encountered by both mothers and fathers in the traditional child-custody arrangement; the general complaints and dissatisfactions most often expressed by the adults involved. *Many of these difficulties are generated by the system itself,* and are inherent in the nature of the either/or concept of custody. For the divorced couple who already feel tense and angry about their relationship, the additional strain created by their custody arrangement causes further polarization. Not only are they upset about the things that led to the end of their marriage, they now find new points of contention and strife which, by their very nature, keep escalating. For instance, the father who withdraws from seeing his children regularly because of the pain involved is roundly castigated by the mother, whose angry resentment simply drives him further away. Thus, instead of helping the divorced family establish a productive pattern for the future, our present practice introduces new problems which weave back and forth between the parents like a bright red ribbon of discord.

Unfortunately, parents in this situation usually blame each other rather than looking to the source of the difficulty. Each adult sees the problem from his or her own perspective, and so finds it hard to recognize that there may be ways to alleviate the strain on one and stabilize the position of the other. When you get right down to it, all of these complaints are the opposite side of the same coin, a fact that becomes obvious when you list the problems side by side:

MOTHER'S VIEWPOINT	FATHER'S VIEWPOINT
1. Overwork, resentment, and worry that the children don't see their father enough.	Separation trauma and depression due to loss of family and children.
2. They see him as Prince Charming, while I'm just a drudge.	I've become a Disneyland Daddy, and my kids are strangers.
3. He runs around and I'm trapped at home.	She has the companionship of the kids and I'm alone.
4. He tries to control me!	She just won't listen!

In the first instance the mother worries that the children don't have enough contact with their father, they lack a stable role model, and she is inundated by the daily problems of raising them by herself. The father, on the other hand, is suffering severely from the trauma of losing his family, finds his life turned upside down, and feels alienated and miserably lonesome for his children. Obviously, if it were possible for him to spend more time with the offspring, they would have the male contact they need, the mother would be relieved of some of the pressure she feels, and the father's life would become less of a nightmare.

But the addition of extra visits and more contact, while an improvement over the present system, is still not the whole solution. In the second complaint the father sees his relationship with the youngsters becoming hollow, superficial, and unrealistic.

Having fallen into the Disneyland Daddy syndrome, he feels compelled to provide unusual and unique entertainment for the kids, while the mother becomes increasingly resentful of the Knight in Shining Armor image he projects for the youngsters. The quality of the time spent together has to change and, by taking on the more natural aspects of normal parent–child interaction, provide the children with a real parent in exchange for Prince Charming. In this way the father experiences a stronger and healthier involvement with his children, the mother feels less dowdy and hostile, and the offspring have a chance to put life with father in its natural perspective, as well as having both adults functioning as parents.

The third problem mentioned, in which the mother feels trapped by her maternity and the father envies her home life with the youngsters, can also be resolved by a better balance of time between parents and children, as long as the quality as well as the quantity is improved. The divorced father who is granted the opportunity to be a responsible and involved parent finds his life has a great deal more direction, suffers less from depression and the sense of personal devaluation, and doesn't experience as much loneliness. The mother who shares the parenting tasks finds she is less martyred by her motherhood. And children who maintain close contact with their fathers have been found to suffer from fewer psychological problems as a result of the divorce.[1]

These are just the first and immediate advantages to such arrangements; if the divorced father knows he is continuing to play an important role in his children's growing up, he is less likely to worry about the mother's influence on the kids when he's not there, less prone to resent supporting them, and less inclined to talk about custody battles and other win/lose situations. And the mother who feels she can count on her ex to help with meeting the children's needs on more than a financial basis invariably finds her own hostilities lessened; as he relaxes and relinquishes the threatening postures of the past, she can do likewise.

The last complaint on the list, that ex-wives won't listen and ex-husbands continue to try to dominate the family, stems from unresolved conflicts left over from the marriage, rather than being a problem that is created by the child-custody system itself.

These difficulties frequently get passed on to the youngsters, however, in the actions and attitudes of the parents toward each other, and sometimes even take the form of needless battles over custody and visitation rights. To the degree that such continuing animosity affects your offspring in an adverse way, it becomes important to find a way to resolve these problems. Only when the two of you as adults have worked out the necessary balance of emotions to establish an equilibrium of dissent will your children be truly secure from the ravages of divorce, and both of you be in a healthy enough state to create new and better futures.

All of which sounds fine; but what can you do now that will help contribute to a more productive future? With all the social attitudes about divorce and child custody reinforcing the either/ or concept, and the personal entanglements between the two of you making everyone snarl, how do you find a way to ease the stresses? To begin with, it's very important that each of you recognize and honor the other's position in the children's lives. No matter who has actual custody, the other parent should be allowed (and encouraged) to spend a good deal of time with the youngsters. Ideally, this means several midweek evenings as well as weekend contact. Many parents who make a point of living close enough to allow the child to go to school from either home are able to devise a schedule which allows for this kind of interaction without getting in each other's way. But even fathers who live farther away will often make extra trips during the week in order to spend time with the offspring in their home. This last situation sometimes poses a problem to both parents; the mother sees it as an invasion of privacy, and the father continually reexperiences the trauma of having to leave the kids behind when his visitation time is up. Several parents I talked with had started with this sort of system, and finally decided that it was healthier and more comfortable for everyone if the noncustodial parent simply took the children for several days out of the week. This way the parent–child bonds are maintained, the children see each parent in normal, daily activity, and yet the adults are able to keep their own distance and go on with their separate lives. In effect these people have developed a shared custody, although neither had started out with that in mind.

There are a number of alternative arrangements such as this

which avoid the difficulties caused by our traditional practice. Some are extensions of very broad visitation rights, and others are outright trade-offs of the parenting function, but all of them result in the maintaining of a family support system for the children, even though the parents are no longer married. Whether it is a question of sharing the youngsters on an alternating-day basis or having them go live with the other parent for a year or so at a time, the end result is the same. Each adult feels that he or she has had a chance to raise the children with his or her own beliefs, standards, and social concepts, and the child gets to know each parent as a real person and reacts to both of them accordingly.

The idea of sharing the responsibilities and privileges of child raising after divorce is not a new one; for several centuries the wealthiest or most bohemian adults who didn't get along have arranged for separate houses, and it wasn't uncommon for the children to spend time with one or the other of their parents at different points in their childhood, unless, of course, they were shipped off to boarding school or were being raised primarily by nannies and other hired help. But for the average American, the possibility of shared custody has only recently come to be looked on as a viable solution to the problem.

Some of the families with whom I've had contact have been sharing custody for as long as seven or eight years, while others have only recently begun to experiment with nontraditional arrangements. These sometimes get changed around to accommodate changes in the circumstances and directions of the divorced family as a whole. But most of the sharing parents I've interviewed have felt very positive about what they are doing, since they believe that the child, as well as the adult, needs to be assured of continuing contact on a relatively normal, everyday basis. So before you make any final decisions about what sort of custody arrangement you want for your family, take a look at what others have been doing.

Long-term Block Time

For most parents this arrangement is arrived at more by accident than design. It's not uncommon for the mother with sole custody to find that as the children approach their teens, they become rebellious, hard to handle, or even frankly out of control. And at this point the alternative of sending such a child to live with the father is often accepted simply because it is preferable to turning the youngster over to Juvenile Hall, or looking for a foster home. Thus the father takes on the parental role as much by default as by intent.

Sometimes this change in parenting takes place because the single mother can't cope with the problems by herself any longer—not necessarily because any of the children are out of hand, but because she is exhausted. Or it may be triggered by the advent of a stepparent, the development of tensions between siblings, or even just curiosity on the part of the offspring, who sincerely want to see what it's like to live with the other parent. Any of these reasons is certainly valid, and such changes often bring the children to a better understanding and appreciation of *both* parents. Nor is it necessary to see such reorganization as being lifelong; some parents agree that it will be for a specific period of time (usually a year or two), and then be reviewed, while others leave it on a more open-ended basis. That is up to the family members themselves to decide, and varies with each situation.

For parents who specifically want to share their children, but who live quite a distance apart, the block-time concept makes the most sense. I know of several who have agreed to alternate years, as long as the children feel comfortable about it. If the youngsters must change schools and social life, the longer term provides them with the opportunity to make their adjustments and develop new friends, as well as complete a full year in one school. It also gives the noncustodial parent sufficient time to embark on long-term projects which the coming and going of progeny might interrupt, such as further schooling, extensive travel, or heavy career commitments.

The disadvantages of this arrangement mostly have to do with the extent of time involved, and a potential conflict about school and social life if the youngster is older. It's hard for a small child to hold the sense of continuity in his or her life with a parent who is absent for a long time.[2] Thus a toddler who doesn't see a parent for a week or two may have lost contact with the emotional and psychological relationship they once enjoyed, and perceive the separation as a form of abandonment. By the same token, it may be hard to reestablish the rapport if the separation has lasted a number of months; even if the intellectual knowledge of the other parent is kept alive by frequent phone calls, letters, and positive talk about him or her, the continuity of psychological parenting from that adult has been interrupted. In effect, the long-term block-time situation becomes an either/or circumstance for the very young child, and probably isn't as good as one could hope for. (Almost all of the sharing parents I interviewed arranged much shorter times if the children were infants or toddlers.) That doesn't mean block time won't work for that age group: only that you have to make a conscious effort to maintain frequent contact between the child and the nonparenting adult.

For the school-aged child, long-term arrangements are usually suitable emotionally, but may cause a problem socially. My own son spent three years with his father between the ages of 10 and 13, and pointed out that because of the organization of the schools, he was a new boy for three out of the four school years involved. (New when he went to his father, new the next year when he moved into junior high, and new to the school he entered when he came back to me.) For some children this can be an exciting and challenging experience, but for others it's pure torture. So you would be wise to find out what the school situation is, and consider how your child feels about it, before making long-range plans of this sort.

There is also the possibility that the older child will develop a very active social life in his or her school and resist losing that simply to go live with the other parent. (As youngsters grow up, the need for constant parental contact naturally becomes less important to them.) I know of one family in which the children, after staying for a year with the father some forty miles away, were so loath to leave the school in his area that they commuted during their last two years of high school after returning to the mother's home. Fortunately, the mother worked not too far from their academic destination, and it was possible to arrange a kind of car-pooling effort to get all members of the family where they needed to go without too much strain.

Winter/Summer

For the child (or parent) who feels anxious about shifting schools every year or two, or for parents who can't find a way to live close enough to the same school district to alleviate this problem, there is the summer/winter system. Although this is not an equal-time arrangement in the strict 50–50 sense, it still provides a more realistic approach to child raising than the every-other-weekend-and-two-weeks-in-the-summer of our current custody practice. It takes into account the stability of schooling, since the youngsters remain with one parent during the entire school year, while allowing enough time over the summer months for them to participate in the everyday pattern of living with the other parent. Since it's very difficult to keep up a party atmosphere for a whole summer, the normalized contact between parent and child is encouraged, and that's what sharing is all about.

The major disadvantages of this system lie in the fact that the summer parent doesn't have a chance to participate in the youngster's year-round growth and activities, and rarely knows what's happening in the child's school life. The winter parent, on the other hand, sometimes misses and resents not having an opportunity to spend vacation time with the offspring. Frequently this can be taken care of by the adult's arranging for his or her own vacation to coincide with the winter holiday of the school so that mutual playtime can be enjoyed.

As in all custody arrangements, it's very important that each parent respect the other's time with the children; if you are the winter parent and you get the kids all excited about going to summer camp, you've certainly overstepped your authority if the children would normally spend that summer with your ex! In general this system works quite well, however, and is often employed by parents who wouldn't consider "sharing" in the more literal sense.

Alternating Short-term Block Time

People with school-aged children frequently decide that keeping the parents within easy reach of the youngsters is important

enough to warrant their both staying in the same school district.
If that's your attitude, you may want to consider the alternate-
month, -week, or even split-week situation. I have seen this work
well for a number of people, the actual frequency of change being
dependent upon the individual needs of the specific families.

In the split-week situation, the children spend the first three
days of the week with one parent, taking the bus or walking
between school and that home on Monday, Tuesday, and
Wednesday mornings. Come Wednesday afternoon they go to the
other home and continue their school treks from that domicile for
the rest of the week. One third-grader I knew was so enthralled
with this arrangement that he took a knapsack to school every
Wednesday, wherein he put his toothbrush, current comic book,
and other immediate needs, and regaled his companions with
stories about his two different homes.

One of the advantages of this arrangement lies in the fact that
the children are often engaged in different activities with the different parents. In one case in which the mother has a small
apartment, she keeps such items as checkers, card games, and
tennis rackets, because they don't take up much room, while the
bicycles, basketball and net, and general sports paraphernalia are
kept at the father's big house. Since gardening, hiking, and fishing
are all activities that are part of the father's life-style, the rough-
est clothes and sturdiest boots stay in the closet there. Although
this is a particularly clear-cut situation, most sharing parents
mentioned that there were specific activities which they themselves didn't share with the children but their exes did.

Many parents who share in this fashion divide the weekends,
thus allowing each adult a day to himself or herself and a day
with the children. Sometimes it is rearranged to an alternating-
weekend system, because of specific activities or interests that
require more time either with the children or away from them. If
there are visiting relatives from one branch of the family, for
instance, the children usually stay with that family during the
whole weekend in order to spend more time with the visitors. In
general, the adults take turns as to who picks up or delivers the
offspring, unless the youngster is old enough to take public transportation. And things such as doctor or dentist appointments are
usually considered the responsibility of both the child and the

parent who has the youngster that day. Most of these things are just a matter of logistics that get worked out between the parents as the need arises.

Every Other Day

Parents with infants or toddlers sometimes work out an every-other-day-and-alternating-weekend arrangement. If the parents both work (and these days most do, by necessity), they find a suitable day-care center and take turns picking up the child on alternating evenings. This has the real advantage of maintaining the continuity of contact between child and parent, since even a very young child retains a sense of familiarity with the absent parent for several days. Because the day-care center is constant, the stability and continuity of daily activity is maintained, and the pattern that is established doesn't interfere with the youngster's sense of security. It does limit the parents to a certain degree, in that neither of them has more than a weekend at a time by himself or herself, but it also allows them to exchange the offspring without having to have personal contact—a situation that is advantageous if the relationship between them is still angry and hostile.

This system also requires that each home have a supply of diapers, toys, and clothes, but since neither parent holds down full-time child care, it doesn't have to be a complete duplication of everything. In most cases of alternating time, I found that there was no specific effort made to provide the youngsters with two of each thing. Certainly it's not necessary. When the children are old enough, they can be responsible for what they want to take with them to the other house, and since there is no competition between the two households, only basic necessities have to be supplied in duplicate.

Preschool Problems

The ages between 2 and 6 seem to be the most awkward ones to handle on a sharing basis. Children at this point are actively involved in the process of discovering the outside world; they want and need space, friends, safe surroundings, intellectual stimulation, and recreational diversions, as well as familiar Teddy bears, a favorite blanket, or a special cup and plate at mealtimes. And they are generally very "reactive" to their environment, often demanding the reassurance of a place for everything and everything in its place. Some parents with children in this age group found that the split-week system just didn't work and longer periods of time, such as several weeks or even months, with each parent were better for both the adult and the child.

In this way the youngster who goes through a noticeable readjustment process in changing households has a chance to settle in, so to speak, during the first few days, and is then ready to spend the next weeks in that home atmosphere.

The need to recognize the readjustment period holds for many children no matter which custody arrangement is being used. The process may last anywhere from several hours to several days; with my own children I noticed it when they returned from their summers with their father. Usually the first evening was full of excitement, questions, and stories and lots of news to catch up on. By the second day there appeared to be a kind of let-down, occasionally accompanied by tears. If there were specific reasons for these emotions, like the death of a puppy over the summer, or a feeling of anxiety about the relationship with either parent, we talked about them. If it was simply reaction to the change in environment, we talked about that too. But by the third day the familiar routines of my home had begun to be reestablished, and everything went fine from then on. Nor is this kind of readjustment limited to children. I know one woman whose husband travels a great deal for the government, and she's long since discovered that no matter how well the trip went, or how glad he is to be back home, he has to pick a fight with her during the first twenty-four hours after he's returned. This has been going on for the last twenty years, and she's learned to shrug it off as being part of his means of acclimating to the change of environment.

Free Access

For those parents who have established a comfortable relationship following their divorce, and so have found a way to live with each other's presence in the children's lives, free access often becomes the most logical way to handle child raising. This requires that you live close enough to allow the youngsters to go back and forth between the homes, more or less at will. For instance, I know of two different couples who bought condominiums at opposite ends of the same complexes; while they themselves don't interact much, the children are always somewhere on the grounds, and a book forgotten at one home can be easily fetched from the other.

This arrangement requires that there be enough communication between both the parents and children so that everyone knows who will be where when. If the children are old enough to recognize the importance of this, and the adults mature enough to keep in touch with each other on a regular basis, there's little chance that the progeny will fall through the cracks somewhere while each parent assumes they are with the other. This question of communication is crucial, however. Few things cause greater panic or wilder scenes than having two divorced parents discover that neither knows where the offspring are; it may all blow over in a hurry when the missing youngsters get home from the library, but the fireworks that take place in the meantime can be quite spectacular!

If the children are reliable, however, and the parents both flexible and open enough to try this system, it certainly has a lot to recommend it. First of all, youngsters perceive the parents working together on a positive basis; if one is recovering from having a tooth pulled, the other steps in and takes care of the kids, or if they both want to go out on the same evening, they can flip a coin to decide who stays home, or share in the cost of a baby-sitter. Secondly, the youngsters learn to be responsible in their own right for keeping the adults informed as to their desires and plans; if it turns out that the children didn't tell either adult about going to the library, both parents will be very likely to impress on them how important that kind of communication is. And thirdly, the offspring feel free and comfortable about being part of either household, without having to make choices or take sides. One of the saddest things about the typical custody arrangement is that children discover that their parents' anger and hostilities are more important than their own love is. When parents can and will work together to allow their offspring to know

and love both of them, the message is one of supportive care and
concern, not personal vindictiveness.

The Birds' Nest and Other Oddities

Once in a while I've run across unique solutions to the question
of how to raise the children after divorce which, although not
common among sharing parents, still deserve mention here if only
because they illustrate how individual family needs and capabilities are.

In the situation of a family with a large equity in a suburban
home, for instance, it is possible to arrange for the children and
the home to stay together while the adults take turns parenting.
Like birds on a nest, the parents alternate times of living in the
home with the children while the other parent stays in a separate
apartment or house not too far away. This is a particularly useful
solution when each parent is adamant about keeping the house,
and neither is willing to compromise. It has several advantages:
the children stay in their own familiar surroundings, with school
and social life continuing as before. And the parents have a
chance to acclimate to being single during those times when they
aren't "nesting" with the youngsters. It provides for a certain
amount of time during which some decision can be made about
the house: whether to sell it outright and have everyone move;
let one parent buy out the other in the settlement; or possibly put
it in the children's name with each parent responsible in some
designated way for the mortgage and upkeep. (This last is a sticky
situation unless both adults are reliable, trusting, and trustworthy. But I do understand that it's worked in several cases
quite successfully.)

There are some specific disadvantages to the birds' nest technique. Unless the family is quite affluent, the only way to have a
non-nest is to share the cost of a single apartment, usually in the
same neighborhood so that getting to and from work isn't a problem. And as most divorcing people discover, sooner or later the
need to create your own individual place becomes something
both very exciting and very necessary. It's hard to do that if
you're sharing the same apartment, even on the alternating-time

basis. Your ex hangs up a new poster, and it becomes an invasion of your privacy; you think you'll buy some new pillows for the living room, and then wonder what to do with them when you're staying with the children. Naturally, if you each can afford your own separate place in which to establish your new territory, those conflicts don't arise. But the average family can only just barely afford two households, much less one each for the adults plus the family domicile for the children!

Another consideration is what to do if either of the parents begins to date seriously and then considers remarriage. How does the new spouse fit into the "every Friday at five o'clock I move from one home to the other" policy? And even if it's okay with both the new spouse and the kids, how will your ex take it? Possibly *not* well.

Basically, therefore, the birds' nest arrangement is most often used on a temporary basis, to help make the transition from single-family to two-family living. It affords everyone time to get used to the change, to explore different relationships with the youngsters, and yet doesn't uproot anyone immediately. The schedule for moving can range anywhere from once a week to a month or more at a time. At a specified time you leave the place you're presently living in, with all dishes washed and sheets changed, and move into the other home. There's no reason why, if it actually fits your family's needs, this arrangement couldn't be adapted to longer periods of time, provided that you all feel comfortable with it.

Another unusual situation I encountered was a case in which the mother of the children ended up renting the cottage at the back of the property while the father and second wife lived in the main house. The children theoretically spent three and a half days with each parent, though in actual fact they were in and out of both places on a very casual, generally free-access basis. Both the parents and the father's second wife found the system had much to commend it, though as each pointed out, there simply wasn't any clear-cut sense of privacy and time when the youngsters were specifically with the other parent. The adults were moderately friendly, but certainly not intimate; the mother maintained her own social life and work, and rarely came to the main house except when there were things to discuss about the kids.

The father's colleagues at work delighted in teasing him about keeping a harem, and refused to believe that wasn't what was happening. But as he pointed out to me, "It may seem strange to them, but when you know and understand how something came about in your own life, it doesn't seem strange to you. The kids think it's great, and as long as we know it works, I guess it doesn't matter what the rest of society thinks."

As you can see from the diversity of styles used by sharing parents, each family has its own reasons for sharing, and its own way of arranging it. Yet there were several fundamental considerations that all mentioned as being necessary for the success of the venture. And while they certainly didn't all agree as to the details involved, each individual family had established its own system to its members' satisfaction.

Communication

The most frequently mentioned necessity was good communication between the adults. Not only did the parents truly believe that what they were doing was important for their kids, they also saw it as necessary for themselves. Knowing that there was another, equally responsible adult with whom to share the problems and decisions of child raising was tremendously helpful. Many who had short-term arrangements reported that they were in phone contact several times a week, although they rarely saw each other in person. Most of them said their conversations were limited to subjects pertaining specifically to their offspring, and all agreed that they appreciated being able to consult with the other parent about things. I myself found this the case when my ex and I were on good terms; the day I was informed that our rented house had been sold and the children and I would have to move during the last month before school was out, it was a godsend to be able to call their father and arrange for them to live with him during that time.

Some sharing parents get together personally, without the youngsters present, in order to discuss how things are going with the children. When my ex and I were sharing, we used to have lunch together every other week, and found that such communication was most helpful. By making a point of communicating even when things were going smoothly, we each managed to keep abreast of what our children were doing, and could foresee problems before they took on crisis proportions. If you have contact with each other only when there are problems to solve, the sound of the other's voice is automatically associated with difficulties, everyone is edgy and guarded, and one or the other of you comes to the situation blind, not having been informed of the background as it was developing. Again, this is a matter of personal preference; if you've been divorced and possibly remarried for a number of years, you are more likely to feel comfortable with each other than if the separation is recent and the wounds still smart.

All of the sharing parents interviewed mentioned that the dissension with their exes had either diminished or been narrowed to those areas which pertained only to the children. Some said that they got on better now than at any other time in their relationship, even though there were still ambivalent or hostile feelings about each other as romantic partners, and a few, who had shared for several years, listed each other as closest friends.

Moving

The second most important consideration for sharing has to do with the parents staying in the same vicinity. Most sharing parents mention that this is either an agreed-upon point, or one that hasn't come up yet, but would be considered from a family-needs point of view if it does. I know of one case in which a man, long seeking employment in a very specialized field, turned down a job offer on the East Coast because his children, who lived with him three and a half days of the week, would be staying on the West Coast. And there is another case in which all the family members met together to discuss how important the career opportunity was, whether the children and both adults could all consider moving to the new locale, or if there was any other, more suitable means of sharing that could be arranged if the parent did take the job some distance away. For the most part, parents of either sex who felt that they were truly involved in the raising of their children didn't consider the subject of a long-distance move something to be decided unilaterally. The typical divorced father who sees his kids only for occasional weekends is much less likely to see such a move as being detrimental to his relationship with the children than is a parent who finds a good deal of pleasure and fulfillment in being a father. That doesn't mean a major move couldn't happen—only that the sharing parent considers it in a different light, since he has more to lose.

Money

The matter of finances is one that varies from family to family. I know of several cases of split siblings in which each adult is financially responsible for the children with him or her, but not for those living with the other spouse. And it is not uncommon for the sharing parent who has all the children to receive some form of support from the other, regardless of whether that parent is a man or a woman. While most of the women I know who pay child support do so voluntarily, some state laws now provide that both parents are responsible for contributing to their youngsters' financial welfare, each according to his or her means. Thus it is possible that more and more judges will be ordering women to pay child support when they can afford it.

Frequently parents work together to meet major expenses such as medical, dental, or educational costs. I met one couple who, after several years of divorce, decided to start saving for the education of their two children. They opened a trust fund to which both contribute equally, with the understanding that it will be used for college by either or both of the children. If the youngster has the requisite grades and interest to attend one of the more expensive schools, the adults will augment the trust to pay for the entire cost of the education; if the child opts for a local community college, his half of the fund will be available to him at that time, but no additional help will be supplied. And if by the age of 21 the youngster has not enrolled in any institution of higher learning, that money reverts to the parents, who will split it equally. These adults haven't seen each other for several years and each has one of the children living with him or her, yet they were willing and able to devise a system which ensures that the children's educational needs will be met.

Celebrations

Another question that comes up is what to do about birthdays, holidays, and vacations. Most sharing families celebrate these things separately, either at different times during the same day or on two different days. Frequently this means two birthday cakes and/or parties, several days of Christmas, or a division of Chanukah festivities. I've known some families who split the cost of a major gift (such as a down sleeping bag, or a much-longed-for stereo) while still holding separate celebrations. And occasionally I've talked with people who all participate in the festivities, even going so far as having joint vacations, camping trips, and the like. This is not a common practice, however, and depends largely on how the adults view the situation. The children seem to thoroughly enjoy having two birthdays and frequently told me in great detail about the different cakes, parties, and gifts involved; they certainly didn't see it as a drawback. This often happens with sole-custody youngsters as well as shared, by the way.

Miscellaneous Details

There are a number of other practical concerns that come up when a couple begin to share their children, most of which are worked out by each couple as they go along. For instance, when the children are with one parent, does the other call to chat, or come by to visit from time to time? Does each parent know and talk about the child's activities with the other, or is there a definite "hands off" policy? How do you handle special occasions such as school plays, ballet or music recitals, first dances, football or baseball games? If there is something one parent wants to discuss which seems to be a criticism of the other's way of parenting, how can that be handled so as not to cause a lot of personal hostility? Should there be an agreement beforehand as to how each parent will act in front of the children when it comes to dating? And how much business is it of the other parent? How do you handle illnesses, physical disasters, discipline problems, school conferences, and the like?

The answers to these and any other questions you may think of are best found within yourselves. They vary from case to case—sometimes having been discussed, formulated, and agreed to in writing at the time sharing was agreed upon, sometimes not even thought about until they presented themselves in the course of living. Different families have found different answers, and it's really up to you to find your own. Whatever works for you works, and there's very little else to be said.

6
Proof of the Pudding

What Happens When Parents Share

Theories and philosophies about child raising, either with or without a mate, are all very fine, but the question "Does it really work?" lurks in the background anytime an unusual concept is put forth. Many is the idea that sounds good on paper, but proves to be woefully inadequate in actual practice. Although the concept of shared responsibility for the raising of children following a divorce obviously solves some of the problems inherent in the traditional method, it generates a whole new set of challenges of its own, many of which are rather unexpected. Yet for the men who are willing to take over the parenting role, and the women who agree to relinquish, or at least loosen, the apron strings, the rewards far outweigh the disadvantages. The adjustments may not always be easy, and sometimes they can be downright comical, but all the parents I talked with agreed that the results make the effort definitely worthwhile.

Men as "Mothers"

So ingrained is the notion that the nurturing, caring, supportive aspects of child raising are limited to the women of our culture, we have no appropriate word to denote such a relationship between fathers and children. "Fatherhood" is seen as being very different from "Motherhood," and one is even forced to talk about fathers' being "mothers." Just as we need a single neutral pronoun so that writers such as me don't have to keep saying "he or she," we need a way to signify the function of mothering on a genderless basis. In the past, the word "husbanding" meant to manage and direct, but nowadays the term is applied mainly to resources or crops, and certainly doesn't have the scope that "mothering" does. I have heard of one case in which the father won custody of his children in court by contending that "to mother" was a verb, and therefore connoted an action, not a sexually defined role—which is at least a step in the right direction. In the meantime, no matter what you call it, there are a number of fathers who have taken over the mothering functions in their families and generally find it both surprisingly rewarding and exasperatingly difficult.

Over and over again single fathers who had actively sought the right to help raise their children by themselves spoke of the changes they observed in themselves. Sometimes this was expressed with amazement, sometimes bemusement, but they all agreed that they underwent a profound and important change for the better. Some were prepared for it, but many were not, and these saw the broadening of their own personal horizons as an unexpected bonus, over and above the obvious benefits of being part of their youngsters' lives.

Most often this was described simply as "becoming more human." In order to be an effective nurturing parent you have to recognize what is needed by your offspring, and that requires a degree of sensitivity and understanding many men were unaware of possessing. Neither background experience nor training in school has much to do with soothing a tearful toddler who has just fallen down for the third time in three minutes. Ordering the frustrated, puzzled, and possibly hurt youngster to stop crying isn't going to help, and runny noses don't get cleaned up by themselves at that age. So the man who finds himself confronted by such problems very quickly discovers inner resources he may not know he has: patience, awareness of subtleties, emotional responsiveness, and a gentle or calming demeanor that may never have been given expression before. In the traditional nuclear family the child with the hurt knee or fearful nightmare runs to Mother for help and consolation, probably as much from habit as from preference. It is Mother, after all, who holds, cuddles, croons, and caresses; as one counselor pointed out, from the cradle on, women are seen as providing pleasure and solace, while men are busy with "matters of state." [1]

"When his mother and I were together, there was nothing I could do for him," one father said. "She knew all there was to know about taking care of children, and viewed my fumbling efforts with a kind of benevolent derision, so I soon gave up trying to do those things for him. As a result, I really didn't interact with my son much when he was small. But it's different now. I've grown so used to being the nurturing parent, I even find I get offended if I'm dating a woman who tries to tell me how to 'mother,' and I resent her interference."

Many men who have felt cut off from their youngsters by the presence of a mother who always knows best begin to discover how rewarding it is to be a parent when they take over the sole responsibility. No longer perceived as primarily dependents and responsibilities, the youngsters start to show all sorts of personal aspects which the fathers had never seen before. "Maybe it's because I'm with them more, in a new way. Or maybe I simply look at them differently," one man commented. "I understand them a lot better now, and they share all kinds of feelings with me—fears and hopes and secrets and such, which I never had time to listen to in the past."

One particularly thoughtful man who became a single father when he and his wife agreed to share their 2½-year-old son found it led him to question all sorts of male-role images he had about himself. Not wanting to see his youngster raised with the same stereotypes, he began to participate more and more in the boy's playtime. "I'd never played with dolls and stuffed toys in my life; those were sissy things when I was growing up. But I didn't want

Steve to be denied those experiences, so I got down on the floor with him and we began to play together.'' And sharing the warm, cuddly, playful things naturally led to the sharing of emotions. ''I could show him how I felt with a hug better than I could say it, both because it was growing easier for me to share my feelings and because words seemed inappropriate for so young a child.''

This willingness to express emotions ran consistently throughout the single fathers' comments. Whether they had sole custody or shared in some fashion, the effect was the same. As long as they had the responsibility of meeting their children's emotional and psychological needs on a daily basis, they came to know not only their children but also themselves better. One father noted, ''My priorities began to shift from work achievements and 'trophy winning' in the business world to the intangible things of the heart. The way my youngest reaches up to take my hand, or the confidence my daughter shows in me when she brings me problems from school is a greater affirmation of my importance than the size of the car I drive or the promotion to an executive position at work.''

Obviously not all single fathers restructure their careers because of their youngsters, but several mentioned turning down a career advancement because it would have required more time on the job and thus interfered with their home lives. Nor were these decisions lightly made, or tinged with resentment. ''I began to see how limited my concept of masculinity was compared with the scope of being not only a professional person but also a full-time nurturing parent. I was able to put aside some of those older and less satisfying goals of success in favor of maintaining a wholeness in the family,'' one man confided with a grin. ''Why should I feel bad about it? A new title on my office door would serve to keep other people out, whereas opting to be with the children brings people closer to me!''

One man I met became so involved with taking care of his preschoolers, and so frustrated at the lack of a good day-care center in his locale, he arranged to go on part-time status at work in order to stay home and start his own cooperative nursery school.[2] ''I can't say that being a single father doesn't interfere with a lot of things I think I want to do,'' he added, thinking about the weekend ski trips and backpacking outings he used to enjoy so often, "but I wouldn't give up parenting my kids just to satisfy those desires."

All of these men were what social scientists term "seekers" rather than "assenters"; [3] that is, they actively sought the opportunity to take part in raising their children. For the men who simply assented to become single fathers, because of either death or desertion on the part of the wife, the outlook was not so bright. Frequently these men felt ill equipped to handle the problems, and martyred at having to assume a role they didn't really want. Just as not all women are good mothers, not all fathers should be single parents; but for those who want to undertake it, it can be a wonderfully enriching experience.

At one point I found myself discussing single parenting with an unusually militant feminist. When I mentioned the idea of encouraging more fathers to take over the supportive, nurturing "mother" role in child raising, the very concept met with a storm of protest. "They don't have the capacity to be gentle, loving, and caring," she announced firmly. "Why, men can't possibly fill that need in a child's life!" Yet it's obvious from my interviews that many men do have that ability, if given the chance to use it. Just as women were assumed to be incapable of understanding mathematics, politics, and economics because they hadn't had the opportunity to develop proficiency in those fields, men have been generally excluded from training in the distaff arts, and so are considered unable to handle them. It turns out, however, that parenting is a genderless job, and there's no reason why more men shouldn't be allowed to participate in it.

Househusbands

One thing that shared parenting invariably brings out in fathers is an appreciation for the problems of single mothers. "How on earth does she do it?" was the query voiced over and over again. One man looked at me balefully and shook his head in disbelief after having his three children with him for a week. "First the youngest came down with impetigo and they wouldn't let him come to the nursery school. He wasn't sick enough to stay in bed, but he couldn't play with the other kids, so I had to find a baby-sitter for him. Then the older children were home because of a school holiday, and I couldn't see leaving them all by themselves, but couldn't find a baby-sitter either, so I brought them to work with me. Hah! That's the last time we try *that* experiment. Finally they're all healthy and back in the classroom, and I'm a nervous wreck, with cancelled appointments and last week's paperwork to catch up on. I had no idea it was all so complicated!''

Quite apart from how you juggle school schedules and working hours, single fathers often find themselves more boggled by the domestic problems they face than by the emotional and psychological aspects of their new role. Because our education of youngsters is so limited, with ''home economics'' being considered more appropriate for girls than boys, many men grow up without any real concept of how one manages a home. It is assumed that they will always have a woman handy to take care of cooking, washing, and mending, getting their shirts ready and their houses spotless. Thus they are unprepared to run their households in anything other than an administrative capacity. All of which may seem rather amusing to the single mother who has been coping with these things and more for some time, but it's rarely funny to the man who has no background for handling domestic crises, and no support group to turn to. ''Somehow,'' one single father said, ''you don't call your best buddy to complain that the spaghetti burned, the seven-year-old spilled milk all over the floor when she dropped her glass, and the ten-year-old cut himself when he tried to pick up the broken pieces!''

Many single fathers rely on their children to help run the household once the initial rearrangement takes place. ''I do all the shopping and most of the cooking,'' one man explained, ''and the children divide the daily chores and once a week do the vacuuming, dusting, and scrubbing. We all take turns on the laundry, and about once a year we spend a weekend doing an old-fashioned housecleaning: window washing, rug beating, and so on. It's not the best-kept house in the world, but it's good enough.''

Some fathers divide the chores on a rotating basis, so that each child takes turns at each task, and in older families it's not uncommon for everyone to pitch in on fixing the meals. Far from blighting the lives of the youngsters, this added responsibility seems to have a beneficial effect. ''I treat them as functioning, capable people, and we all work pretty well together,'' one man said. "It sure helps build a sense of family unity if the kids realize we have to work together, and I'm not going to knock myself out at the office and then do all the domestic things when I get home. That may be all right for some women, but not for me." (Most men, not having been raised with the self-sacrificing ethic of women, find the sharing of family tasks to be both natural and desirable—an attitude many single mothers could learn much from.)

How well any individual single father does naturally depends largely on his own approach to the problem and who his children are. I recently had occasion to contact a man whom I had interviewed some time ago, and found him to be harried, bemused, rattled, and generally running from pillar to post. This was quite a contrast to the calm, collected young father I had originally spoken with, and when I mentioned that fact he burst out laughing.

"During the first year, when the kids were smaller, I really thought I had it licked. The housework was a cinch, I had everything all nicely organized, and frankly, I found myself wondering why some of the other guys I knew had so much trouble getting it together. But now we've got Cub Scouts, Little League, soccer teams; you name it! Time for orthodontia, for teaching the kids to take a hand in the cooking, for getting them chauffeured to their different appointments. My Lord, I've had to drop out of almost everything else I was doing, just to be able to meet the home schedule, and it's killing me. And on top of all those other things, I keep running into problems I never dreamed existed. I mean, I know what to say to a mechanic who isn't doing what I want him to with my car . . . I just tell the S.O.B. where to get off. But what do you say to a den mother who's giving you trouble? That takes a whole new vocabulary, and I haven't mastered it yet."

Fortunately, most single fathers (and mothers as well) develop a kind of humor that carries them through. I don't know whether that's a necessary ingredient for making your custody arrangements work or not, but among the single parents I talked with, those who handled it best also had the ability to see the ludicrous side of things—which helped make it entertaining, if not always easy.

One of the least easy aspects of being a single father seems to be having the responsibility of a teen-aged daughter. As one counselor pointed out to me, nothing makes a grown man quail so much as being confronted with the task of raising a young girl to womanhood. Some such men attempt to turn their daughters into miniature housewives, expecting them to handle all the domestic chores, on the theory (or rationalization) that this is good practice for the future. Others treat them simply like comrades and buddies with whom they share the work; and still others make a particular effort to be sure the girl doesn't feel that she is a "substitute wife." "At fourteen, she's still a child, still young and full of play and the need to run around and experience the world without having to take over the adult role of homemaker," one father told me, "and I make a real point of not putting her in that role."

All of which is fine; but how do you handle dating, questions about sex and menstruation, moodiness and depressions on her part, and your own overprotective, stern-parent reaction within yourself? Among the fathers I've talked with, those who shared custody were particularly grateful for the mother's involvement with the child at this point. And for those who didn't share, female relatives, steady girlfriends, or even friendly neighbor women generally came to the rescue. Most fathers feel conflicts about raising a teen-aged daughter alone, but many have done admirable jobs. Certainly it is not beyond the realm of possibility.

Sharing Mothers

While the sharing father is discovering his capacity to relate more closely with his children, the sharing mother is usually surprised to discover how well she does *without* them. No longer constrained to adjust her activities around the needs of the family, she now has both time and energy to investigate the world on her own terms, while still maintaining a comfortable relationship with her youngsters. It is, as one woman told me, "the best of both worlds. I have the pleasure of being an involved parent, and at the same time can see myself as something other than nursemaid, housekeeper, and disciplinarian. And the children see me differently now. I'm no longer simply part of the furniture!"

Indeed, it is not uncommon for shared youngsters to begin to view their mother in a new light, especially if they have lived with her in a single-parent home before the sharing arrangement took effect. The overexposure to each other which plagues both children and single mothers begins to diminish as soon as the living pattern changes, and if the woman becomes involved in career, school, creative projects, or some other activity that is exciting and fulfilling in its own right, she takes on an added dimension which the children may not have seen before. "Because I'm a more balanced person, I'm a better parent," one woman said, "even though at first I couldn't believe that giving up full-time control of the kids would lead to my being a more effective mother."

Nor is it just a matter of Mama's becoming a more interesting person than the children had thought. The aura of magic which once surrounded their Disneyland Daddy tends to be dispelled, so that they see him in a more realistic way, and their appreciation of Dear Old Mom often increases proportionately. (Few mothers get caught in the Disneyland Daddy trap, possibly because they rarely have the finances or compulsion to spend extravagantly in order to entertain their kids.) Consequently, the children are less quick to shrug off their mother's philosophies and talents. "I thought you used to be too strict," one youngster confided in her mother, "until I started living with Dad." And a much younger child caroled, "I promise to eat my salad every day, as long as you don't burn the potatoes like Daddy does." This ability to see each parent in a clearer perspective is often reflected in the comments of teen-agers: "There are advantages and disadvantages in any family, and having two different homes has made me see that more clearly, I think. I feel I understand my parents better now, and in the end it all balances out. I wouldn't want to have to choose one over the other."

Another change that many women encounter is the increased enjoyment they find in being with their children. Just as the single mother is generally taken for granted by her offspring, they in turn are often thought of as "always being underfoot." No matter where she turns or what she plans, she has to take them into account. But sharing mothers reported they looked forward to being with their children in a way they'd never experienced before. Instead of relying on communication consisting mainly of do's and don'ts, many women found they made a point of conversing with their youngsters. "We see each other now because we want to, when we want to," said one mother who had moved out and left father and children in the family home. "And that in itself makes a big difference. I'm really able to sit down and talk with them, and we have a lot more to share and catch up on because of our time apart."

Nor is the change in relationship limited only to the offspring. Most mothers found that their exes were far less hostile, certainly more cooperative, and in some cases, quite frank in their expression of admiration for the job the mother had done in the past. "It's as though we are friends for the first time," one woman reported. "I guess he can relax and be more positive about our interaction now that he isn't threatened by my influence on the kids." From my own experience I know this can result in a much-appreciated lessening of tensions, and if you are sharing in some alternating pattern, you would do well to establish as good a rapport as possible while he has the children and is feeling good about it.

Adjustments

Shifting from full- to part-time motherhood is bound to require some degree of adjustment, though how easy or difficult this is depends largely on the woman herself. For those mothers who willingly agree to a short-term alternating system of sharing, there appear to be few hazards; they are more involved with the logistics of who-is-where than with the question of why-have-they-gone. None experienced feelings of guilt, rejection, self-doubt, or loneliness, and while a few wondered if the unconventionality of the situation would prove harmful to the children in the long run, they all noted that they were more sensitive to this question than the youngsters themselves were. One sharing mother summed it up with a grin: "Sometimes I think I'm a kind of social pioneer doing something very good and important . . . and sometimes I think I must be crazy!"

Mothers who gave their consent for the children to move

some distance away for long-term sharing mentioned that loneliness was occasionally a problem. "The first few months were really hard," one woman wrote. "I missed my daughter terribly. Only the thought that it was good for her to be with her father kept me from going back on the agreement." If there were several youngsters and the family decided on a split sibling arrangement, loneliness was much less a factor. Although most mothers miss the absent child, they don't feel abandoned or rejected. And if contact is kept through letters, phone calls, and visits, there is no sense of having "lost" the child. "Knowing that next year we're going to trade back again is a big help," one young mother reported. "And in the meantime my son and I are enjoying each other's company in a totally new way. This is the first time we've lived together without his sister, and it's been great."

Yet in spite of the many advantages of sharing, some women refuse to consider the idea because they equate the absence of their offspring with desertion, rejection, and guilt. If a mother is afraid of sharing because she sees it as losing the children, she'll tend to view the idea as some invention of the devil, and if she is full of unresolved angers toward her past partner, she may simply deny him the chance to share out of spite and vengefulness. Her desire to maintain control over the children, regardless of why, outweighs all other considerations, and she sets herself up for an untold amount of grief and difficulty not only from her ex-husband but possibly from the youngsters as well. When a woman locks herself into the either/or position of sole custody, she may find her husband heading back to court in an effort to get custody for himself, or the children demanding that they be allowed to go live with him, either one of which situations is guaranteed to bring out all the negative emotions she's been trying so hard to avoid.

In my interviews with nonsharing mothers who did not have custody of their children it became obvious that the problems they encountered were the result of how the children had come to be living elsewhere, not the simple fact that they weren't with her. There are several basic reasons for youngsters' being with their fathers, over and above sharing, and each of them generates its own difficulty for the mother. The amount of pain and confusion involved in adjusting to these situations is directly proportionate to the stubbornness with which she fought the change. If it is something that is decided without your permission, such as the court's awarding sole custody to your spouse, the effects will be much more harrowing than if you've agreed to a form of sharing, no matter how hesitant you feel about giving your consent.

Mothers Without Children

Although the courts have been notoriously biased against fathers during the last fifty years, that situation is gradually changing, and it isn't hard to locate mothers whose children were "awarded" to their opposing partner. When this is the case guilt, self-recrimination, and the sense of having been victimized by an unfair system all play a part in her reaction. Not only does she bear the scars of the court battle itself; she also feels the stigma of having been adjudged the less fit parent. Like the father who loses a custody fight, this mother is quick to blame poor attorneys, biased judges, and prejudiced investigators. Yet more than one such woman has added, "You know, in the long run I think it's been for the best."

Many offer rationalizations about the welfare of the children: "He's better able to support them," or "He's remarried, so now they have a 'normal' home." And sometimes the child is blamed: one woman said, "Since she wanted to play power games, and told the judge how much she'd rather be with Daddy, I'm better off without her." Most of these remarks sound like making the best of a bad situation, particularly if the woman is bitter and hostile and refuses to establish any kind of consistent visiting schedule with the children. Just as the divorced father frequently withdraws from his youngsters because of the pain of the separation trauma, the mother who has lost custody often finds that the anguish and confusion she experiences override, at first, her desire to see the children. Filled with regrets, depression, and feelings of worthlessness, some such mothers go through nervous breakdowns, others resort to alcohol, and a few simply vanish in an effort to put all that misery behind them— none of which bodes well for the youngsters.

Fortunately, most of the mothers I spoke with had come to grips with the situation and been able to reestablish positive relations with their offspring, once they regained some of the self-esteem they felt had been stripped from them in the legal battle. Most went on to create new lives for themselves, and a few were able to incorporate regular and constructive visiting arrangements with the kids. How long this adjustment takes depends largely on the woman and on the circumstances of the individual case. For some such mothers it is a matter of several months or a year, while others actually lose contact with their children for five or ten years, particularly if the father remarries or moves to another locale. One mother, who lost her child when he was 5 years old, went on to build a comfortable career during the next decade, and was bemused to discover that when her now teen-aged son came to spend the summer with her, the relationship that developed was far superior to that which the child had with his father. "I guess I'm sort of an adult friend and counselor to him now," she said. "He'll ask my advice about things he won't even discuss with his dad, and lots of times I say the same thing I know his father would, but he takes it from me."

Losing custody of your offspring in the courts is certainly not the end of the world, but it is a heavy blow for any mother or father to sustain, and is bound to have an effect on the parent–child relationship which may take years to overcome—all of which should be kept in mind if you're thinking in terms of a custody battle.

Some mothers are without their children because they set out on their own while the youngsters remained behind with the father. Although this is not a common occurrence, it has received a large amount of publicity in recent years, and such women are often unfairly branded as "runaway mothers." Yet in spite of the negative judgment this culture makes of their actions, the number of women who leave home is gradually increasing.[4]

Women walk out on home and children for any number of reasons. For some it's the only way to end a bad marriage; for others it's the best means of exploring their own potential; and in a number of cases, it's based on the fact that the father is, in both their estimations, as good a single parent as the mother would be, or better. The levels of guilt, doubt, regret, and difficulty of adjustment depend largely on how the separation is handled and what sort of relationship is maintained with the youngsters.

For those women whose marriages have included a history of

physical abuse, the act of departing without warning may be the only way of ensuring that they can walk out the door with their skins intact. Fear, dread, and desperation lead them to steal away quietly, leaving only a note behind. These are not women who are running away with lovers; they have simply decided that they have to take control of their own lives, and so make a bolt for freedom. A few lose contact with their children completely, either by their own choice or because the father refuses to allow them to communicate with the youngsters, but most get back in touch with their families as soon as they are themselves somewhat settled, and are gradually able to work out a visiting arrangement for the kids. How much guilt they experience depends largely on how successful they are in reestablishing contact with their children. None of them intended to desert their offspring, and all mentioned that worry about the effects of their action on the youngsters was of more importance to them than any personal sense of guilt. They were not so much worried about what society might say about them as they were about the cultural assumption that all children need full-time mothers in order to grow up healthy and well adjusted. Many voiced the sentiment that this attitude is simply part of our sexist upbringing and has no basis in actual fact, but all noted that it contributed to their uneasiness, at first, about their decision. "I didn't want my daughter to be pitied as the child whose mother had run away," one woman explained. "She says she understands why I left, and that's very important to me."

In many other cases the mother's departure was much less dramatic. "My husband and I had talked it over for months," a woman attorney related, "and I finally sat down and explained to the children that I was going to be getting an apartment nearby, but we'd be in touch every day or so by phone, and they could come over on weekends or in the evenings. They took it better than I had expected, and after four years I think I can safely say it's worked out very well. Guilty?" she added. "Why should I feel guilty? I'm a much better parent this way. He's the one who always wanted a big family, and he's better equipped to raise them than I am."

All the mothers I talked with who had left home maintained close phone or letter contact and saw the children regularly, and many contributed to their financial support. In essence, they took on the role of the divorced father. For some this was a temporary situation: they hadn't been sure about dissolving the marriage and wanted some time away from the family setting to think it over. (This is chancy, however, as such a departure may be used against you if there is an eventual custody battle. If you and your spouse are considering a trial separation, it would be wise to draw up a legal contract which includes an agreement that your leaving will not be prejudicial. Fathers sometimes move out for several months at a time, and it is rarely assumed there is anything deviant in this behavior. But let a mother leave home, even for a month, and she runs the risk of being called "unfit" by a court of law.)

The mother who takes the initiative in leaving the nest has one great advantage: she made the decision herself. Usually she has some career objective in mind, though occasionally it is a question of needing time alone to determine what she really wants to do or be. Almost all such mothers put their energies into improving their own lives, and thus have an impetus to keep them going. Missing the children, and sometimes feeling lonely for them, is seen as simply a natural consequence of the situation. This is something most divorced mothers experience from time to time, though it is less of a problem for the sharing mother than for the one who is distinctly a noncustodial parent.

Rejection

One of the hardest situations to cope with arises when the child opts to go live with the father because of friction with the mother. This most frequently comes about where sons are concerned, though more and more one hears of daughters' moving to their father's care because of difficulty with their mother. This leaves the woman feeling not only guilty, but also rejected; somehow she's failed to provide what the child wanted or needed, and so is being replaced by the other adult. The youngster goes tripping off to the other household, full of happy hopes and expectations, and the mother remains behind, filled with confusion, hurt, and sometimes anger.

When my son went to live with his father, I breathed a sigh of relief—and then felt the world fall out from under me. Our relationship had been fraught with scenes, tensions, and angers on both sides, and I was delighted that the boy saw the solution for himself; the last thing any mother should do is threaten to send a child to his father as a form of punishment! Yet though I couldn't see any other way out of a situation that had become well nigh impossible for both of us, the sense of failure was all but overwhelming. We got the move accomplished during the next week, and for the month that followed I walked around like a zombie. All the rationalizations in the world couldn't touch my misery. Finally, in the course of meeting with the family counselor who had suggested the move, I began to realize that no matter how hard I tried, I couldn't be a dad to that kid. And my son knew it, all the while he was angry and hurt about not having a father, so that his own feelings of disappointment were compounded by guilt about being mad at me. This is a very common problem, particularly with pubescent children, and the youngster gets caught in a double bind that only increases the difficulties.

How well any individual mother handles this situation depends largely on how she views the move. After my son, Chris, had been gone for a year, my daughter, Tasha, opined that she would also like to go live with her father, but was afraid that I would take her departure as hard as I had taken her brother's. Interestingly enough, when expressed as an honest desire to get to know her father better, coupled with the fact that she missed her brother, her suggestion didn't leave me feeling either guilty or rejected. I knew we had a good relationship, and she wasn't seeking to escape a negative home environment. Consequently, I saw it as a broadening of her world, something she wanted to do not to get away from me, but because she needed contact with her other parent and his decidedly different life-style. Thus she left for what was agreed would be a year's stay, with my blessings and good wishes. And while I missed her occasionally and looked forward to having both of the youngsters visit on holidays, there was none of the grim depression that I had experienced before.

It's not always possible to approach such a change with this attitude, even if you consciously realize that it's best for the whole family. Where conflict between the parents runs deep, and there is a residual sense of loss and betrayal, having a child announce that he or she wants to go live with the other parent may open up scarcely healed wounds. One mother whose youngest chose to live with her father because of tensions and squabbles with her siblings has found that even two years later she cannot talk about the situation without her eyes' filling up with tears. Although there is frequent visiting, and the other youngsters have stayed in the maternal nest, this woman's feeling of rejection is hard for her to deal with. Intellectually she accepts and even acknowledges the improvements in the family relationships since the move, but emotionally it still hurts. All in all, however, I think it's fair to say that while the adjustment may be hard to make, in the long run it generally proves to have been worthwhile.

Unexpected Advantages

For most of the women I talked with, finding themselves free of the prescribed definition of "mother" led to a noticeable change in attitude about themselves as people, and as women. No matter how much we may have enjoyed being mothers, and been able to integrate that aspect of our lives with careers and the desire to have an adult personal life of our own, the fact remains that being a full-time traditional mother limits both our opportunities and our experiences. Once a woman is willing to come out from behind her apron and stand as a whole, separate, and specific individual, her horizons begin to expand and she has the opportunity to shape her own life according to her own lights.

At first the loss of the maternal role may seem to leave a big hole in the fabric of your daily living. I found that when the children went to stay with their dad, I would check their bedrooms in the late afternoon to see why they were taking such long naps, and when they got older, I'd continue to listen for their arrival at dinner time or wonder whether I was supposed to have picked them up after school. This wore off for me within a couple of days, however, and the more I practiced sharing the children, the easier the adjustment became. I eventually likened my maternity to a cape which I could put on or take off—never discarding it, but not always enfolded by it, either.

Getting used to the extra time you have is one of the first and

most immediately noticeable aspects of relinquishing motherhood, even temporarily. Although you may have never resented
the continual disruption created by offspring, the fact that a
once-cleaned house stays neat and clean for days on end may
come as a real shock. If you're tired at the end of the day, there's
time to take a nap without feeling guilty about not rushing to get
dinner on the table before Junior goes to Scouts. And discovering
that Saturdays can be made up of something other than the
weekly food shopping, laundry, housecleaning, and children's
activities is often a major revelation, as is the fact that you need
not leap out of bed on Sunday morning to fix breakfast, but can
enjoy a leisurely cup of tea while you read every inch of the
newspaper if you wish. Dating, partying, or general socializing
with friends and neighbors becomes a casual "Do I want to or
not?" decision, rather than a question of logistics as to who will
feed the youngsters and how much baby-sitting time you can
afford. And if you have any long-range plans or hopes, such as
schooling or travel or a big creative project, not having to drop
everything in order to make the PTA meeting can be a real
blessing.

Nor are the benefits of taking time off from the single-parent
role limited to the immediate present. Children have a remarkably
consistent habit of growing up and leaving home, and the more
you can practice letting go of them, the easier it will be when that
day finally comes. That is not to say that you won't feel it in the
bottom of your stomach when the youngest one moves out, but
you will have a good deal more conviction that you can function
without them if you've done so at various times when they were
younger. Whatever other reassessments you may go through at
that time, at least you already know that you can make a good
life for yourself on your own.

There seems to be a sort of mysterious strength that parenthood gives some mothers. I heard one woman describe a kind of
continuous uneasiness that settled over her during the first month
after her daughter went to live with the father. "Somehow, I
avoided going back to the apartment in the evening, not just
because I was lonely or missed her, but because it seemed as
though she was a kind of talisman which would ward off bad
things." Although this doesn't make much logical sense, it was a

feeling several other mothers reported. And I myself found that for the first time in my life, I was nervous in the house alone at night after the children had grown up and left home. It was not so much that they had provided any actual protection, but rather the sense that as long as the whole family was together, nothing frightening could happen.

Parting

Unless you are sharing on some prearranged schedule, the act of saying goodbye to your children when they go to live with their other parent can be traumatic for everyone. (This holds true for fathers as well as mothers.) Be sure the youngsters know that your door is always open. Some parents take a child's departure so hard that they become cold and hostile, insisting, "If you don't want to live with *me,* you can just pack *all* your things and leave!" This kind of attitude generally comes from a bruised ego where the adult is concerned, but it can upset the children deeply. No child wants to hurt his parents, and many children will go to extreme lengths to keep from doing so. To make the youngster feel guilty about loving and living with the other parent is both unfair and immature on the part of the adult, and puts an unnecessary strain on the relationship for the youngster. Many children understand that such behavior is just pure selfishness on the parent's part, but that doesn't keep them from being hurt by it. So if it's at all possible, make a point of reassuring your offspring that you don't take their living with the other parent as a betrayal; that you wish them well, and that you look forward to seeing them on visits, talking on the phone, or exchanging letters while they're living elsewhere. It doesn't matter if the tears are running down your cheeks when you say it: as long as the warmth and assurance of your love is not conditional on their choosing between their parents, they'll understand and appreciate you for it.

Is It Worth It?

Naturally, shared custody avoids many of these problems, and each family should decide for themselves whether it's appropriate for their future. What works for one doesn't necessarily work for another, and sometimes it's a trial-and-error situation until you find the right mode of sharing. Many of the people who have been willing to try it, however, have found it to be an excellent solution to the problem. More and more magazines are carrying articles on the subject,[5] and Miriam Galper's book *Co-Parenting* provides a number of very direct first-person accounts of sharing situations. By all means look them up in the library. And don't forget to ask around in your own community; you might be surprised to discover how many sharing parents there are near you. Most such people are both willing and eager to pass on information about their own experiences, and will give you tips about what did or didn't work for them. The situation is much more common than is generally recognized by the professionals; there are an awful lot of divorced parents who are really trying to look after their children's needs first!

SHARING IDEAS

Make a list of the different types of sharing you would be willing to discuss, and evaluate their usefulness to your family. Specify the drawbacks and advantages you see in each type of arrangement, and don't hesitate to explore new ways of sharing that you two come up with between yourselves. It's your family, after all, and you're the only ones who can truly assess what is most important to your individual case.

If you each follow the form shown below, you'll have an easier time of comparing your two different lists.

TYPE OF SHARING	ADVANTAGES	DISAD-VANTAGES

FEARS ABOUT SHARING

Everyone has some doubts or questions about any contemplated custody arrangement, whether sharing or otherwise. Complete each of the sentences below which are appropriate for you. *Do not* include insults against your spouse; it's important that everything you put down be a true fear or consideration on your part, not as an assumption about what you think he or she might be likely to do.

After you have both completed this exercise, you may find that by sharing it with each other you'll have a better understanding of the fears and hesitations between you.

I like the idea of sharing the children because _____

_____, but I'm afraid it won't work because

_____ .

Shared custody won't work for us unless _____.

I'm willing to consider sharing on a _____ basis,

provided that _____.

I think sole custody to _____ is the best solution
because _____.

I would be willing to share if _____.

7
Stumbling Blocks and Stepping-stones

The Divorce Process Itself

Considering both the logic of sharing children after divorce and the positive results reported by people who have shared, why isn't this solution to the problem used more often? Probably the fact that all our social conventions have upheld the either/or, win/lose attitudes about both divorce and child custody has had a lot to do with it. Then too, lack of information must be taken into account; most of the parents I talked with had worked out their own arrangement without having heard of anyone else who shared. But on the much deeper, more personal level, there is also the animosity of the parents to be considered. When you're going through a great deal of pain and depression because of your onetime partner, it's hard to think in terms of finding ways to cooperate with that person. As one woman said, "All I want from him is to have him fall off the face of the earth! How do you expect me to talk about sharing when he's just shattered everything I thought mattered?"

Such sentiments are certainly not uncommon, particularly during the initial stages of divorce, and may well be justified from the parent's point of view. Society sees the dissolution of marriage as the erasing of a past bond; the marriage itself is said to be "breaking up," the children now come from a "broken home," and there are all sorts of personally disastrous connotations involved, such as "broken promises" and "broken hearts." It's interesting to note that our entire culture supports and encourages efforts to "come together," yet does so little to teach us how to separate with grace and inner dignity. From cradle on we are admonished to make friends, make contact, achieve intimacy, find our "other half" and establish some form of "togetherness." Nowhere do we learn how to let go, be alone, and explore our separateness as a positive thing. Even the words for coming apart are made up of negative prefixes placed before a term for unification: disconnect, disassociate, uncouple, unravel, detach. Certainly this attitude is carried over to the act of dissolving a marriage and, when added to all the personal disappointments involved, creates a climate of negation and hostility.

The advantages to be found in such a circumstance are almost entirely overlooked. Gettleman and Markowitz have written an excellent book on the subject, titled *The Courage to Divorce*, in which they point out:

> Both lay and professional writers . . . emphasize the ways that divorce ends family ties, and . . . ignore the ways in which divorce *positively restructures* family relationships. (emphasis added) [1]

Thus we tend to view divorce as a tragedy, rather than a transition, and a series of stumbling blocks instead of stepping-stones to a more productive future. Divorce actually involves a major change in life direction, a rearrangement of living patterns, and reorganization for the future. And as with any time of growth and reassessment, it is full of both hopes and hazards. How well you handle it will have a great deal to do with how your children are affected in the future, and warrants some consideration on your own part.

Understanding the Problem

In the past there has been a tendency to view divorce as an event, rather than a process. That is like saying the wedding made up the whole marriage, and whatever happened to the couple before or after was more or less incidental. Anyone who has been through a divorce knows that the actual day in court is just one of the midway points along the line. The pressures and changes in the people that led up to the decision to dissolve the marriage may have taken months to come to fruition, and the arrangements and adjustments made afterward will affect the rest of *all* your lives. It takes time to work through the various emotions encountered in ending the old and beginning the new, and each member of the family will be deeply touched by it psychologically in one way or another. The studies of both Wallerstein and Hetherington indicate that the average divorcing family experiences at least one full year of difficulties, when both children and adults have trouble dealing with many aspects of living. And often it is only by the end of the second year that positive adjustments begin to be felt and everyone seems to be on some sort of new, and—thankfully—more even, keel.[2]

Unfortunately, some people make a moderately successful adjustment to being single again, but still retain so much anger toward the opposing partner that they can't achieve an equilibrium of dissent, and so continue to badger each other through their offspring. When parents are unable to complete the psychological changes involved in divorce, they are likely to use the children as a means of getting even. Indeed, it has been found that the majority of custody or visitation disputes, either at the time of divorce or during the years following it, come about not so much because of the needs of the children, but because of the *parents' problems between themselves.* Meyer Elkin, who was instrumental in developing the Conciliation Court system, has commented that in working with about three hundred Los Angeles families with this sort of conflict,

> It became apparent . . . that custody/visitation problems are usually not the real issue . . . but are old wars being fought out on new battlefields.[3]

Such parents are simply using their children as an excuse to perpetuate their squabbles because one or both of them have not been able to finish up the divorce. Thus an antagonistic wife refuses to let the father have a normal interaction with his children, or an irate husband opts for a custody battle in order to prove to his ex that he can still call the shots in her life.

Certainly it is clear that those couples who continually return to court to fight with each other over the children may be legally separated, but they've never managed to effect an emotional divorce; they see their divorce as a license to continue fighting. Such couples are now as preoccupied with reacting to each other negatively as they once were with looking at the positives during courtship. I know of a case in which the adults were married for a total of twenty-five months, and in the five years since their separation they have returned to the courthouse more than thirty times! (So far this grand show of hostility between the parents has had little or no effect on the custody arrangement, the child has lived the greater part of his life in a warlike atmosphere, and the legal fees and attendant costs for the father alone have come to almost $60,000.) One judge, in looking at such a situation, burst out with the comment "These people are using the courtroom as a trysting place, only they're exchanging billy clubs instead of billets-doux."

Fortunately, most parents recognize the futility of this sort of behavior, as well as the damage that it does to the children. Yet the problems of accepting your divorce may be both deep and difficult. Working through the different stages of divorce and coping with the emotional turmoil you're going through can seem like an endless form of nightmare. Take heart: it's all part of the process of achieving a constructive divorce. Remember, it's not something that comes about overnight, simply because you cease to be married, any more than living happily ever after came about just because you got married to begin with.

The Stages of Divorce

Psychologists are only now beginning to study the dynamics of the divorce process. Toward this end, Kenneth Kressel and Morton Deutsch have published a study in which they list the various phases of divorce as seen by a number of therapists who work with divorcing people.[4] They note four distinct stages: the predivorce time, when the future of the marriage begins to be in doubt; the decision period itself; the time of mourning once the end of the marriage has come about; and the establishment of "reequilibration," or what I call the equilibrium of dissent.

There are specific emotional responses involved in these four stages, and while each person will express them in his or her own way, the pattern of indecision, anger, loss, and healing is evident to some degree in every constructive divorce.

The predivorce phase generally involves dissatisfaction, uncertainty, and vacillation on the part of both partners. It may be relatively brief, or long and drawn out, with both people changing their minds frequently and neither really willing to make the decisive move. Some couples stay in this situation for years on end; but once one of the partners concludes that divorce is a necessity, the second phase has begun.

The actual confrontation of an impending divorce usually brings with it hostility, pain, and confusion on a massive scale. Whereas the first stage is generally characterized by disappointment and disbelief (and the hope that *something* will make the relationship better), anger and frustration are the major components of the second phase. The appearance of this anger on the part of each partner seems to be a healthy sign, as it signifies that your own defenses are rallying. No longer wallowing helplessly in the depression and despair of a bad marriage, you are willing to face the difficulties of uncoupling, albeit with rolling pin and hammer in hand mentally. You may still be deeply hurt and frightened, but you're also willing to take a stand on the subject of the future.

The third stage, which usually comes about after the actual separation but may take place anytime before, during, or after the legal divorce, contains not only anger and depression, but also sadness, guilt, rejection, and a sense of loss so deep that the whole process is often likened to a time of mourning. This is the period when a thousand details and memories from the past crop up, all colored by your present regret, resentment, and recrimination. You may carry on hundreds of silent conversations in your head, develop a huge case of self-pity, or be unable to think of your ex without sorrow, anguish, rage, and misery. It is a normal part of getting unmarried, but unless you are able to work through both the griefs and angers, it is easy to get stuck at this point and find yourself becoming bitter, vindictive, and vengeful. Like a wound that won't heal or a record player that gets stuck in one groove, the whole thing drags on and on and there seems to be no end to it.

There are no clear-cut lines between these different phases; as with the colors of the rainbow, your reactions will overlap and bleed into each other. Different people respond to these stages differently, and the length of time needed to move from one step to the next often varies between the two partners—a fact that frequently causes further tension, unhappiness, and guilt. One person may continue to attempt a reconciliation after the other one has fully accepted the need for the divorce, or you may both be so caught up in the hostilities of the decision itself that you feed each other's anger and neither is able to move into the mourning period. Or one may be stuck in the grieving process, and so be unable to accept the positive as well as negative aspects of the situation. When this happens, the person involved doesn't complete the divorce psychologically, but clings instead to all the pain and sorrow and injustices of the past, neither resolving the problem nor getting free of it. Working through these various stages is vitally important to the well-being of the individual adults as well as the children involved, however, as each step is part of the necessary transition from a bad marriage to a constructive divorce.

Eventually, unless you really enjoy holding on to all that misery, the adrenaline will diminish, the wounds get a final licking, and the scars begin to fade. It is at this point that you start to move away from the past and the sense of life and living returns to the present. At last you're not only free to go on with your own life, you can feel comfortable about letting your ex go on with his or hers.

There will probably always be areas of touchiness and sensitivity in each of you, but you will have learned how to avoid opening the old wounds, and you'll both stop dwelling on your own personal sore spots. Once you've completed the divorce process, your reactions and responses to the children's other parent become appropriate to the present situation. There may be lingering defenses and new disagreements, but they won't be as likely to flare into huge bonfires that threaten not only your own but also your children's peace of mind. You will have established your own truce, your ability to recognize and accept a "coparenting" relationship with your ex, and your personal equilibrium of dissent. Thus you can go about your separate lives while still functioning well for your children.

Letting Go

All of which may sound fine in theory, yet seem all but impossible while you're in the actual throes of divorce. It helps if you have a little perspective on the emotions going on at this time. Although the problems which have led to your decision to go your separate ways are bound to be unique to each couple, and the way each of you personally copes with the stages of divorce will be individual, there are several dynamics and reactions that come into play just *because* of the decision to end the marriage. They may show up in any one of the first three phases, but their eventual disappearance is a sure sign that the fourth stage has been completed successfully. Though they pertain to you more as partners than as parents, how you deal with them will be reflected in your attitudes about child custody.

Psychologists, social scientists, and lawyers will all tell you that there is no more turbulent time in a person's life than that encountered in going through a divorce. It is not uncommon to experience great swings of emotion, from relief, exhilaration, and even gaiety to deep depression, morose guilt, and flaming anger, sometimes all in the course of one day's time. The more passionate and emotional the marriage was, the more passionate and emotional the divorce is likely to be; if yours was a fairly calm and rational union, you may even accomplish a calm and rational divorce, at least on the surface. Yet whatever other feelings are involved, a sense of anxiety and fear about the future is likely to be part of your reaction. This fear can lead to unexpected outbursts, sudden changes of mind, or a general sullenness, but it is rarely expressed in words or actions that are direct reflections of the sadness or depression you're experiencing. Thus you may feel totally debilitated and vulnerable inside, but confront the world, and particularly your opposing partner, with an enormous amount of defensive hostility and bitterness.

There are specific reasons for this kind of behavior, contradictory as it seems. It is often observed that as people reach the end of a long project they tend to feel let down, devalued, and depressed. No matter how successful their work has been, they will negate their achievements, look with cool distaste at their past involvements, and discount all the positives that went before. This is a common phenomenon, frequently observed in women whose children are growing up and leaving home, among men who are about to retire, and even in persons with terminal illnesses, who are in the process of letting go of living. There seems to be a need for some kind of withdrawal, of disengagement, as though one has to say, "Ah, it wasn't important anyhow" before being ready to give up that activity.

This tendency to downgrade the positives of the past is seen over and over again in people who are divorcing; not only do you feel all the pain and sorrow of the present situation: you look bitterly on the past and reject whatever was of value in the relationship. Perhaps this is necessary in order to accept that the relationship is ending; to cling to all the good things is to make the separation unbearable. Unfortunately, these devaluating tactics are rarely understood, either by the person who is experiencing them or by the other partner who encounters a sudden barrage of angry and sometimes unfair denunciations. When these feelings start to be exchanged by divorcing couples, they tend to spark further conflicts; each feels additionally insulted, humiliated, or enraged by the other's comments, and new grievances are piled on past aggravations.

Yet ironically, the divorcing partners are rarely ready to let go completely. No matter how much each protests that he or she just wants to be free and finished with the whole thing, there is still the secret security of knowing that, until the last sheets are divided and the final agreement signed, the marriage is not entirely ended.

This sometimes leads to what an attorney I know calls "the

cuckoo-clock complex." He had a case in which both parties had agreed to a full and complete division of the property, bills, assets, and child custody—all the details that generally foul up the contemporary divorce. These people, with eminent good sense and willingness to work together, had ironed out everything, they thought, and all the attorney had to do was write up their agreement. All went very smoothly until the last item on the household list, which was a cuckoo clock. "It's mine! Your grandmother gave it to me when we got married." "Oh no you don't! It was my relative who bought it, and it'll stay in my family now that you're leaving." Heated words led almost to blows, and both parties marched out, each intent on a court fight that had started over a $100 cuckoo clock! The attorney offered to buy a new clock for whoever would give it up, but neither would listen. Eventually, after retaining a second lawyer and scheduling the whole thing for a hearing before the judge, the couple resolved their differences on the courthouse steps. This entire maneuver had cost them considerable time and money, to say nothing of abraded feelings and lots of recriminations, but it had also postponed that last, final parting.

This is not an unusual story; most attorneys can tell you of cases in which one item became so important its actual value was blown all out of proportion. Why? Probably because it was the very last tie from the marriage. No matter how much you want to move into the present and future of your life, letting go of the past can be very frightening, and if you can postpone it by disagreeing on the final step, you won't have to face it for a little while longer.

Thus some couples end up provoking needless battles to stay in contact, at the same time heaping endless insults on each other because they can't bear to remember that it was once a good relationship. Long-hidden hurts, unexpected accusations, and sudden intractableness come to the surface when least expected, leaving both partners feeling rejected, misunderstood, and unfairly attacked. And all too often these chaotic reactions and responses are translated into battles over the children.

This doesn't mean you shouldn't have all those conflicting feelings, or that you should stifle or suppress them. They may be part of the normal, if uncomfortable, process of your own disengagement. What it does mean is that it may help both of you to cope better if you understand what is going on, and that it is *absolutely essential* for each of you to see to it that your personal adult reactions to each other be kept separate from your parental responsibilities to your offspring. Waging war with your ex over the cuckoo clock may be something both of you need to do in order to "consummate the divorce," but that's very different from using "possession" of your children to get revenge on your partner.

To want to dissolve the marriage contract is one thing; to attempt to wipe out all that went before by denying the positive elements is quite something else. Just as you can't break the bond between parent and child, you can't tear up the memories, achievements, or present results of the years spent together as a family. Any sustained effort to do so denies your own living experience and cheats your progeny of their heritage, since you're also attacking *their* memories, their perception of the other parent, and their very existence! If you need to bicker, harangue, and defy each other, do it on your own time, and about your own subjects. Although the youngsters will naturally feel some of the effects of it, they won't be used as weapons, and their future stability won't become the ransom for your personal vendetta.

Divorce as Reorganization

It would be nice to think that everyone who divorces will work through the various phases of the process and eventually turn what had been an emotional swamp into a delta land, nourishing growth. Obviously, it doesn't always work that way. Yet for the family with children it's not just a question of what would be nice, but rather what is most important for the youngsters. Although spouses sometimes come and go, parents are indeed forever. There's one set per lifetime, and even when they no longer live together, they never cease to be parents in the eyes of their offspring. The children's definition of what a parent is (good, bad, or indifferent) will be based on their own experiences with you, and no amount of paperwork, legal decrees, or physical absence is going to change the fact that you are *both* their closest relatives.

For your youngsters the separation will mean one very specific thing: the pattern of their daily lives will change. The issues that have caused you to decide to go your own ways may or may not be understood by the children, but the end result is a restructuring of the family as a whole, and that's what they will perceive and react to. If both of you can acknowledge this fact, and are willing to consider your divorce as a *rearrangement* rather than the ending of your relationship, you'll be able to avoid some of the worst hazards where child custody is concerned.

When looked at in this light, divorce can be seen as a transition period during which the parents move from the nuclear-family system to one in which each adult is allowed the freedom necessary to create a separate future, while at the same time acknowledging the other's right and duty to be an actively involved and supportive parent to the children. The relationship between the past partners undergoes a major change and evolves into something new: no longer mates, you have become co-parents. Hence you'll need to reassess your attitudes about each other, and be willing to look at your relationship from this new perspective. This holds true regardless of what form of custody you use.

Unfortunately, divorcing couples too often become frozen in regard to each other, and continue to interact and respond to old stimuli instead of developing this necessary new relationship. Jacqueline Larcombe Doyle has commented on the frozen quality of divorce relations by likening them to a still picture taken in the midst of a dance.[5] The couple involved, whose past relationship has been full of the fluid, moving, constantly changing patterns of any human interaction, are suddenly caught in the moment of request and rejection, appeal and denial that comes about at the time of separation. Thus both are transfixed not only in the way they see themselves but also in their picture of the partner, in the hostile, threatening, pleading, or despairing posture encountered at the time of parting. These images can last for many years, with guilt, fear, rejection, or despair becoming the predominant characteristic of self-definition, while the partner is forever seen in the stance of that one frozen moment. That life goes on, that the interaction between these dancers will realign itself into a new pattern, and that completion of the first three stages of divorce can lead to a healthy and constructive approach to your new relationship are not understood. All you know is that you have been deeply hurt, and have no way to recover your own sense of balance as long as the other partner is perceived in that still-frame memory.

This ability to allow the other person to change, both in himself and in your perception of him, is necessary in all human relationships, and especially in marriage and divorce. It is not uncommon to hear divorcing partners exclaim, with mystification and sometimes sincere puzzlement, "He (or she) is simply not the same person I married." This is, of course, a very valid comment; few people remain untouched by the interaction of marriage, and divorcing couples have tended to grow and change in ways that each mate finds uncomfortable or hard to accept in the other. By the same token, divorce itself brings about many changes, and the person with whom you are a coparent will be different in many ways from the one you confronted at the end of the marriage. By the time you have completed your psychological divorce, you'll be able to let go of the old images and expectations, and recognize your past spouse as a separate person with whom you now share the responsibilities of parenting in a new way.

This need to see each other in a new context is one of the fundamental aspects of achieving an equilibrium of dissent. It ties in directly with the last of the common complaints from divorced parents, mentioned in earlier chapters. The mother, protective of her new independence and feeling vulnerable and guarded in her relations with her ex, continues to see him as a threat to her security and the creator of difficult situations. And the father, who may or may not wish to share his newfound insights with her, still feels compelled to meet his responsibilities to the family by advising them about what to do, how to do it, and when. (Sometimes this manifests itself as a comment in retrospect, so that the information comes out as a form of criticism of what has been done, rather than a command for the future; in either case it is likely to be met with a stone-wall type of resistance and righteous wrath on the part of the woman and children.) In either event, each assumes that the other is coming from the old position of discord, and so reacts with the same old angers and animosities. Neither is able to consider the other in the context of their *new* relationship, and so each maintains the polarized hostility typical of the divorce process itself.

Moving out of these old positions will help you to overcome the past associations, expectations, and automatic assumptions, and be well on the way to establishing an equilibrium of dissent. Both the marriage *and* the divorce will be concluded, you'll have achieved psychological "closure" on that period of your lives, and each can concentrate on the present need for coparenting. Kressel and Deutsch sum the whole thing up as follows:

> The successful divorce should . . . leave each parent with a balanced view of the other, and of the marriage and with a sense of psychological closure . . . The constructive divorce . . . is one in which psychic injury to the children is minimized, principally through the maintenance of a good coparenting relationship between the former spouses. In particular, children should be free of the apprehension that loving either parent will jeopardize their place in the affections of the other.[6]

Working It Out

In looking at ways of achieving a constructive divorce, Kressel and Deutsch point out the need for *cooperative negotiations* "undertaken with a healthy sense of one's own needs and a spirit of fair play."[7] This is particularly true when child custody is involved, since the negotiating of a reasonable custody arrangement becomes the foundation for the entire family's new structure. Therefore the need for establishing a "good coparenting relationship," both for your own sakes and for those of the children, can't be emphasized too strongly.

It is not uncommon for one or both of the parents to feel so helpless, hurt, and vulnerable, or so guilty for wanting to end the marriage, that he or she passively accepts whatever the other partner or attorneys suggest. When this happens and the settlement is made *without both people actively participating* in the decisions that affect their offspring's lives, there is a high probability that later on the passive parent will move into the angry stage of divorce, become dissatisfied with the original agreement, and initiate a court battle to change the arrangement. Some fathers, on encountering this situation, simply disappear from the scene, leaving the children without any contact whatsoever. Either response is going to be disastrous for the youngsters, and is certainly not part of a constructive solution to the problem.

The process of working out a custody arrangement between yourselves can be therapeutic in itself, and if you are at all willing to do so, that in itself will help create a more balanced situation for everyone concerned. By becoming actively involved in the reorganization of your family, you are confronting and dealing with the divorce decision, and taking responsibility for how the future develops. The very act of working together in this manner provides you *both* with an opportunity to create a fair and constructive arrangement for your children, at the same time establishing and defining your own new relationship as coparents. Thus you are less likely to remain "stuck" in one of the incompleted phases of the divorce.

That doesn't mean you won't experience a fair amount of pain and frustration and sometimes anger with each other, but that would be there anyway. And if you can turn the energy of that anger toward resolving your conflicts between yourselves, everyone will benefit. It has been said that we are an "anger-phobic" society: that is, we are afraid of anger both in ourselves and in others. As a result, we often fail to realize its healthy aspect and the tremendous amount of energy it makes available to us. Anger, provided it is not twisted into spite, vindictiveness, or hatred, can be the impetus necessary to take action, to express dissatisfaction, to clarify your thinking and improve the situation. I strongly suggest you both read *The Angry Book* by Dr. Theodore I. Rubin and *The Intimate Enemy* by Dr. George Bach and Peter Wyden. Learning how to fight fairly, argue constructively, and generally turn your grievances against each other to productive ends is bound to be one of the most useful skills divorced parents can acquire!

Getting Help

All of this information about the dynamics of divorce should give you a strong enough background on the subject to begin to consider how you want to proceed with making your own decisions. This is a major step, a life-changing rearrangement, and it deserves to be made carefully and with much thought. Don't feel you have to rush through it, just to get free of the tensions of your present situation; jumping to a bad decision because you don't want to face the problem of working together to create a good one will only leave you with future battles and a lot of scars.

Many psychologists mention that they see children and adults whose major problems are immediately traceable to an uncompleted divorce, either their own or their parents'. If such people had been able to work through the difficulties of divorce with professional help, many years of distress could have been avoided, and those youngsters' childhood memories would have been far pleasanter! Even if one or both of you have been living with an uncompleted divorce for years, it is still possible to work it out, and not only improve your own relationship as coparents, but also protect your children from further pain at the hands of your own frustration.

Up until recently there have been very few programs for training people specifically for divorce-therapy work, but the need is now being recognized professionally, and divorce clinics and workshops are being set up across the country. These are oriented not toward getting couples to reunite, but rather toward helping them achieve constructive divorces. Nor do such counselors see their clients as being "sick"; they concentrate their efforts on helping to resolve the areas of conflict that are causing the most trouble, and often enable the parents to come to a much better understanding between themselves.

If you have been going to a family counselor before deciding to divorce, don't stop seeing him or her just because you've decided to terminate the marriage. Too often people drop family counseling as soon as they've contacted an attorney, figuring that the decision to divorce puts an end to the usefulness of the therapist. Since the dividing of property and making decisions about custody are at least as harrowing as the troubles that went before, you'd be very well advised to have the help and guidance of a therapist during this time. A good divorce therapist can work with both of you to help get your arrangement settled, and can often mediate where the attorney may only aggravate the situation. A growing number of family-law attorneys are now working with family therapists and/or child psychologists to help divorce clients find a reasonable way to separate. If you don't know of any family counselors who act in this capacity, ask the attorneys you interview whom they would recommend, and whether they make a practice of working as part of a divorce team in this way. Certainly such an approach provides a better understanding of how your children are reacting, and will undoubtedly ease the tensions where you yourselves are concerned.

Another source of professional guidance to consider is the Veterans Administration hospital in your area. If a member of your family is a U.S. veteran, chances are you will qualify for family counseling under the new program the V.A. is presently developing. This particular service looks at the family unit as a whole, and will attempt to work with you in finding the best way to handle your reorganization. This is an excellent approach, and since V.A. services are available across the country, many divorced or divorcing parents should be able to find the help they need.

Whether you decide to negotiate your own custody agreement between yourselves or with the help of a divorce therapist, remember that you, as parents, can probably find a better solution to your situation than any outsider can. You have a better understanding of your family's needs than either attorney or judge, and leaving it up to them is avoiding your responsibility to your offspring. So you'd do well to sort out which are personal problems between the two of you as adults, and which are family needs and considerations. The steps in the next chapter will be relevant to looking at the family needs no matter which custody arrangement you're considering, and they are useful regardless of whether you are presently divorcing or planning a custody rearrangement long after the actual divorce.

The apparent key to a constructive divorce and consequent reorganization of the family lies in how the parents react. It has been stated that a divorce is a disaster to the children only if it's a disaster in the eyes of the parents, and that seems to be borne out time and time again in interviews. So keep in mind that if you are able and willing to make a reasonably constructive adjustment, the children will feel more secure and everyone will benefit in the long run. It's up to you.

8
Step by Step

Establishing Family Priorities

More than one couple have stood in the midst of their marital wreckage each swearing that no matter how reasonable and cooperative he or she is being, the other is bent on the total destruction of any remaining shred of respect, trust, or cooperative endeavor. How in heaven's name are you going to reach any kind of accord when the opposing partner is out to sabotage every effort you make? You'll probably both agree that you want this situation to harm the children as little as possible, and then get into a screaming melee over what is the least destructive way to go about it. (Don't feel bad; a divorcing couple can always find something to fight over, even it it's only the way the other one says "Hello.")

Yet the fact remains that you have two problems to contend with simultaneously: how to reorganize the family and keep from committing mayhem while you're doing it. It's like being a juggler on a tightrope: if you concentrate on your feet, you're likely to drop your balls, and if you concentrate entirely on your juggling, you may land splat in the sawdust! A successful resolution is possible, if you take it one step at a time. Any flying leaps may prove to be disastrous, and while this approach may seem slow, it's much safer for all concerned.

Family Priorities

Once you can view your separation or divorce as an attempt to find a better living arrangement which will lessen the pressures between the adults and still provide the children with the necessary parental support they require for growing up, the solutions you are seeking become *family* solutions. They have to take into account the needs and desires of each of the family members, since the welfare of one reflects on the welfare of the rest. Thus if one parent wants to exclude the other from all but minimal contact with the kids, both the children and the parents will suffer. And if one of the adults wants to go back to school and spend the next three years moving into a better career position, insisting that parent must also take over sole custody of the youngsters will hurt the rest of the family. What you need to do, then, is consider the needs and desires not only of the children, but of each adult as well, and try to find a solution that provides the best possible balance for everyone. In this way the divorce will afford the adults as much space and separation as necessary, and still allow them to function as a supportive family system for the youngsters.

Therefore, instead of making unilateral decisions about how to restructure your family, it's wise to have several discussions on the subject over a period of time. You don't have to decide everything at one sitting, and it may be that in looking for the most suitable arrangement for everyone, you'll discover a number of different possibilities that need to be thought over and explored. Don't hesitate to discuss each new idea; talking about it needn't commit you to a particular solution, and while nothing is going to be perfect, knowing that you both agreed to try the system which seemed to be most appropriate for your family needs as a whole will make it easier to live with later on.

This sort of conference is best held between the two adults at first, in order to determine just what forms of custody you're willing to consider, and on what terms. This is a time when you can honestly begin to establish your new relationship, as well as looking at the children's future. And if either of you is feeling cranky and hard to get along with, you can always put the discussion off for another day, when tempers are less snappish. (Naturally, if you keep hiding behind this excuse to avoid dealing with the problems that need to be solved, you won't get anywhere. If you find yourself postponing these conferences on a regular basis, you'd better reconsider what your motives really are; it could be that you're trying to put off accepting the separation altogether.)

Since providing your youngsters with a balanced upbringing is one of your primary concerns, it's just as well to look at this aspect of restructuring your family first. The questions of who will live where and how much money will be supplied by whom are the details that must be considered in order to make the best arrangement possible. They can be dealt with, however, at a later date, after you have determined what the basic family needs are, and assessed who can give what to which child. Once the family's priorities are established, the practical aspects of how to implement them often fall into place without any undue fuss.

Parental Involvement

In the two-parent family it is expected that both parents will contribute to the children's lives, each in the area of influence he or she feels best equipped to handle and deems most important. Thus you have a parent who is good at physical skills teaching them one thing, while the other parent may concentrate on social graces or emotional support. Unfortunately, this division of parental interests and talents is largely overlooked in the traditional child-custody arrangement, which cheats the child out of the non-custodial parent's contribution to his upbringing and development. That doesn't have to be the case in your family, however.

It's long been accepted that different people fulfill different needs in each other, and this holds as true between parents and offspring as it does between friends. One parent may have a closer bond to the youngsters where intellectual stimulation is concerned, while the other parent may be more involved with the creative side of living. Or you might be the better picnic planner, model-airplane builder, and general recreational genius, but not as good a guide to financial affairs as is your ex. The first exercise at the end of this chapter is designed to help you determine what your own parental strengths and priorities are, as well as giving you a chance to recognize and allow for those areas in which your opposing partner can be more helpful to the children. By all means use this to look at what you and your ex each provide for the children, which responsibilities can best be delegated to whom, and in what areas you can share. And if you think of other subjects not covered in that list, feel free to add them.

It is not uncommon for people to assume that in order to be effective parents, they must agree on how to raise the kids. While it is true that two totally different approaches in the same household are likely to confuse not only the progeny but the adults as well, the fact is that putting different emphasis on different aspects of child rearing can be a particularly helpful thing in the divorced family. Using the list of parental-influence areas, arrange the subjects in a list of your own, with the most important ones at the top and the less vital things at the bottom. This will give you a basic outline of what your priorities in child raising are, and when you and your ex get together to begin looking at ways to reorganize, you can compare your two lists. Chances are they won't be identical; but instead of their being a source of contention, you can use this difference to the children's advantage. If your ex places more stress on something in which you have only limited interest, let that become an area of strong involvement where he or she is concerned. The fact that you don't rank it among your first priorities doesn't mean the youngsters won't profit from it, and if the other parent sees it as important and wants to provide it, by all means encourage that. In this way you'll both have a chance to see that your children get the things you each consider most worthwhile, neither one will worry that something of value is being denied the offspring, and you'll each gain experience in cooperating for your children's benefit—all of which are important steps in learning to compromise with each other as divorced parents.

Sometimes the difference in priorities is quite clear-cut, and can indicate how best to arrange for time sharing. For instance, if religious education is not one of your paramount considerations but it is important to your ex-husband, it would be natural to have the children spend those days or evenings which relate to religious observance with him. On the other hand, if you are very much involved in their physical development, encouraging them to go out for sports or arranging for weekly gymnastic meets or ballet classes, and your spouse doesn't see that as a high priority, it's logical for you to fulfill that part of the parenting function on the long-term basis yourself.

Naturally there will be large areas of overlap in your lists, and this is where the definition of how much you influence your children in these different matters may be helpful. You can explore that part of the exercise on your own; if you and your ex start comparing these things and find that it only leads to arguments about how you evaluate yourself and each other, you're not using it properly. The idea is to help you discover where your involvement with the youngsters is strongest, not to give you new ammunition for more personal fighting!

Parental Agreement

Now is an excellent time to come to an agreement about not undermining each other with the children. This is always a worry for the noncustodial parent, and an early agreement that each of you will respect the other's place in your offspring's lives will benefit both you and the youngsters. Although most of the parents I interviewed said that they tried hard not to comment negatively about each other to the children, many admitted that it occasionally happened. Some apologized to the children when it happened, some called and apologized to the other adult, and a few did both. All said that recognizing it might happen, and agreeing to try to avoid it in the future, were very much part of their agreement right from the start. Discussing this between yourselves and taking an active part in reassuring each other that it won't happen intentionally will help to establish a workable rapport between you, and cuts down on the fear that either of you will cast stones at the other's parenthood.

One of the most important things to keep in mind, both now and later, is that yours is not the only way to raise the children. Kids are remarkably resilient creatures, and can accept a broad range of experiences, provided that they aren't made to feel guilty about them or to worry that one or another way of doing things is "wrong." Even if your ex is much stricter about house rules— insisting that everyone be in bed at a certain time, behave in a specified manner at the dinner table, and complete all chores before being allowed to engage in recreational pursuits—although you may cringe inwardly at such rigidity, the children will probably accept it quite calmly *as long as you don't stir up trouble*. By the same token, a casual approach to chores, mealtimes, and how much television is watched isn't going to corrupt your darlings forever.

Most cases of parental conflict over details of how one parent does things as compared with how the other does them are superficial excuses for expressing unresolved feelings involving a deeper (and more personal) anger. I know a mother who claimed her ex was absolutely unfit to have the children overnight because he let them have chocolate cake for breakfast. And in another case, the father was convinced that his past wife's dating of other men was detrimental to the offspring. These are obvious cases of rationalization; each resented the other's action, and so concluded that it was harmful to the youngsters. That the children showed no sign of malnutrition in the first case, or that the mother was discreet and certainly not being promiscuous in the second, was overlooked by each parent in their continual effort to prove their exes a bad influence. The children in each case were not nearly as concerned as their parents; cake for breakfast was an occasional lark, not a steady diet, and the mother's need for adult companionship was accepted as perfectly normal in her youngsters' eyes.

So don't panic if you each want to be involved with your kids in many of the same areas, but with different philosophies. There's always more than one way to do things, and letting your offspring experience that for themselves isn't going to hurt them in the long run. You can certainly explain how you think it's best to handle a situation *without* coming out and saying the other parent's solution is wrong. And as long as you each reaffirm with the children that the other parent loves and cares for them too, and simply shows it in a different way than you do, you aren't undermining that relationship. All of you will feel more secure and comfortable about not getting caught in the middle of a conflict over how things "should" be done, each adult has the opportunity to help in raising the kids, and the children gain a broader insight into what it is to be an adult human.

Most sharing parents (and many who have sole custody as well) report having a "When in Rome, do as the Romans do" policy firmly established with their children. Thus they not only agree with their exes not to undermine each other's authority, they also make it clear to the youngsters that they will not get involved in petty squabbles. When my children would return from their father's with some tale of woe, I could listen, assess just how important the matter was, and if necessary call him to talk about what our child was experiencing. For the most part such complaints were of a minor sort, dealing with bedtimes or lunch money or other small aggravations. If I agreed with his stand on the subject, I told the children so, and if not I simply resorted to the "When in Rome" rule. I didn't have to agree with him in order to support his right to interact with the youngsters in his own fashion, and I certainly wasn't going to foment trouble for either them or myself by taking sides and causing a scene over something that was basic to his nature. (If it was something that disturbed the youngsters deeply, I made a point of talking it over with him; sometimes there were circumstances I was not familiar with, or consequences that he had no way of knowing about before. Such conversations are never particularly easy, as they may smack of criticism, but only once did we get into a major hassle; the rest of the time the exchange of information was more productive than not.) Children can handle the "When in Rome" concept very well, as long as you are clear about it yourself.

This is also a good time to think about major catastrophes; agreeing to keep each other informed immediately about such things as broken arms, severe illnesses, or the need for a parental conference in the event of a major disciplinary situation is an excellent idea. You don't have to agree about little things in order

to be supportive to each other and the children when the big
issues come up.

Parent–Child Relationships

While you and your ex are discussing the various aspects of parenting and how best to reorganize your family in order to provide
for them, you should also consider any particularly strong emotional bonds that may exist within the family already. Although
one assumes that siblings will stay together, this doesn't have to
be the case if there is some strong reason for one child to go with
a specific parent. In the past it's been a frequent practice of the
courts to allow pubescent boys to live with their fathers, on the
assumption that they specifically need paternal guidance during
the time of becoming young adults. It's gradually being recognized that this need is not limited *only* to sons, and that not all
fathers are well equipped to handle adolescent children; but the
practice of acknowledging that the special relationships between
individual youngsters and their parents should be taken into account is certainly a valid one.

Nor do these considerations have to be limited only to the
strong, positive bonds. If one of the children is going through a
stage in which he or she has a particularly difficult time getting
along with a specific parent, it's ludicrous to expect that child to
be comfortable with that adult in a single-parent family. Or if
there is a lot of tension and rivalry between siblings, it might be
best for all concerned to separate them, so that one or more live
with the father while the others stay with their mother.

These bonds are much more difficult to define than parental
priorities are, and it will be up to you as sensitive and aware
parents to recognize and discuss how they affect your decisions
about restructuring the family. It isn't time yet to ask the children
about their feelings; that can come later, once you've established
between yourselves some idea of what is possible. For now it's
enough that you look at your family as a whole and decide if there
are strong and compelling reasons for certain pairings between
children and parents, or between siblings.

Many families are so homogeneous in their emotional makeup

that the children feel equally comfortable with each parent. If that's the case for you, don't feel you *have* to find defendable reasons for having one or another of your children with either of you. The fact that you are both their parents, and as such want to participate in their raising, is sufficient.

A word of caution: This is no place for your own ego to get involved; to fight over who needs whom is just a waste of time. You can both handle this best by sticking to your own feelings and defining your own relationships with the youngsters, rather than evaluating your spouse's. Comments such as "Well, you never did understand Lisa" will only muddy the water and make for bad feelings. So when you're dealing with this aspect of your discussions, give the devil his due and allow your opposing partner to express his or her feelings without taking umbrage at them. And remember that your ex is the children's parent, not their spouse! The fact that that person didn't fill your needs as an adult mate doesn't mean he or she can't be a perfectly adequate parent to the children.

Adult Needs

In the past one sometimes heard divorced parents criticized as being selfish, egocentric, and more interested in their own happiness than in their children's welfare. If anything, many parents whose marriages are ending tend to be overanxious about their children on the one hand, and unable to think about what they themselves want in their lives on the other. This frequently causes them to focus almost exclusively on the youngsters, and they become so engrossed in fighting over what is best for their offspring, they feel guilty about considering what is best for themselves. Yet if the restructuring of your family pattern is going to be successful, it has to take into account the specific goals, hopes, plans, and needs of the two adults as well as the children. And the better an idea you have of what you want your future to include, the more readily you and your ex can discuss it.

If you don't have any particular direction in mind at the moment, that's okay. But if you do, if you've thought about going back to school, or taking a leave of absence from your job, or beginning a new career, this may be a good time to bring it up. Any of these things will affect what happens to the children, after all, and with a little cooperation between the parents, can provide further guidelines for decisions about child custody.

Among the divorced parents I've interviewed, those who felt they had the best arrangements for their children worked together to a fairly large degree. If a husband wanted to take a leave from his job and go to school, for instance, the wife would waive a certain amount of the child support he was expected to pay, on the condition that after he was through and established in a new job, he'd take the children while she went to school, or catch up on his back child support so that she could have the time to write her book, start a new business, or whatever else she wanted to do. Often this sort of cooperation came about after the divorce was completed, when the two of them had established an equilibrium of dissent, and emotions were no longer quite so volatile. But, for some couples, recognition of the need to work together for everyone's welfare is part of the reorganizing process right from the start.

This doesn't mean you have to agree automatically to whatever your ex is proposing, or that he or she should necessarily concur as soon as you voice a thought about your own future. Just being willing and able to listen to and consider these things is enough to begin with. How much weight they assume as you come closer to deciding on what to do next is up to the two of you. Because people in the throes of divorce often go through sudden and radical changes of interest or direction, it's very possible that the thing you thought you wanted yesterday will have nothing to do with what you work for tomorrow, so don't feel you have to decide everything all at once. But do get into the habit of listening to any proffered ideas, be willing to consider them from several points of view (the eventual effect on the other adult, the immediate effect upon the children, and what your motivations are for objecting to them), and get your own ideas well enough organized to be able to express and explain your reaction. This kind of communication, if handled tactfully and without bullying or bribery, can help to establish the sort of trust and respect which makes divorced parents of the same children a lot more comfortable about their relationship.

Needless to say, if immediate remarriage is one of your hopes and plans for the future, talking extensively about it with your ex is not going to improve your relationship at all! But you should pay him or her the courtesy of at least mentioning it tactfully; no one is as justifiably enraged as a rejected spouse who has not been informed that the children will have a new stepparent. In most instances, newly married couples want to have at least a period of several months together before considering taking on children, and if this is the case, you can assure your ex that you aren't using your new status as a means of appealing to the court to get full custody. Although I interviewed many families in which one or both of the parents had remarried, and found them to be some of the best examples of positive divorce and successfully "blended" families, expecting that to come about immediately after the divorce is a bit unrealistic. So if you find yourself in this position, bear with it. Time and future efforts to establish a reasonable rapport among all of you can eventually smooth things out. Don't, whatever you do, get the kids involved in it; trying to woo them into a new family environment or turning them against their now remarried parent is only going to lead to misery for one and all, and will escalate what may be a difficult time into an outright disaster.

Special Considerations

There may be some special, outside consideration that needs to be taken into account. For instance, if you have a child with a major medical problem, you'll probably want to stay in the area closest to the doctor or hospital where the child is being treated. By the same token, one or all of the youngsters may be heavily involved in special schools, community activities, or advanced sports and resist strongly the idea of any change of residence that would disturb their present situation. These things must be examined and their importance weighed in the light of what the whole family needs. If the children are old enough to have a voice in what they want their future to include socially, bring up these questions when you talk it all over with them; they'll appreciate your concern, and you may find that you've under- or overestimated the importance of these things in their lives. These are the sort of details that the members of each family need to look at for themselves, and then act on accordingly, so don't be afraid to discuss them.

Now that you've explored the various philosophical, psychological, emotional, and social criteria that are important to your family's future, it's time to begin to look at how you can incorporate those things into your reorganization. After you have pretty well established who should live with whom, and been able to work out some pattern of responsibilities for allowing the most normal interchange between children and parents, the next question is how you go about realizing those desires. And that, of course, is what the following chapter is all about.

PARENTAL INFLUENCE
(Based on the work of Dr. Melvin Roman)

On a separate piece of paper, make a list of the areas of parental involvement noted below, arranging them with the most important at the top, the least important at the bottom. There will probably be some which you group together as equally important, but try to make the list as balanced as possible; they can't *all* fit at the top! This will provide you with an outline of what things you hold as high-, medium- and low-priority items. Get together with your opposing partner and compare your lists as a means of beginning to see who can best provide what for the various children.

FINANCIAL AFFAIRS   RELIGIOUS DEVELOPMENT
PHYSICAL DEVELOPMENT   INTELLECTUAL DEVELOPMENT
MORAL OR ETHICAL DEVELOPMENT   CREATIVE DEVELOPMENT
EMOTIONAL DEVELOPMENT   RECREATIONAL ACTIVITIES
MANNERS AND HOW TO BEHAVE   BEING PART OF A FAMILY
ROUTINE DAILY CARE AND SAFETY

If you wish, make another list of your own involvement with your children in these different areas, rating them from 5 points, as a high level of influence, down to 1 point if you have little or no input on that part of your youngster's life. You may wish to make up such a list for each child, as parents often interact with their individual offspring in different ways.

Which of these areas do you most enjoy sharing with your children? Which would you like to be more involved in? Which are you willing or desirous of cutting back on? Does your ex want to contribute more strongly in any of those areas? Are you willing to let him or her do so? Are there any places where your opposing partner is less involved and you can take up the slack without too much difficulty? What areas would you like to have him or her be more involved in? How can you make that possible?

9
Putting It All Together

Creating Your Own Custody Solution

Once you've had a chance to look at the various things that are important in the reorganization of your family, and explored some of the options that are available, it's time to get down to the nitty-gritty of how to implement those things which you agree you want in your futures. This means examining the finances, talking it all over with the children, deciding where you go from here, and finding a way to tell the rest of the world about it (including your own parents). Some of these areas are touchy or difficult, but all must be dealt with, one way or another. They are the details that will help you through the transition, and should be respected as the cornerstone of the new family structure you're designing.

Financial Facts

Money, or the lack of it, crops up again and again in the course of divorce settlements. Nor is this surprising; what was recently used for the maintenance and support of a single family must now be spread over two households. And unless you're very wealthy, you'll probably find that there just isn't enough to go around! Time and again attorneys mention the fact that divorcing couples just don't realize how much their life-styles will have to change, and are therefore shocked and angry when confronted by the necessary adjustments demanded of them. If you are in the middle of preparing for the dissolution of your marriage, and have been able to work out the various other factors involved in your custody decision, now's the time to set aside a quiet evening to go over the family budget.

As already noted, money holds a lot of symbolic meaning for many people, and the division of it, particularly when there is a lot of distress and acrimony between the parties, can lead to bloody battles and major declarations of war. If you're the kind of wife who decides to run out and charge everything in sight in a last, vengeful shopping spree which you assume *he'll* have to pay for, you may have quite a surprise coming when you discover that his attorney has already counseled him to close all the accounts. Or if you're the sort of husband who tries to hide your assets, secreting the savings accounts in your own name and declaring that financially you're in such a slump that you can't pay anything more than bare-minimum child support, you're depriving your youngsters by your own selfish and punitive attitude. Chances are such people will end up spending a fortune in the courts in order to fight over pennies, and while this is better than fighting over custody, it seems a sad waste of time and family resources.

Interestingly enough, however, money is seen as being only tangentially important for most people when it comes to custody matters. In my research with parents who had some form of shared custody, I found that economics had little to do with the way they felt about sharing their children. The majority of families were in the middle income range, and some of them had a great disparity between the income of the husband and that of the wife. Yet they generally found ways to work it out to everyone's satisfaction. Not surprisingly, the most unusual solutions were found among the noticeably poor and the specifically wealthy; the first because they were used to being ingenious and the second because they could afford to buy whatever was required to make their sharing arrangement work. (In the case of the birds' nest, that might include three separate households; one for each spouse, plus the family "nest" for the children.)

At any rate, 80 percent of the men interviewed voiced strong opinions about the need to keep custody and money separate. Many made comments such as "Children are human beings, not possessions" and "There is no way to equate love of your youngsters with division of the bank account." Of the 10 percent who felt the two subjects were intertwined, apologies were generally proffered, such as "Sad but true: whoever gets the kids, gets the cash," and the remaining 10 percent ignored the subject. These comments came from both custodial and noncustodial fathers, and aren't simply the reflections of complacent housewives living on child support. (That situation has always been more myth than reality anyhow, and with the present attitudes of the courts, it's almost nonexistent nowadays.)

Most fathers don't resent supporting their children if they can see how the money is spent, and feel assured that it isn't simply being used by the mother to improve her own lot. This is an understandable reaction; but when you're going over the cost of raising the children, it's important to take into account the time and energy spent by the parenting adult as being an essential, if nonmonetary, contribution. The average housewife and mother spends almost ninety hours a week on domestic and maternal chores. So the father who begrudges the fact that his ex stays home to take care of young offspring might do well to consider the expense of providing comparable care if she weren't around. (A recent study to determine how much it would cost to pay outsiders to perform the various tasks of a housekeeper-mother showed that the charges would come to more than $225 *a week* for such services![1])

There are three basic areas of monetary information that the court is going to be interested in, whether you do your divorce by yourselves, settle out of court with the help of attorneys, or go through the process of asking the judge to divide things up for you. You might as well look at them now and write them down, both for your own information and so that you know what to tell your attorney. If you and your ex are more or less on speaking terms, it's wise to pool this information and then look at how much expense the different custody arrangements would entail.

Expenditures

These are the daily, weekly, monthly, and occasional expenses necessary for running the whole family. If one of you has been keeping a budget book, or some other form of records, by all means make a Xerox copy of it so that each of you can have one. This is important in establishing not only how you have been living, but what the future is likely to contain as well. If Junior went through four pairs of tennis shoes in the last twelve months, you may hope that he's either going to quit growing or become more gentle on his feet, but there's no real assurance that he isn't going to need an equal number in the future. Many men have little notion of how much it costs to feed a family, just as some women don't know what the insurance premium on the car amounts to, and the process of going over these records will help acquaint both of you with what you'll be dealing with in the coming months.

There is a sample budget form at the end of this chapter which is based on the financial statement required by the Santa Clara County Superior Court in California. Use it as a guide for noting what your family's actual costs have been, and then make up a comparable list for the future; don't forget to include dental bills, the children's allowances, and the cost of maintaining the car. The fact that you're rearranging your life-style doesn't mean these things won't require attention in the future.

Your projected budget should also reflect the changes in residence, the number of people in one place (which will affect the size of apartment or house necessary, as well as the amount of food they'll need), and any other expenditures that are likely to arise because of your reorganization. For instance, if you'll both be working outside the home for the first time, you'll need to know what to expect in the way of child-care expenses. You'd be well advised to contact several day-care centers, nursery schools, or baby-sitters in order to find out not only how much money is involved, but whether there's a waiting list, and so on. Making a random guess about the cost is likely to leave you with inaccurate information, and you're going to have to find out about these things shortly anyhow.

Items such as transportation should include not only the up-keep of whatever vehicles you currently have, but also the additional costs if a second car is necessary, or the estimated commuting fare if one of you will be using public transportation. It's wise for you and your spouse to work out these budgets together, so that the separate households will be completely represented. Be sure to use a pencil, not a pen, for the future amounts, as you'll probably have to make a number of revisions when you begin trying to fit the various allocations into the actual amount available.

Income

The court may ask to see tax returns, paychecks, or even company books for as far back as five years if you get into a battle over money. But for your immediate purposes, you need look only at what is coming in presently. It probably won't be nearly enough. If either one of you is changing jobs, in line for a raise, or going to work for the first time, keep that fact in mind—but don't count on that money until you are sure it is available. Birds in the bush won't fill hungry children's stomachs, and it's always unwise to plan on something which isn't yet a reality. This is particularly important for women, who may be expecting to command a higher salary than will actually be offered, and for men who are assuming a promotion will come through. What you have now is what you have to work with, and wishful thinking alone won't change that.

Debts and Assets

Your attorney and possibly even the judge will want to see a complete list of personal and real property owned by each of you, and by the children, either jointly or individually. This includes your house, car, furniture, stocks and bonds, savings accounts, checking accounts, retirement plans, insurance of all kinds, and so on. How it gets divided depends on how much you are able and willing to settle things between yourselves, or on the judge if you can't work it out. If you have much property, by all means consider hiring an appraiser. Before you actually set out to make your dissolution legal, it's wise to have a pretty good idea of the worth of the house, your equity in it, the amount of debts, and whether or not those debts should be split between you or paid out of the community funds (if any) before those get divided. You have several options on this, and would do well to get some professional counseling, from either a financial expert or your attorney, or both, before deciding how to handle it. Naturally, if all you have is a five-year-old station wagon and a secondhand dresser or two, you can probably make your own division without professional help. But if you have any doubts about the value of the things you have purchased during the marriage, be sure to look into having them appraised. It's one of the first things an attorney will recommend if you decide to fight over the matter, and if you're not going into battle, you'll both feel reassured by having an outside, professional opinion on the subject.

Another area in which you might benefit from professional advice is that of taxes. Many couples reported working out various arrangements for filing tax returns which turned out to be advantageous for all concerned, provided that they shared in the money coming back from the government. A well-informed attorney or a certified public accountant can tell you what will be most profitable in your specific case, if you're willing to cooperate between yourselves.

Dividing Up the Pie

The process of deciding who gets how much for what needs is one of the most hazardous aspects of dissolving a marriage. Traditionally the battle lines are drawn with the woman demanding control of the children and the man doing everything in his power to hide and protect his finances. This is, of course, a direct reflection of the traditional mother/children–father/money division, and it's a large part of what this book is intended to help you avoid. Just as the man who swears to "get the kids" in order to punish his wife doesn't deserve much consideration in negotiating, the woman who overreaches in her material expectations and tries to ruin her husband financially is not only selfish and vindictive: she can expect a fierce and nasty battle to ensue. Such fighting is both needless and harmful to the children, and can cause bad feelings between the partners which often last the rest of their lives. If you've been able to look at and deal with the questions of child custody reasonably, you should be able to handle the money aspect as well. For the man who knows he's got a cooperative ex when it comes to contact with the youngsters, it's much easier to be responsible and cooperative where the finances are concerned. And the woman who knows her ex isn't out to "show her" by withholding funds for the children is much more likely to feel comfortable about sharing them with him. So in the same way that you should look at all the emotional and psychological aspects of parenting your youngsters once the separation takes place, you should also consider all the ramifications involved in dividing the monetary pie.

Once you have a fairly clear idea of the financial condition of the family, go on to the Proposed Expenditures page and start trying to find a way to fit the pieces together. If it's possible to stay within your present income, by all means do so, even if you have to stop having the poodle trimmed professionally, or the car washed by someone else. You must each be willing to make concessions not only on what you yourself can give up, but also on what the other person needs. The man who refuses to acknowledge his ex-wife's need to have baby-sitting funds when the children are still small is going to find he has to deal with a shrew and a fishwife whenever they have occasion to talk. And a woman who insists she must have so many things that her ex can't afford to rent a decent place for himself is likely to find that he's left town entirely and she has no help from him of any kind!

It's bound to be a hard time for everyone, emotionally, psychologically, socially, and financially. Don't forget that if one or the other of you is unduly deprived by the financial arrangements, it's going to affect the children eventually. You may both be feeling that you're constantly battling the wolf from the door, but it helps to know the other is doing the best he or she can to hold up the other end of the bargain, and there is much less likelihood of either's denouncing the other to the children when the burden is shared.

If you are a man who is feeling particularly edgy on this subject, I suggest that you read some of the works on women, divorce, and economics, to get a more accurate picture of what your children may have to face. The women and children of divorce are often among the most poverty-stricken groups in the country, and while you may be railing at the idea of sending any money at all to your ex, remember that it's your children who are going to be hurt if your anger at her ends up depriving them of a reasonable childhood.

How you handle the various details in your specific situation is pretty much up to you; as mentioned earlier, every couple I've talked with have arranged their own system if they are sharing the children. And there was no bitterness expressed about child support by fathers who either shared custody or had very broad and extensive visiting arrangements, even though some paid alimony as well as child support. (I have not gone into the subject of alimony here because it varies so from state to state, and is less directly related to child custody and raising than is child support.) It's certainly reasonable to conclude that the man who continues to be actively involved with his youngsters is less prone to begrudge paying for them.

Don't hesitate to consider different ways of sharing the financial burden. I know of one case in which the mother, who has moved to a small apartment and is a student at college, comes to the family house every afternoon to baby-sit and do the housework. Her ex pays her a salary, and deposits the necessary withholding tax in the bank, just as he would for any professional housekeeper. Because this is strictly a business arrangement, and she is no longer his dependent, he can deduct her salary from his taxes as part of the cost of child care. She claims it as earned income, not as alimony, which she would have to pay taxes on anyway. She needs the part-time job, the children have a chance to be with both parents regularly, and he's getting a more loving and concerned type of child care than would be available otherwise. (The IRS assures me this is not fraudulent in any way, provided the whole matter is handled in a businesslike fashion.)

If you can't come to a basic agreement on these money matters, you would do well to consult an attorney and try to work out some settlement with his or her help. Among those people I've known, some were quite able to agree on custody questions while haggling over everything else. For goodness' sake, don't let your financial disputes destroy whatever accord you've reached about the children! It's not necessary, and it will be very detrimental to everyone if you do.

Bringing In the Children

By now you are probably pretty well along the path of having your future organized, or convinced you'll be waging war for the rest of your lives (or maybe both). In either event, you each should have an idea as to the practical standing of your finances and some fairly strong notion as to what kind of custody arrangements you're willing to consider. And this is the point at which you'd do well to consult with the children.

Telling children about an impending rearrangement of their lives is always sticky. Although they may have known you weren't getting on well, the actual idea of divorce may not have occurred to them. Children are often both marvelously sensitive and aware of what's going on, and at the same time totally naive about what the results are likely to be. If you already have friends or relatives who are divorced, the notion that their parents are separating may not be such a shock to them intellectually. Emotionally, however, they are likely to perceive it as a terrible, threatening unknown: something new and frightening is entering their lives, and they will need as much emotionally supportive reassurance as you can provide.

The restructuring of their family will deeply affect your children, and you should show them the respect and courtesy of talking it over with them, once you have all the pieces of the puzzle in hand. You should never discuss an impending rearrangement with youngsters unless you are sure it will happen. Casual speculation about *what if* Daddy and Mommy separate is pure self-indulgence on the part of the adult, and can drive your offspring up a wall. So be certain that you intend some definite action in the near future before bringing it up with the kids.

Children, although largely egocentric, are completely at the mercy of the adults in their environment, and in that sense are quite powerless. It's been found that very few couples talk over an impending separation with preschool children, and even parents of teen-agers sometimes withhold the information of a planned reorganization for fear of creating a mood of misery and depression before the actual event takes place. Yet this silence causes a sudden and unexpected shift in the children's world; one day both parents are together, and the next day one of the adults has moved out! The youngsters are presented with a fait accompli over which they have no control, and for which they have often had no preparation. Frequently, this results in exactly the kind of insecurity and worry the parents were trying to avoid.

The more you can include your youngsters in the final decisions about custody, about who moves out and where he or she is going, the less unknown and distressing the whole process will be for them. If you are both feeling very defensive and angry (as opposed to sad and vulnerable), you may want to talk these things over with them separately. But if you can possibly manage a joint conference, by all means do so. It can make a world of difference as to how the youngsters perceive the restructuring of their universe; experiencing the fact that their parents are not excluding them from future plans can do much to alleviate initial fears.

This is no time to go into the whys and wherefores of your own connubial conflicts, and laying blame on each other is only going to confuse and frighten the children more. There are several excellent books on the subject of divorce from a child's viewpoint which I have listed in Suggested Reading. Whether you use these as actual tools for discussing your situation with your offspring or not, they will certainly give you a number of worthwhile insights into the handling of the problem.

If you have already agreed to the specific rearrangement you are going to use, at least at the beginning, make it clear to the kids what it is you are considering. But if you are open to discussion about various forms of sharing, make that clear to them also. This is not to say that they should in any way feel that they are choosing between parents; to put children in that position is to run the risk of warping them for the rest of their lives! But *if you are sharing* there is no question of either one of you being cut off from your progeny, and once you establish that fact with them, a discussion of their feelings and considerations about which arrangement feels best to them now can be very beneficial (and informative).

However you handle it, it's tremendously important that everyone have a chance to talk about and decide on the forthcoming rearrangement. Even if you have already decided what the custody situation will be, you need to discuss not only what to do, but *how to do it* with the youngsters. Make sure that everyone knows what the arrangement is, and whether it's for the immediate future only, or projected as a long-term thing. In one family, when the mother remarried, the father took all the children for the first month. When she and her new husband were more or less settled, two of the children went to stay with them for two weeks while the other stayed with the father. This switching around and trading off continued during the whole summer, giving each child and adult a chance to see who fitted in most comfortably where. At the end of the summer the adults got together and discussed their different reactions and feelings, and once they were more or less agreed on priorities, held a family conference so that everyone could be in on the decision. These parents had been divorced for several years and had reached an equilibrium of dissent, so there were few causes for emotional outbursts. Such arrangements are possible if you're both pretty comfortable with each other, or you may want to hold off and use this sort of trial method after more time has elapsed.

Remember, custody decisions, either in court or between yourselves, are not binding for life; what works now may not work later, and the children should have the option of expressing their own feelings on the subject as time goes by. Some couples have yearly reviews of their situation, though usually such re-evaluations are handled on a much less formal basis. It's not uncommon for the offspring to bring up the subject of a change in living arrangements if they feel they can talk comfortably with their parents. Even preschoolers have been known to sit down and explain that they want more time with their other parent, and such requests should certainly be listened to and talked about with the child, as well as the other adult. (This is assuming, of course, that it isn't just an angry outburst that will shortly blow over.) It may not be possible to rearrange things at that point, but at least the youngster has the reassurance of knowing that you care and understand how he or she feels.

If you are planning on some form of sharing, now is the time to get across to the children that they will have *two equally valid homes;* this is important whether you are just now divorcing, or are rearranging an old custody agreement. Regardless of which method you decide to use, it must be clearly understood that the first time they get upset at one home they can't just pack up and move to the other house. Your parental authority needs to be maintained and respected, not only for your own sakes, but also for the youngsters'. Some people actually set up contracts with the children about this, so that everyone understands what is happening and what is expected of them. This may seem an odd way of handling it, but it helps to eliminate misunderstandings and incomplete communication. And during a time of stress and confusion, it's best to have as much clarity and understanding as possible.

Children's Reactions

Many parents try to present an impending separation as casually as possible in the hope of avoiding terribly debilitating emotional scenes with their children. One youngster mentioned that his parents kept saying "It's all right, there's no reason to be upset; we both still love you" while his stomach turned to jelly and he tried to stifle his tears. In actual fact there was a great deal to be upset about, and having his parents deny the normal expression of his fear and sadness was no help to the youngster at all.

To deny the expression of the child's pain (and/or your own) is to deny him or her the right to participate in being part of the family. There may indeed be a big tearful scene. When my son announced that he wanted to go live with his dad, I agreed, recognizing that the paternal authority and support were necessary for him at that point. And once it was agreed to, we all dissolved in a puddle of tears. The two children and I must have gone through a whole box of Kleenex, sitting on my double bed and reaffirming how much we would miss each other. Yet no one said "Don't go . . . stay here," and when the flood subsided we all felt better for having shared our sorrow and pain at the separation. We were finally able to dry the tears, set about fixing dinner, and start packing his things once the initial emotional reaction was experienced and acknowledged. Sharing sadness, without feeling that you *have to "make everything okay,"* is a very important part of being supportive, and frequently acts as a kind of catharsis.

Children who are seeing the family structure undergo a major revamping are going to be sensitive to any and every change around them. Fears and distress about their relationships with their parents will make them doubly alert and apprehensive about their own position in the family, now that the two-parent structure no longer exists. This is true regardless of the age, though it generally manifests itself differently according to the emotional development of the child. Little ones sometimes regress to earlier stages of behavior, and take to wetting their beds or using baby talk. School-aged children may have nightmares and worry about disasters they fear will befall them or someone they love. And teen-agers will frequently become even more rebellious and demanding. This kind of reaction may start to show up as soon as the separation occurs, or it may be delayed somewhat; young children often seem to deny the situation, taking it all very calmly and not expressing much on the surface. That doesn't mean they aren't deeply affected by it, however, and as every book on children and divorce will tell you, their emotional reaction is bound to show up one way or another.

Even children as young as a year feel sad and terrified over family separations. And it is terror that's involved for them; the younger the child, the more incomprehensible the whole thing is. There is a deep sense of woefulness and disorientation evident in the story one father told about his toddler son's return to the family apartment on the first weekend after the mother and child had moved out. Unable to verbalize his feelings, the child took his father's hand and led him to what had been the nursery, pointed to the spot where his own crib had so recently stood, and began sobbing in the most heartbroken fashion. The father picked him up and cuddled him, and the two of them stood there with tears running down their cheeks, each acknowledging the pain and finding solace in a big, warm hug.

Much of the children's fear has to do with the unknown future: what's going to happen now? If Daddy can leave so easily, does that mean that Mama will leave too? Where does the departing parent go when he or she is not with me? Will I ever see him again? Did I cause this to happen by being bad, and if so, can I get them back together by being good? Many of these things can be talked about in the ensuing months; they may not be vocalized for some time, but if you are able to establish a good, strong communication with your offspring, chances are they will express their fears sooner or later.

Of course, some worries can be headed off right from the start if the child and the moving parent maintain close contact. Some parents arrange for the kids to go along on apartment-hunting expeditions, help set up the new household, and generally feel part and parcel of the continuing life of the noncustodial parent. This seems to have several positive effects. First, the children continue to feel included in that parent's life. They can visualize what he or she is doing, where he lives, how he fixes meals, and so on, when not with the youngsters. And they are reassured that no one is going to abandon them by just disappearing into the void. Secondly, it makes the explanation of a reorganization of the family structure obviously valid. They not only hear that both parents will continue to love them and interact with them; they actually experience it right from the beginning.

It is not uncommon for children to try to bring their parents back together; few, if any, of them (with the exception of some teen-agers, who are much less in need of the family structure) want their parents to divorce. Yet just as you shouldn't involve children in the ways and means of separating unless you're positive that's what is going to happen, neither should you be swayed by the youngsters' efforts to effect a reconciliation. Countless parents who decided they couldn't stand the sight of each other have been coerced into burying the hatchet by a manipulative child playing on the adults' sense of guilt, worry, and confusion about how the kid will take the separation. Usually this just means additional months of marital misery for both, and the whole thing explodes again in a year or two, sometimes with more acrimony and viciousness than before. So as long as you are convinced that your marriage has ended, don't feel you have to "stay together for the children's sake."

Friends and Relatives

Well-meaning as they may be, and important as their support may seem to you, getting friends and relatives involved in either a divorce or a rearrangement of child custody often proves to be more hazardous than helpful. If they don't have tons of very unprofessional legal advice, they'll certainly have all sorts of opinions about custody, and more than one grandparent has added to the problem by taking sides, propagandizing the grandchildren, and haranguing the beleaguered parent. If you have any concern at all that your own relatives will become intrusive in your situation, better leave them out of it until all your decisions are made between the two of you.

Much depends on the family background and history. If there has never been a divorce in the family, and yours is the first, chances are you'll feel additionally terrible about the whole thing. Not only are your own emotions about your ex flailing around inside you: there's the further sense of failure, shame, rejection, and disgrace that you may fear from your folks. Some parents are very supportive and understanding, but others turn out to be outraged, either at your behavior, at your spouse's actions, or at what they are afraid will happen to their own relationship with the children. This fear of losing contact with their grandchildren is often very strong, and you would do well to reassure them from the outset that their link to the future is not going to be severed.

If your children and their grandparents already enjoy a warm relationship, by all means encourage it to continue. The children will benefit, provided that the grandparent doesn't interfere with the youngster's own place in the rearrangement by taking sides, asking a lot of prying questions, or indicating a strong disapproval of either parent.

Nor should this reassurance be limited to your own parents; many divorced people who have made a point of keeping in touch with their in-laws develop a cordial and respectful, if not necessarily close, relationship. Frequently a single mother says with pride, "My mother-in-law and I couldn't get along ourselves, but after all these years she really compliments me on how I've raised the children." Such comments are the result of the divorced parents' honest effort to make sure that the marital strife between them doesn't poison the relationship of the new generation with the past, as well as the grandparents' good sense and wisdom in staying out of the parents' hair.

The understanding grandparents, who can enjoy the second generation of offspring without meddling in the parents' affairs are surely blessed in a special way. They not only have the continuing pleasure of being with their grandchildren, they know they can provide a place of refuge; a solid, safe, untroubled spot where the youngsters can get away from the pressures of domestic strife if the parents are still bickering. If you are such a relative, remember that the best thing you can offer your grandchildren is a neutral and respectful silence on the subject of their parents; those children need a place of unquestioning warmth, understanding, and compassion, where they can forget about the hassles of their parents and enjoy the company of their elders. And in the long run, not only they but their besieged parents will appreciate you the more for it.

If you, as a divorcing couple, are fortunate enough to have parents as wise and supportive as this, you may find that they will be a help during the initial stages of your reorganization. Many is the single parent whose mother or even grandmother steps in to help him or her take care of setting up housekeeping with the youngsters. And for the children whose divorced father is licking his wounds in some distant town, the presence of a caring and interested grandfather can be a godsend. Not all such relatives are willing or able to provide positive support, of course, but if your families include members who can and will help stabilize the situation without causing further conflict, by all means consider that among your options.

Much of your parents' reaction to your domestic realignment will probably depend on how close you were during the marriage. I know of one situation in which, although the husband's mother was eventually told of the divorce a year or two *after* it happened, she never informed the rest of the family. And since there is a good deal of distance, both physical and emotional, between the older family members and the West Coast divorced family, no one else knows that the nice young couple out West aren't still married! Yet while that situation may seem a little strange, it's nothing compared with some of the other stories I've heard.

In one case the man and wife divorced, amicably, and he took over the parenting role while she went back to school. There was no fighting or hassling over the kids; everyone, including the ex-wife, felt good about the arrangement. And then the man told his mother. The grandmother called every relative she could find, sent delegations of cousins and such around to dissuade him from such an unthinkable arrangement, and ended up not speaking to her son, all because she couldn't believe that he wasn't denying the children's mother the opportunity of raising the children! No amount of reassurance from her daughter-in-law could persuade this matriarch that she was not looking at some terrible wrong that needed to be righted, and the result has been a total stalemate.

Nobody wants to have to cope with misplaced outrage on the part of an older relative; but neither should you be swamped with oversolicitous concern and a constant harping on old grievances. The mother who continually tells her divorcing child what a no-good the ex-spouse is may well be doing more harm than good, and should politely but firmly be asked to keep out of what is, after all, not her affair. There is enough pain and conflict without having someone else's good intentions incessantly prodding at the wounds.

Nor is this a problem encountered only by women, although fewer people assume they have the right to tell an adult male what to do. Usually it is friends who begin pressuring the divorced father. This can range all the way from an incredulous "You mean you let her have the car? Boy, are you dumb!" to the long and generally inaccurate commentaries of an armchair attorney who keeps asserting that your lawyer sold you down the river. You'll probably run into all kinds of tips on how to avoid paying alimony, whom to hire to "get the goods" on your wife, and where to find an attorney who will "get you off scot-free." Not only are these suggestions of dubious value to begin with: if followed they could so polarize you and your ex that it becomes impossible to achieve any sort of accord where the children are concerned. This is the kind of advice that you specifically don't need, and you'd do well to brush it off and forget it; inflammatory rhetoric, whether from personal friends or published authors, is certainly not going to help you restore your own sense of balance, and may damage whatever progress you and your opposing partner have already made toward a peaceful settlement of your differences.

What you really should have at this point is friends (and/or relatives) who understand that you're going through an extremely difficult process, that you want and need pleasant and positive companionship, and that any talk about your problems should be considered simply as your letting off steam, not as an invitation for them to take sides. While many people want to remain friends with both partners of a divorced family, others may be prone to take a very partisan view of the whole thing, and delight in passing on opinions, rumors, or general gossip in the misguided belief that they are keeping you "informed." If you are trying to cope as best you can, and have managed to establish any sort of rapport, however fragile, with your ex, letting other people stir up further trouble is just plain foolhardy. So avoid these people like the plague; you have enough difficulties already, without having bystanders who have nothing at stake louse up what you've worked so hard to develop.

Now What?

At this point you should have all the information you need in order to decide how you want to restructure your living pattern. You know what you both want for your kids, as well as for yourselves. Your resources have been inventoried, and you are aware of the various options for implementing your desires. Now it becomes a question of how best to put these into practice. Should you try to keep the house, and if so who will be responsible for it? How much space will you need in the second household, and which of you will live there? What are the children's desires, and can they be accommodated, given the emotional and financial circumstances? Can one or another of the grandparents help in any way, and how do you both feel about that? Can you afford two cars, and if not, how can you arrange transportation? What level of involvement can you tolerate with your ex, and how much are you willing to keep your personal antagonisms from affecting the children? What do you disagree on, and how rigid is your position on those matters? If you are set on retaining sole custody of the children, how much visitation is going to be possible, and what can you do to facilitate it? (In cases where the parents can't be in the same room without fighting, the children can be picked up and returned at the house of a friend or relative, so that the spouses don't have to have actual contact. Or if the children are old enough, public transportation may be a solution, or you may agree to begin and end each visit at the public library or some other neutral spot.)

These are all things that must be considered and dealt with, and you'd be far wiser to settle them between yourselves than to turn them over to the legal system, which is at best impersonal and disinterested, and at worst a source of further dissension. So work out as much as you can in private, and if necessary, look for professional counseling to help you handle the emotional adjustments necessary.

How Well Do You Know Your Kids?

Although parents tend to assume that they both know and understand their offspring more intimately and better than anyone else, chances are that there are many aspects of your youngster's way of looking at and appreciating the world that you've never thought about. Take a moment to check over the list. *Don't* sit down with your child and ask him or her about these things, as that will take on the appearance of being a test, and he or she might consider it as undue prying on your part. But do start thinking of your offspring as separate people in their own right, with very individual responses to the world. And if you establish a chatty, general communication level with them, give them a chance to tell you about these things in their own ways; just because Sally looks great in pink, it isn't necessarily her favorite color, and although you may have bought them *Winnie the Pooh* for three Christmases running, don't be surprised if you find their favorite book is actually *Charlotte's Web*! Also, never argue or contradict them about any of these things; their favorite memory may be of something that was a totally miserable time for you, but they have a right to perceive their experiences and feelings in their own fashion.

CAN YOU ANSWER THESE QUESTIONS ABOUT
YOUR INDIVIDUAL CHILDREN?

Favorite color?
Favorite food?
Favorite song or musical group?
Secret hiding place?
Earliest rememberable dream?
Greatest guilt?
Secret name for himself or herself? (Don't be hurt if your child never tells you this; that's what secrets are for.)

Favorite fairy-tale character?
Favorite flower?
Favorite animal?
Happiest memory?
Worst nightmare?
Best triumph?
Does he or she have an imaginary companion, and if so, what's that companion's name?
Recurring daydream?

Does he or she have a fantasy about growing up to become an astronaut, a pirate, a doctor, movie star, race driver, veterinarian, or perhaps a jockey? Something else?

What kind of animal would he or she like to be? (For that matter, what animal would *you* like to be?) Why?

APPRECIATION

On a separate sheet of paper complete each of the following sentences:

I appreciate that my ex

_____

_____

_____

And I wish he/she would also

_____

_____

_____

Time Management

Write a few words or sentences about the following:

1. What you do best
2. What you do most
3. What you do least well
4. What you most dislike doing
5. What you wish you did more of

What does this tell you about the way you presently handle your life, and how can you improve it for the future?

Life Direction

Take ten minutes of time to be alone and comfortable, and let yourself imagine all the things you'd like to do with your life if you could. This is a purely enjoyable time, with no restrictions on the ideas you want to explore, but they must be things that *you* would do, not things that you want *others* to do for you, or to you. When you've finished, ask yourself why you aren't doing them, and what you can do to make it possible to achieve your dreams. (There is no point in explaining all the reasons why you can't do these things, unless you are willing to consider how those limitations can be changed.)

FINANCIAL FORM

MONTHLY EXPENDITURES OF ENTIRE FAMILY	$
Rent or mortgage payments (residence)	
Real property taxes (residence)	
Real property insurance (residence)	
Food and household supplies	
Utilities	
Telephone	
Laundry and cleaning	
Clothing	
Medical	
Dental	
Insurance (life, health, accident, etc.)	
Child care	
Payment of child/spousal support from prior marriage	
School	
Entertainment	
Incidentals	
Transportation	
Auto expenses (insurance, gas, oil, repairs)	
Auto payments	
MONTHLY TOTAL	

INCOME	Husband	Wife

Gross monthly income from:
    Salary and wages, including
        commissions, bonuses, tips, and
        overtime
    Pensions and retirement
    Social Security
    Disability and unemployment
        insurance
    Public Assistance (welfare,
        AFDC, etc.)
    Child/spousal support from prior
        marriage
    Rents
    All other sources (specify)

    _____

    _____

    Total Monthly Income, Gross

Itemized deductions from gross income:
    Income tax (local, state, and federal)
    Social Security
    Unemployment insurance
    Medical or other insurance
    Union or other dues
    Retirement or pension fund
    Savings plan
    Other (specify)

    _____

    _____

    Total Deductions

Total Monthly Income, Net (subtract
    deductions from total monthly
    income, gross)

FAMILY DEBTS AND OBLIGATIONS
   (in both names)

Creditor's name	For	Monthly payment	Balance
_____	_____		
_____	_____		
_____	_____		
_____	_____		
_____	_____		

Other (specify)

| _____ | _____ | | |
| _____ | _____ | _____ | |

Total

DEBTS

There are several different ways of handling the payment of family debts following the decision to divorce: each of you can take responsibility for paying off specific obligations, according to an agreement reached between you; or you can pool all the bills and agree to pay them off from the money available in the family assets as a whole, provided there are any. How you decide to handle that is up to you, but you would do well to consult a professional if you have any questions or doubts about the fairness or advantages of either system.

INDIVIDUAL DEBTS AND OBLIGATIONS	Husband	Wife
Creditor's name	For	
Total		

ASSETS

If you have more than one savings account, insurance policy, real estate holding, etc., make a separate list of these on another piece of paper and enter the totals on this form. Remember that your attorney will want to see such a list as well.

	Joint	Husband	Wife	Children
Cash on hand				
Money in checking accounts				
Money in savings accounts				
Money in credit-union accounts				
Money in any other accounts or deposits				
Retirement or pension fund				
Life insurance cash value				
Value of stocks and bonds				
Value of real estate				
Value of all other property				
Total Property				

FINANCIAL SUMMARY

	Family	Husband	Wife
Monthly family expenses			
Monthly income, net			
Monthly obligations and debts			
Total balance of family debts $ _____			
Total assets			
Total children's assets $ _____			

PROPOSED BUDGETS	Husband	Wife
Number of children living with		
Rent or mortgage payments		
Real property taxes		
Real property insurance		
Maintenance		
Food and household supplies		
Utilities		
Telephone		
Laundry and cleaning		
Clothing		
Medical		
Dental		
Insurance (life, health, accident, etc.)		
Child care		
Payment of child/spousal support		
School		
Entertainment		
Incidentals		
Transportation (auto expenses or public transportation)		
Installment payments (insert total monthly amount according to who takes which bills)		
Legal fees for divorce		
Total Proposed Budget		
Total Income Available to Each		
Proposed Child Support Necessary to Balance Budget		

10
You've Agreed to *What?*

Professional Responses

It is not uncommon for parents who are considering ways of sharing their children after divorce to be looked at as though they had taken leave of their senses. Friends and relatives are often puzzled and ask why you are separating to begin with if you are each going to continue parenting the youngsters, and professionals generally throw up their hands in dismay and present you with all sorts of arguments as to why or how it won't work. Oddly enough, these arguments have little or nothing to do with what sharing parents actually experience, and in researching this aspect of the child-custody subject, I found an enormous gap between what the professionals expect and what is actually going on "out there" in the world. Sometimes this discrepancy is funny, and sometimes sad, but it's certainly worth examining further.

Most attorneys try to dissuade their clients from even exploring the idea of joint physical custody, and none make a point of suggesting it to clients. (The legal terminology is "joint physical custody"; "shared custody" is a general phrase indicating any form of sharing, whether legally sanctioned or not.) Nor are lawyers the only ones who assume that sharing won't work; many psychologists take a dim view of the concept, and until recently most popular books on the subject of children and divorce neglected to mention it at all. A few authors comment on it in passing and suggest that it might be possible under special circumstances, and one comes out and states flatly that parents who share their offspring must be doing so for very neurotic reasons! (I can't help noting that I have included some of these books in the Suggested Reading list because of other insights they provide. I trust that you, the reader, will recognize that none of us can find the best solution for you; we can only pass on information about what we have observed. Since a large part of my research involved people who were satisfied with some form of sharing, I hope you will consider it among your options, and then make your own decision yourselves.)

There appear to be several reasons for this professional hesitation where shared custody is concerned, most of which are based on cultural assumptions. To begin with, there is the concept that if two parents can't agree to stay married, they must be enemies. (Unfortunately, this expectation is further bolstered by the adversary nature of our legal proceedings.) That the agreement to separate is just as valid as an agreement to remain together is generally overlooked entirely. This attitude appears most notably in Goldstein, Freud and Solnit's book *Beyond the Best Interests of the Child,* which is predicated on the assumption that divorcing parents will most probably be so vicious toward each other, they can't possibly work together for their children's benefit! (That book has contributed a great deal to the understanding of the parenting function, and has provided the courts with a legal definition of "parent," but the authors' conclusion that after divorce one parent should be given complete control over the youngsters while the other one simply disappears is deplorable, to say the least.)

Many lawyers have told me, in all seriousness, that expecting a divorcing couple to share peacefully in the rearing of their progeny is just plain crazy. Yet this attitude says more about the attorney than about shared custody itself. Whenever I hear a lawyer start lecturing on how shared custody doesn't work, I remember the day I spent listening to those arguments in every office I went to, and then had dinner with two divorced parents, their two mutual children, and the two second-marriage spouses, all at one big table. That family (and where the children are concerned, it is one family; when it's just the adults, then it's a two-family situation) has worked out a split-week, shared-cost, mutual-responsibility pattern that is a delight to behold, and the children seem to be completely comfortable with parent and parent, parent and stepparent, or stepparent and stepparent. These people aren't "crazy"; they simply never accepted the idea that divorce has to cut the children off from either of the grown-ups' love.

One of the main reasons for the legal professional's assumption that sharing isn't feasible lies in the fact that divorce attorneys spend most of their time on cases in which the clients are unable or unwilling to reach a settlement of their own. Frequently these people are acting out the unresolved battles of their marriage, and have no intention of reaching any agreement. Thus they appeal to the professional in the hope of getting public vindication through the courts. On the other hand, the couples who are willing and able to work out a solution to their problems themselves don't demand much of the professional's attention; in some states these people don't have to hire attorneys at all. Therefore, since family-law specialists are mostly involved with the fighting, angry, bitter, vindictive members of the divorce population, it's little wonder that they consistently told me divorcing couples just don't have the maturity, stability, or desire to make shared custody work.

Psychologists have a similar kind of situation; they are most often confronted by the divorce disasters, and so have had very little exposure to those cases in which the parents have arrived at a positive solution to the custody question. Consequently, their views of divorce and custody matters tend to be biased in the same way as lawyers' are, and because they lack any real information about the positive practicalities of sharing, they hesitate to recommend it.

In addition to this expectation of hostility between the parents, most professionals express concern about specific aspects of sharing which they see as detrimental to the children themselves. These arguments are based on incredibly narrow assumptions, however, and often have little or nothing to do with the way people actually handle shared custody. In fact, many of the things that the professionals caution against are more likely to come about in the sole-custody situation than in a sharing arrangement.

The Yo-Yo Theory

The most frequently heard claim against shared custody is that it makes a "Yo-Yo" out of the youngsters, forcing them to shuttle back and forth between homes regardless of their own feelings and needs. This assumes that the parents are unconcerned about their progeny's welfare, and are more intent on keeping to an inflexible timetable than on trying to find an arrangement which allows for reasonable time in each home. Indeed, one occasionally hears the statement that such arrangements are purely for the parents' convenience, and don't consider the needs of the children at all! Among the sharing parents I talked with, nothing could have been further from the truth. Sharing involves not only cooperation but also coordination, and there are times when trying to handle everyone's schedules make an airport controller's job look easy. Yet parents continue to work these things out because of their belief that the children have the right to live with each of them; they take the youngsters' desires into consideration and are willing to be flexible in how the sharing evolves as time goes by. If a child expresses, either verbally or nonverbally, distress with the present arrangement, a new order of things is looked for; after all, the whole point of sharing is to provide well for the offspring.

By comparison, sole custody imposes a much more arbitrary system on the youngsters when it comes to visitation. Several children mentioned the fact that they resented not being able to participate in regular Saturday classes or activities with their friends, since every other Saturday must be set aside for the visiting parent. "It's not that I don't want to see him," one child said. "It's just that I'd like to be able to have him be part of my regular life, instead of a special occasion that interferes with the other things I want to do. Sometimes I feel guilty about feeling this way . . . it's like I have to choose between being with my father or with my friends, and I wish I could have them both."

Then too, the typical visitation schedule makes no allowance for the number of children involved. The same amount of time is doled out to the noncustodial parent regardless of whether there are one or ten children to be visited. As a result, the children of bigger families get even less of their visiting parent's attention, a situation both parent and child are quick to mention.

The Question of Loyalty

Many people assume that children who are shared will be caught between conflicting loyalties and life-styles. Henry Foster, past Chairman of the American Bar Association Family Law Section, has been quoted as saying:

> A servant can't have two masters. With joint custody the child is put into a double bind. Psychologically, it is better to have authority vested in one parent.[1]

Yet most psychologists agree that double binds come from the parents' attitudes, *not from the structure of the custody arrangement*. Provided that each parent honors the other's right and responsibility to care for the youngsters, the question of divided loyalties simply doesn't come up; because each home is recognized as valid by both adults and children, there need be no conflict. Among the children I talked with or have read the comments of, having two separate homes is no problem. It is well established, understood, and accepted that each parent has authority in and over his or her home, and that they take turns or share in such things as teacher–parent conferences, disciplinary problems, and outside activities and recreations.

This question of divided loyalties is much more likely to be present in the sole custody situation. Being forced to live with one parent, while expected to relate to the noncustodial parent on a "sometimes" basis, can cause all sorts of grief within children. Not only do they feel guilty about loving the parent they don't live with: there is the constant fear of appearing to take sides. And if the parents each want to dominate the youngsters, the either/or aspect of sole custody gives them one more thing to fight over. Arguments about visitation, disputes over holidays, or out-and-out attempts to wrest custody away from each other are certainly fostered more by the win/lose structure of traditional custody than by the win/win situation involved in sharing.

Manipulation

Another frequently mentioned concern is the possibility that shared custody promotes manipulation on the part of either the youngsters or the parents. This too seems to be more of a theoretical problem than an actual one. As long as there is frequent communication between the adults (and in most sharing situations there certainly is, unless the arrangement is for long-term block-time schedules, and the distances involved are considerable), there just isn't any opportunity for manipulation on the part of the child. If the youngster comes home with some outlandish tale about the other household, a simple phone call can clear up whatever misunderstandings, misinterpretations, or general misinformation is being passed on. This holds true even in cases where there is sole custody; it's easy for children to react to what they *think* is happening, without understanding the subtler reasons behind adult actions. So the parent who is confronted with reports of injustices in the other household should always keep a cool head and check out what's really taking place before deciding it's time to send in the Marines.

In addition, a child who tries to play the parents off against each other with threats about preferring to live with the other adult has no ammunition in a shared arrangement. "I want to go live with Daddy!" may strike panic in the heart of the sole-custody mother, but it carries very little weight when that's exactly what is going to happen next week or next month.

In many ways, intentional manipulation of the parents is much easier when there is sole custody. I know one young woman who, when she went to visit her father during the summer, arrived on the scene with a freshly bought and partially smoked package of cigarettes. Since she was underage, her father took her to task for it, only to be blithely assured that "Mama lets me smoke." By the time the visit was over and she returned to her mother's house, she could quite truthfully look aggrieved at her mother's consternation, and reply "Oh, but I've been smoking at Daddy's all summer." This sort of manipulation is not possible when there are close communication and shared responsibility between the parents.

Parental Dependency

Finally, many psychologists argue that sharing custody prevents the parents from adequately completing their own psychic divorce. They say that continued contact, particularly if it is in a positive vein, will keep the parents dependent on each other and possibly reinforce the idea in the children's minds that there will be a reconciliation.

There may be some justification for this argument where the children are concerned. It's important for the parents to establish that there are now two separate, but equal, loving homes, and to keep this clearly in mind from the start. Most children carry secret fantasies about reuniting their parents even when it is obvious to everyone, including the kids, that such a thing would result in mayhem. That desire will probably be there no matter what custody method is used; if you are careful not to play on such hopes, and to respect each other's separateness when dealing with your offspring, it shouldn't be any greater problem with shared custody than it is with sole custody. (Some parents have found that an increase in activities with the presently noncustodial parent helps to alleviate this kind of pressure if the child's fantasy about reconciliation stems from missing the other parent.)

Whether or not sharing hinders the completion of the divorce between the parents depends largely upon the individuals involved. Among those parents I interviewed, this question was brought up only once, and that by a psychologist who was herself doing a study on custody. Her comment seemed to be purely speculative, rather than being a specific statement of her own feelings, and I attribute it more to her professionalism than to any doubts within herself. A few sharing parents mentioned that they found the necessary contact with their past-love-lost to be more harrowing than they had expected, and so worked out ways to minimize personal encounters and kept their communication limited to the children. You'll have to find out just how much contact you can comfortably tolerate, and adjust the schedule accordingly.

Some parents make a firm rule that the children are not to carry information about each other's love life back and forth, while others don't seem to mind hearing about new flames. Naturally, if there is a serious or projected long-term relationship which will affect the children in the form of a stepparent (legal or otherwise), the other parent should be informed. But that is the case in all custody situations anyway, and is not necessarily made more painful by sharing.

As one parent pointed out, there is a big difference between being *dependent* on each other and knowing that you can *rely* on your coparent when problems arise. Many others reported that discovering they not only could trust their opposing partner to be a good and fair parent, but were also trusted by that person was a tremendous help in developing their coparenting relationship. It gave them a chance to see the reorganization as a positive solution for all concerned, and proved they could work together in providing a natural support system for their youngsters instead of continuing the negative behaviors that had led to the divorce.

Motivation

There are two arguments against shared custody that do warrant consideration, both involving the question of good faith. Among those people who had tried sharing and found it didn't work (and I did run into a small number of them), the final evaluation on at least one parent's part was that the sharing had been agreed to in order to maintain closer contact with the ex, and thus negate the actual divorce. In this particular case the mother took an apartment directly across the street from the family home, and used it as a position for spying on her past spouse's activities. The children were quizzed after every visit; she herself popped in un-announced from time to time, ostensibly to retrieve articles left behind; and the situation soon became intolerable for the father. It is probable that this woman would have done the same thing even if she'd been awarded sole custody, so one can't necessarily blame the sharing arrangement. She simply used that as an easy excuse to rationalize her behavior. It is well to note, however, that trying to use a shared-custody system as a means of keeping tabs on your ex will probably lead you back to the traditional either/or arrangement in short order.

The second area of potential problems is related to our legal system. One reason that lawyers don't like to suggest shared custody lies in the fact that the courts presently tend to grant sole custody in preference to joint custody, regardless of how long or well sharing has been working. And they always hesitate to change a child's home situation unless there is real reason for concern about the youngster's welfare. These two attitudes make it possible for one parent to have the children for an agreed-to six-month- or year-long period of sharing, and then file for sole custody with the courts on the grounds that the offspring should remain in their present location. There is certainly a possibility that the courts will agree, regardless of the original agreement to share. Naturally, therefore, the attorney sees shared custody as weakening his client's position in the long run if there is any chance that the opposing partner won't stick to it.

Along the same line, lawyers also point out that joint physical custody would allow either parent to legally take the children out of state, and then initiate sole-custody proceedings in the new locale. Because the custody laws differ from state to state, there is no guarantee that the new state of residence will uphold the findings of the original court. There has been a nationwide effort to implement the Uniform Child Custody Act, which would insist that each state honor the orders of any other where child-custody matters are concerned, but to date only twenty-one states have ratified it. And, as one lawyer gleefully assured me, "That leaves twenty-nine other states I could advise my client to move to!" Hopefully this mess will be corrected in the near future, as our present situation sometimes gets so tangled that the same children are awarded to opposing parents in different states.

Both of these legal cautions are valid, but they assume that one of the parents is not really willing to share to begin with, and is only agreeing to it as a ploy to achieve other ends. Any contract is only as good as the faith of the persons who make it, and it seems likely those parents who don't trust each other enough to honor the principles of sharing wouldn't consider it a viable solution anyway. But for those of you who wish to arrange for some kind of joint custody and feel the need of specific assurance about these things, there are several steps that can be taken.

Precautions

If you are very doubtful about your ex's intentions where the offspring are concerned, you may feel that giving him or her equal opportunity to raise the children in a block-time arrangement is running the risk of losing your own right to interact freely with the kids. Usually this kind of suspicion runs in couples; that is, each adult is nervous about the other. Some parents who feel particularly vulnerable prefer to set up a split-sibling system so that each is reassured that the other won't start any unnecessary battles for fear of losing contact with the offspring who aren't presently living with him or her. In order to afford the youngsters more or less equal time with each parent, they exchange kids periodically, and alternating weekends and midweek visits give the children an opportunity to spend time together themselves. Naturally, if there is only one child, or if the siblings are very close and resent the idea of being parted, this kind of arrangement isn't practical. But where the youngsters are comfortable with it, this solution works very well.

Another way to handle the problem is to include a paragraph in your custody agreement which specifies that neither parent shall remove any of the children from the present county of residence (except for short visits) without a ninety-day notice to the court *and* to the other parent. This allows enough time to negotiate some change in sharing, or to file for sole custody if that is what you are determined to do.

There is no way to guarantee that shared custody won't result in a court battle, any more than one can assume that sole custody must create a legal conflict. So while sharing doesn't necessarily mean you won't ever face a custody conflict, neither does the award of sole custody mean you can't share. Many of the sharing parents I talked with can't even remember what their original agreements were; these people are less interested in maintaining paper power than they are in providing well for their offspring. In the final analysis, the question of whether or not to share your children boils down to how much you can trust each other, and how sincere each of you is about maintaining a fair and equitable agreement. If you feel confident that neither one of you will drag the rest of the family through the devastations of a court battle, sharing can work as well for you as it has for countless others, and all the professional arguments to the contrary should be taken with a grain of salt.

New Approaches

Changes in our entire social structure have led to the reevaluation of marriage, of women's roles, of parenting in general and fathers in particular. And the last few years have seen an increase of interest in the subject of child custody following divorce; psychologists, law experts, and social scientists are beginning to question many of the assumptions that have been taken for granted for so long, and to look for ways to improve our present system.

For years it was accepted that divorce was a tragedy for the children involved, and the resultant single-parent home was considered "broken," "abnormal," "socially deviant," and bound to be unhealthy. This was the social expectation, and much of the early research on the subject indicated that not only the researchers but also the children and parents studied saw it that way themselves. Most of the literature about the psychological effects of divorce concentrated on negative cases and ignored those in which there were a healthy resolution and completed psychic divorce. It has been only during the 1970s that professionals have begun to realize that there are a number of stable single-parent families producing healthy kids, and we should look at how they do it, rather than studying cases which are defined as maladjusted at the outset.

Recent studies tend to disprove, or at least seriously question, the belief that children with divorced parents are more likely to be delinquent, have sexual problems, be underachievers, and in general suffer lifelong social maladjustments and emotional disturbances. Dr. Richard Gardner points out that

> most psychiatrists agree that divorce *per se* does not necessarily cause psychiatric problems to develop in children. In fact, the child living with unhappily married parents more often gets into psychiatric difficulty than the one whose mismatched parents have been healthy enough to sever their troubled relationship.[2]

One study which compared seventh- and eleventh-graders from divorced families with their counterparts from undivorced homes found no appreciable differences in their emotional well-being.[3] And Gettleman and Markowitz, the psychotherapists who wrote *The Courage to Divorce,* noted that they have seen a number of cases in which the children of embattled parents experienced relief and a resurgence of positive attitudes once the adults finally decided to end their marriage and cease fighting over it.[4]

This recognition that divorce can create a more positive situation for the children as well as the parents has led to an interest in different forms of postdivorce family structure. Although research in this area is still in its infancy, and the results of the various studies probably won't be available until sometime in the 1980s, it means that the idea of shared custody is beginning to be acknowledged as a potential solution to the problem.

Nor is professional interest in this subject purely a regional thing; just as there are sharing parents in all parts of the country, one finds professionals throughout the nation becoming more and more outspoken in defense of this solution. Dr. Melvin Roman of New York has been a pioneer in presenting the idea to conferences of psychologists and attorneys alike, as has Jay Folberg, a member of the law faculty at Lewis and Clark College in Oregon. Dr. Virginia Church of California, who is both an attorney and a psychologist, has long been an exponent of shared custody, and classes geared to teaching family counselors how to implement the "Two-Home Family" concept have been taught by Isolina Ricci in Colorado, Utah, and California.

Thus the idea of sharing in the raising of children after divorce is now being validated not only by the parents who are using it, but by concerned professionals as well; what has too often been classed as "unworkable" or "impractical" in the past is gradually being verified by those who are willing to study how such systems work. And the advantages of such arrangements for the children are reported over and over again. Isolina Ricci has summed it up concisely and well as follows:

> If parents think they have a family, they have one. If parents think they have a broken home, they have one. When children believe—because their parents believe—*that they have two intact homes where they belong and are wanted*, they gain the security of continuity, as well as a sense of their parents' commitment to their parental roles.[5] (Emphasis in text)

The French author de Tocqueville once commented that revolutions are simply society's way of ratifying changes that have already taken place among the people. Certainly that observation seems to apply in this situation, although on a nonpolitical level. As more and more families report that alternative custody arrangements work well for them, the professionals are beginning to take note of what the parents themselves have discovered. Hopefully, even the legal system will acknowledge the potential positive results of joint custody. It may not work for all families; but for the thousands who wish to restructure their living arrangement in such a way as to allow their children the most freedom to love, associate, and interact with each parent, it's a beginning. Not only does the process of arranging for shared responsibility in child raising help the couple complete their divorce: it also provides for a richer and more stable future for the children.

11
Children at Risk

Problems to Consider and Disasters to Avoid

All children, regardless of their age or situation, are affected when their parents decide to end the marriage. The infant may not consciously feel the effects of it until he or she gets older, and the grown youngsters who have left home and created lives for themselves may not react strongly on an emotional level, but all will respond in one way or another. Not all the reactions are negative, and some are more obvious than others, depending largely on the child's own makeup. But for the offspring who will be living in the restructured family, there are a number of hidden hazards, not the least of which are the emotional stresses their parents are experiencing.

During the different stages of the divorce and restructuring process, the children involved are considered to be "at risk." That is, although they may not in fact develop long-term difficulties, the separation and custody arrangements *may* create a climate which is adverse to the youngsters' needs. And because of their particular vulnerability at this time, these children may not have adequate ways of dealing with their distress.

One of the most crucial factors mentioned over and over again in studies of children going through divorce is the parents' "diminished capacity" to provide a secure, supportive, and caring environment for their offspring. It's not uncommon for the parents who are themselves in the midst of so much turmoil to overlook what would, in more stable times, have been obvious signs of depression, regressive behavior, or general inability to cope on the part of the youngsters. Too often these problems and demands for extra attention and reassurance come at a time when the single parent is least able to fulfill the offspring's needs. With so many other things pressing in on them, it may be understandable if newly separated parents are cranky or distracted; but that doesn't help the child whose world has fallen apart. And in most of the studies on children of different ages, the findings indicate that the youngsters were notably the worse for wear at the end of the first year largely because of *the parents' lack of recognition of the youngsters' plight.* (It's also noteworthy that almost all of them had regained their balance and made up whatever ground they had lost in emotional, social, and mental growth by the end of the second year, when both parents and offspring seem to have been able to work through the different stages of divorce.)

One father, who felt that the separation was not handled well where his children were concerned, looked at me sternly and said, "For goodness' sake, tell your readers to stop and think! If they are going through hell, what must their offspring be feeling? If you can get the parents to let go of their own pain for a little bit, and try to imagine what the children are experiencing, they'll find ways within themselves to help their youngsters through this crisis. But they have to be aware of it, and recognize that they aren't the only ones coping with the situation." Sadly enough, this too rarely happens. Adults, caught up in the storm of their own dissolution and trying to keep from letting the acid of their acrimony spill over onto the kids, may accidentally end up blocking the youngsters out completely. So try taking his advice; every so often put yourself in your offspring's shoes, and see where you can be more helpful in reassuring them of your love, your understanding, your support. You will not only be helping them through the immediate difficulties of adjusting to the separation: you'll also be teaching them how to be caring, concerned, and nurturing parents in their future years.

Unfortunately, the emotional ups and downs of the separation are not the only risks children of divorce encounter. Although it is estimated that only 10 percent of divorce cases involve a custody battle, 10 percent of one million divorces per year adds up to a lot of heartbreak and pain. Considering that these legal actions are initiated by the parents, and not the children, it's no wonder that the youngsters caught in such situations feel victimized and torn by a system that polarizes the family into armed camps. The statement "When angry parents go to war with each other, the first casualties are the children" is more than borne out by the comments of the youngsters who have been through the experience.

The Child's View of a Custody Battle

Throughout this book I have referred to custody fights as being vicious, inhumane, and in the long run, pointless. In many ways they are similar to civil wars, which are notorious for their cruelty and terrible aftermath: the two adults go through a psychological meat grinder, while the children are, as Dr. Roman says, both battered and "bartered." And I speak not only as a social observer, but also as a mother who went through it, and, in retrospect, realizes that the relationships so assailed have been irreparably warped.

One articulate young man looks back on the two-year battle that occurred when he and his sister were both just reaching puberty, and calls it a form of not-so-temporary madness which somehow invaded his parents and drove reason, sensitivity, parental awareness, and concern for the children they were fighting over right out the window.

"With my grades, I could now be going to Harvard, Yale, Princeton, any school I wanted to, if my parents hadn't used up *all* the family assets (including my college fund) on a game of revenge between themselves. Instead I'm applying for scholarships, working to augment them, and thinking that both adults did a very poor job of meeting their responsibilities, all just to salve their own egos."

In this case, both parents armed themselves with a battery of private psychologists who set to work, along with the court-appointed specialist, to ascertain with whom the children should stay. The continual interviews and questions and hours of probing and prying led the sister to retreat from the world of conflict to such a degree that one of the professionals reported that as far as he could tell, the girl was mute.

The children were individually questioned, tested, observed, and queried about their home life, their schoolwork, their feelings concerning the divorce and their own future, and all to no avail. "I began to feel that I could have said anything at all and it wouldn't have mattered," he lamented. "Each professional had his or her own bias, his or her own technique, and his or her own conviction as to what the outcome should be. And though they all declared they wanted to know how we *really* felt about the situation, no one was listening. I knew right from the beginning what I preferred, and why; I loved both of my parents, but I had already made up my mind which one I needed to live with. Yet no one heard me. I came to feel like a rat in a cage, trying to honestly communicate but being turned into an experimental object by the very people who professed to have my best interest at heart."

(He also pointed out that even the simplest divorce costs approximately $400 these days. At one million divorces per year, that comes to $400,000,000 couples spend to separate. When one sees an estimated 10 percent of such parents paying up to $10,000 or more to have their attorneys slug it out in court, the overall cost of divorce becomes astronomical. And it's particularly sad when one thinks of how that money could have been spent for the youngsters' welfare!)

Although I spoke with only a few children who had undergone this trauma, they all mentioned the same feelings of helplessness, sadness, and the annihilation of their own humanity. "When you're treated like a *thing* that everyone is scrapping over, it's hard to remember that you really are a valid person" was one comment. "And no matter how much they tell you they're doing it for your sake, and because they love you, it doesn't take very long before you realize that even when you beg and beg them to stop this insanity, they just keep right on, like machines. Not only that: when you ask them to stop, they start crying that *you* don't love *them,* and you end up comforting the adults who are causing you so much pain!''

There are several different reasons why people begin custody contests. Sometimes each parent is out to "get" the other, in which case both of them see a custody battle as a chance to call down the other while continuing to defend themselves with righteous indignation. Sometimes it comes about because the noncustodial parent is using it as a weapon against the custodial adult, and that parent feels compelled to defend himself or herself, regardless of how distasteful it may become. And sometimes it is a strategy used by the attorney in order to try to assume a stronger bargaining position for his or her client.

Remember, an attorney for the parent *does not represent the child,* and in fact may be cautioned not to take the child's welfare into consideration during a custody battle. A Formal Opinion of the Professional Ethics of the California State Bar states that if a California attorney discovers that to win custody of the minor child for his client would be detrimental to the youngster involved, he must not in any way convey that information to the judge who has to decide what is best for the minor.[1] Furthermore, the attorney with such knowledge may not even ask the court to appoint a third lawyer for the child, since such a request might cast suspicion on his own client and so prejudice the judge. Although this opinion is not binding on the members of the bar, it clearly points out one of the worst hazards of resorting to the adversary system for settling custody disputes.

If you find that it's impossible to avoid a custody battle, don't involve the children in the actual proceedings except in the most minimal way. Many judges insist that the youngsters concerned must leave the courtroom when it is time for the hearing, although they may want to talk with them privately in chambers. But this is actually only the final round of a progressive battle; generally there have been depositions taken prior to the actual court appearance, and children should never be allowed to sit in on those, either. Granted, it is their future which is at stake, and you may feel that it's better for them to experience firsthand the unreasonableness of their other parent, rather than hearing anything from you secondhand. But regardless of how much you want their moral support, or how curious they are to attend such proceedings, it will only upset the children more to watch their parents call names, make accusations, and generally display the most reprehensible sides of their characters. Even if the youngsters agree with your position and want to stay with you, they will be caught in the loyalty bind of having to face down the angry, hurting, and possibly vindictive parent on the other side. (One father refused to speak to his teen-age children for years because they had been present at the depositions required when *he* instigated a custody battle even though they had said they preferred to stay with their mother. He dropped the fight on the courthouse steps, but remained angry and hurt about what he claimed was his youngsters' "sneering" attitude during the deposition. Naturally, his reaction hurt the children deeply.)

So whenever possible, leave the children at home. In fact, if you can arrange to have them go stay with neutral friends or relatives during the duration of the war, it would probably be an excellent idea. Remember, in the long run a custody battle severely victimizes the children involved, creates lifelong hostilities and distrust between parents and children, as well as between the two adults, and squanders the mental, emotional, and financial resources of the family.

In Devastation's Wake

Although custody battles are generally very negative experiences for children, there is one thing worse. Because of the stress of the either/or concept of our present system, some parents resort to the practice of stealing their own youngsters and disappearing from sight. Child snatching, as this is called, is the most extreme example of what happens when the win/lose system is pushed to its limits. It is based on fear, vengefulness, frustration, and a breakdown of belief that any system of help can make the situation better. Often it is the irrational response of one parent trying to cope with the unreasonableness of the other. There is about it an air of desperation, of guilt and righteousness and the brutal disregard of anything other than one's own desire to have exclusive control of the children. It is complex, heartbreaking, and horrible all at once, and it's a growing problem which needs to be recognized and remedied.

Sometimes in a moment of blind fantasy, you want to believe that by running away with your youngster you can leave all the sordidness and pain behind with the other parent, and create a new life in some other place. I once heard a young father, who stood at the back of the room at an Equal Rights for Fathers meeting, ask for the chance to speak and then admonish us loudly *not to turn around to look at him.* (Fear of recognition is an ever-present aspect of the child snatcher's life.) In the surprised silence that followed his request he sobbed out the story of having snatched his 3-year-old daughter several weeks before. "I couldn't face taking her back. I knew I just couldn't cope with my ex's snide remarks and taunting accusations, with the loneliness of the next two weeks, with the fear I wouldn't be allowed to see her next time around. So when it was time to go back, I headed out of town instead. I hadn't thought about it beforehand or anything, I just did it. I had my paycheck in my pocket, and stopped by my room to pick up a few clothes and things, but we've been on the move across the country ever since. The baby cries for her mother a lot, we've stayed in cheap motels or slept in the car, I don't have a job or any idea what to do next. I'd like to be able to take her back, and try to explain what happened . . . why I did it. But I know my ex would grab the kid and slam the door, and I'd never get to see my daughter again, ever. Or maybe I'd be sent to jail. I don't want to hurt my girl . . . I never meant to hurt her. But every day I keep on running I feel more like a criminal, and I wonder where it will all end and *can anyone help me —anyone at all?*"

I wish I could say that someone was able to give the young father a solution to his problem; that there was an agency which would, as a third party, call the mother and help to negotiate some sort of agreement whereby the child and the mother could be reunited and some understanding worked out between the parents for the future. Unfortunately, no one in that room could suggest anything more than his contacting an attorney, which he felt loath to do and had little money left for, and I don't know the ending of the story.

Not all child snatchings are as impulsive as that, however. Many are planned for months or years in advance, with full knowledge of the potential consequences thereof. In 1974, Seward Prosser Mellon was granted sole custody of his two daughters in Pennsylvania. Their mother snatched them from him and took them to New York, where she started custody proceedings of her own. Then, in 1976, three of Mellon's hired men snatched the girls from the school they were attending and spirited them back to their father. Interestingly enough, New York went on to award the mother custody *after* the father had resnatched the youngsters, so as things presently stand, each state has given custody to the parent who resides therein, and the children must be constantly aware of the fact that any stranger may be a kidnapper paid to whisk them away again.

This sense of fear and apprehension pervades the snatched child's life, and often continues even after he or she is grown. In a long and exhausting interview, a grown man who was snatched as a child recounted his experiences to me, occasionally breaking into a sweat and sometimes staring for long periods of time at the floor as he told his story. In his case, as in many others, it was the resnatching that was so traumatic.

Usually the first move is made during a visiting time; in this particular situation, the father had carefully arranged everything including passports in advance, and both he and the children had landed in Israel before the custodial mother even knew they had left California.

The father was a well-paid professional and had no problem getting work, finding the family an apartment, and hiring a housekeeper. Although the first few months involved a certain amount of tension and confusion, fear of reprisals and guilt about not being in touch with his mother diminished as the boy settled into his new life.

One day when he and his younger sister were home from school with colds, a pair of strangers appeared at the door, announced they were looking for a gas leak, and proceeded to search the home. Although they left, the boy felt apprehensive, perhaps because it seemed odd to have these workmen come barging in at the dinner hour. Having made sure that the father wasn't on the premises, and that the cars were in readiness, the two strangers (who were members of the Israeli secret service) came bursting through the door and made a lunge for each child. The young girl fled to the balcony, where she hid in terrified silence, while the boy broke away from his captors and raced out of the building and down the street. "If I'd only known the Hebrew word for 'kidnap,' I might have gotten some help!" he ruefully remembers. As it was, he could only scream for help in English before his burly pursuer finally caught up with him, dragged him back to the waiting car, and threw him on the floor of the back seat, where he was covered with rugs and blankets to muffle his shouts and hide him from view. The two cars, one containing the mother, the other the children, sped directly to the U.S. Consulate, where they were granted asylum. After a fair amount of reshuffling and confusion, it was decided to drive to another city where the chances of getting a plane for the States appeared more certain. As they were leaving the building the father drove up, recognized his ex-wife, and proceeded to ram the first of the two cars. The second vehicle, with its cargo of mother and youngsters, roared around the wreck and made it out of town at top speed. The boy had no idea how badly his father might have been hurt in the accident, and didn't learn for many months that he had been heavily bruised, but not seriously injured.

After a quick debriefing in Washington, D.C., the mother and offspring flew back to California and the boy went back to his former school the next day as though nothing untoward had happened. Contact with the father was completely cut off, and they didn't meet again until the child was grown.

"The last thing I saw as I ran out of the apartment was the clock, which said six-twenty. To this day, if I wake early, or simply glance up at a clock in a restaurant or a store, and see the hands at the six-twenty position, whether it's morning or night, I get a knot in my stomach and think I'm going to vomit. I used to have nightmares for the first three years or so, but those have more or less gone away, although I still can't stand having anything like a blanket over my head. Sometimes I get angry, though usually I just feel sad when I think of how twisted my parents' love became . . . but mostly I keep thinking, 'No child should have to go through that.' "

Nightmares, recurrent terrors, and general trauma run

through the stories of both snatched *and* snatchers. A young father who was given custody of his two small children discovered that their mother had taken them and vanished the afternoon he was supposed to pick them up. For months he wandered around in a daze, not knowing if they were dead or alive, and scared that he would never find out. At last he got a phone call from his ex–mother-in-law, saying that the children were healthy and happy and didn't ever want to see him again. During the next year he spent a fortune trying to locate them; occasionally he would get a long-distance call, but never anything he could trace. He appealed to all the legal and law-enforcement agencies he could find, only to discover that no one would help him; child snatching is not a federal offense. Legal Aid couldn't do anything for him, and the two private detectives he hired didn't turn up anything for more than a year.

During that time, the father vacillated about what to do if he did find them. On the one hand he was convinced that he was the better parent, and on the other he worried that if he tried to establish any form of contact with his ex, she would disappear again. He even went so far as to correspond with "Mean Gene," a nationally known figure who makes a living resnatching children. (This man, who calls his work "vigilante recovery," has been quoted as counseling parents, "Use violence if necessary, because you're going to be accused of it anyway." [2]) The father finally decided that the trauma of being abducted by a stranger would be more than he was willing to subject his youngsters to, so when at last the phone call came saying that the wife and children had been found in the Midwest, he had to decide whether he would attempt to snatch them himself or not.

"I went back there, still uncertain about what to do," he said. "I had two private eyes with me, and the three of us followed her and the children for four full days, learning what her pattern of behavior was, watching for and talking over when and how to get the kids. At last we decided I should meet them at the school grounds first thing in the morning, after she left them off and went to park the car. [She worked at the same school.] I stood in the shadows at the top of the stairs, sweating, heart pounding, with a mouth like cotton. They didn't come up the stairs as usual, so I had to run after them, and when they turned around and I bent down to pick them up, one on each arm, *they didn't know who I was!* I kept saying, 'I'm Daddy,' like an idiot, while I started walking as fast as I could toward the car. Just as we got to it, the six-year-old began to scream, and as we slid into the back seat and slammed the door their mother appeared, running across the school grounds with her face contorted in an awful shriek. The windows were all closed, and the doors locked, but I still have nightmares about that silent scream as she pounded on the car. The little ones were howling hysterically, I was trying to calm them, a fellow teacher had run up and was attacking the windshield with his briefcase, and somehow the driver managed to get us under way. For a moment I thought my ex had thrown herself across the hood of the car, and I was terrified she'd fall off and get run over. . . . It was horrible; more horrible than anything I had imagined beforehand, and I still get sick when I think about it.''

That father made his way out of the town with the use of several car changes, and returned to his home area, but not to the life he had been leading. For the next six months, he and the children lived with friends in the country; he was extremely vague, but from the primitive conditions he mentioned, it was probably a transient farm workers' camp. ''It was both a good time and a bad one,'' he commented. ''We were basically in hiding, with me using a different name and watching everyone and everything. When my ex had them, she made the youngsters wear wigs and use false names; I wasn't going to lay *that* kind of trip on them—the situation was crazy enough as it was. But it was good, too, in some ways. Although they missed her considerably, and I often wondered if I'd done the right thing, we grew close again and now have a really stable, loving relationship once more. I enjoyed working in the outdoors, life was simple, and I gradually began to feel we could come out of hiding.''

That was a year ago. I had the distinct impression that the name he now goes by is not his original one; I know that he made contact with me by phone, and the only way I could reach him to confirm our date at the park was through a post-office box registered in the name of a men's organization. His promising career has probably been completely scrapped, his fear of letting his ex even visit the children is logical, and his worry about how the children have been affected runs through all his comments on what happened.

During our morning at the park the youngsters played, laughed, and generally seemed to be enjoying themselves while we grown-ups talked. He had explained to them who I was and what we would be discussing, and after thinking it over the children decided they really didn't want to talk about it themselves, but wouldn't mind if he did. Aside from a few long, speculative looks on the part of the older child, they never referred to what I was doing there, and after I thanked them for sharing their daddy with me that morning, they waved goodby with friendly grins. Yet as their father said, sadly, "Who knows what's happened deep down in their psyches? Or how it will affect their own adult lives? Who knows . . . ?"

This appears to be the profound reaction of most parents who participate in child snatching. Arnold Miller, the founder of Children's Rights, Inc., who snatched back his own son only to have him stolen a second time, has now concluded that he wouldn't do it again, just as the fellow interviewed had. While righteousness and fear, worry and consternation may carry you into such a project initially, the realization of what actually happens to the snatched child seems to have a very sobering effect on even the most ardently determined parent. And just as the child lives with the remnants of fear and nightmares for the rest of his or her life, so too the parent continues to wonder, "Did I do the right thing?"

When the young man who had been snatched agreed to the interview, he made it clear it was for one reason only: "I really don't want to go back and relive all those things," he said. "But if reading about my experience and my pain can keep even one parent from snatching one other child, it will be worth it to me. No one should have to live with these things!" And his parting comment seemed to sum up all the children's reactions: "Whatever is necessary to change the system should be done . . . truly, *there has to be a better way!*"

12
Making
It Legal

The Role of Attorneys in Divorce and Custody Matters

Once you've decided to dissolve the marriage and looked at the various options available, your next consideration should be whether or not you need an attorney, and if so, on what basis. Just as there are many alternatives to the classic mother/children–father/money division after marriage, there are many different capacities in which an attorney can be helpful in your divorce. It is not always necessary for both parties to have separate legal representation, just as it isn't always necessary for divorcing parents to contest custody. Your individual case may be better served by having a *consultation* with an attorney, rather than retaining him or her to fight for you in court, particularly if you and your ex are pretty well in agreement about what you want. Or you may wish to use an attorney who is skilled in arbitration, or agrees to some form of mediation to help you reach an agreement. Before examining the details of these different options, however, let's look at the typical divorce client–attorney relationship and its effect on the divorcing parents.

There are few aspects of divorce more fraught with dissent, disillusionment, and dissatisfaction than those having to do with lawyers. Over and over again they are blamed by clients, therapists, and even other attorneys for escalating the problems between divorcing clients. I have heard attorneys charged with all manner of things (sometimes fairly, sometimes not), and have read statements by divorce lawyers which literally turned my stomach considering that the remnants of the family involved must live with the results of these people's decisions for the rest of their lives![1] I have also found attorneys and judges who are well aware of the problems created by the legal system itself, and are willing to look at ways to improve the situation. Many of these concerned and caring professionals brought up suggestions for this chapter, recognizing that the best way to change the system is to encourage the individual parents to avoid the most obvious problems. By fully understanding what you want, as well as what you are doing and why, you can keep from being caught in a system which claims to look out for "the best interest of the child" and then proceeds to pit that youngster's parents against each other mentally, emotionally, and financially.

Client Dissatisfaction

It can hardly be an accident that 80 percent of the time the divorced client comes away from the courtroom feeling angry, bitter, exploited and ill used, and helpless to do anything about it! In all probability, a large part of the disenchantment expressed by these clients stems from the need to find a scapegoat. In any win/lose system the loser has to develop excuses for not winning, and the disgruntled client often finds it easier to blame his lawyer than to admit that perhaps he didn't have the strongest case to begin with. "If only I'd had a *good* attorney . . ."; "He didn't even mention that my ex had done this and that"; and "He was so anxious to get on to his golf date with the judge, he didn't take the time to fight for my rights!" are common complaints of the person who has lost his or her case in court. In the light of the emotions involved, this may be an understandable reaction, but these accusations usually relate more to the client's disappointment than to any objective reality. In fact, the attorney may have done an excellent job in salvaging whatever he or she could from an *antagonistic judge,* and thus have served the client very well indeed. But because the client is unversed in the actual practice of our legal system, and because he wants to believe his case is better than the other parent's, in his eyes the whole thing smacks of unprofessional and unethical conduct, collusion, and a conspiracy between lawyers to build fat fees.

Dissatisfaction with the divorce attorney is so widespread, however, that one can't chalk it up to either sour grapes on the part of *all* clients or total ineptness on the part of *all* lawyers. It becomes clear that there must be some basic misunderstanding between the client and the professional; somehow, the consumer expects something other than what he gets, and ends up feeling even more outraged when presented with an enormous bill after the battle is waged.

Why does this happen? How come there is such a disparity between what the client thinks he's going to get and what the lawyer actually produces? It results not from misrepresentation, usually, but because the client has little awareness of the limitations and strictures within which the attorney has to operate, and consciously or unconsciously he puts the lawyer in a position no one could adequately fill. As one attorney sadly pointed out, "The client tends to look to the law for relief from painful emotions, and doesn't understand that the courts can't provide that. He or she expects miracles when the best that can be hoped for is some kind of equity."

Client Expectations

Typically when a marriage is coming to an end, one or the other of the adults will decide to go to an attorney for some general legal advice. Sometimes this is agreed to by both parties, and sometimes it is simply an exploratory move on the part of one, who wishes to find out what all would be involved in arranging for the dissolution. Often it is meant only to be a fact-finding expedition, rather than the first step in filing for dissolution.

Emotions are high at this point, and the extremely vulnerable consumer walks through the office doors looking not only for legal information but also for relief from all the tension, confusion, and doubts that are so inherent in rearranging the family structure. Is this really the best thing to do? How does one go about it? What will be the most productive situation for the children? How can we keep from losing all the equity in the house? What sort of grounds does one need to get a divorce in this state anyhow, and what are the local attitudes about child custody? Am I being reasonable to consider divorce, or just neurotic? Do I have to bring charges against my spouse, and if so, what kind of proof do I need? Can there be charges brought against me, and if so, what can I do about that? Is there any way to untangle this whole mess fairly? And what can an attorney do to help me?

What the attorney usually does is sit in his or her office, which is designed to afford both comfort and confidence to the client, and listen to the long, sad outpouring of all the no longer bearable hurts, misunderstandings, arguments, and disappointments that have brought you there in the first place. He or she will be listening carefully, maybe taking notes or asking discreet questions, and his concern is very flattering and reassuring. Obviously this is both a businesslike and caring person, and you begin to feel better immediately. The end of your struggles may be closer than you thought, and with this professional to calm your doubts, handle your problems and take care of the legal aspects of the situation, you can finally relax a little. He or she will be your counselor, decision-maker, rescuer, or maybe even hand-holder, at least figuratively if not literally. So you heave a big sigh of gratitude; you've found someone to advise you on all the sticky things and be your champion during this time of peril and despair.

Generally the client walks away from the first meeting feeling relieved, believing that he or she has just arranged for the services of a guide dog to help get through the maze of paperwork, technicalities, and logistics of the financial arrangements, and to represent his or her interest where the question of child custody is concerned. But it's possible that he or she has hired a very efficient, highly trained and expensive guard dog who's been taught to attack on sight in defense of the client's rights, rather than to help both parties resolve their problems and complete their reorganization.

Escalation of Hostilities

Considering the emotional and psychological needs of the divorcing family, it's little wonder one of the most frequent and bitter
observations of divorced people is that the initial visit to a lawyer
made things worse, not better. "We were working it out pretty
well until she went to an attorney who turned her head all
around!" and "It seemed to me we were settling into being divorced parents okay, and then he found a new lawyer and hit me
with a custody battle out of the blue!" are examples of comments
heard time and again. Often it is the attorney who gets blamed for
this change in attitude, whether or not such blame is warranted.
Since the shift in position from first to second stage of divorce
usually coincides with the introduction of the professional, which
was cause and which was effect is often hard to say.

During the typical family divorce, if one partner goes to see a
lawyer and then comes back to report, "*My* attorney thinks I
should get such-and-such," the relationship between the spouses
will probably do a complete nose dive right then. The other
spouse is likely to feel betrayed, threatened, defensive, and
ganged-up-on because an outsider is being brought in on the
scene, and is taking the side of the opposing partner. (Interestingly enough, husbands usually get furious at the attorney, whom
they see as a meddling interloper intent on lousing things up by
encouraging the wife to become more difficult, while wives blame
the husband directly for picking the nastiest and most aggressive
lawyer available. This seems to be a further reflection of the
cultural belief that men are authoritative, all-powerful, and to be
held responsible for whatever happens; they hire people to get
things done their way. But women aren't considered to be that
responsible for their own attitudes, and so are characterized as
being weak-minded and easily misguided.) In any event, retaining
an attorney is often seen as a declaration of war, whether or not
the attorney sees it that way, and the situation has started to shift
from that of a family in need of legal help in its reorganization to
that of two separate and warring individuals who are about to
divide up the spoils. Everyone starts to get defensive, guarded,
hostile and frightened. Tempers flare, a second attorney may be

hired by the other spouse, and the escalation of hostilities has begun.

Conflict of Interest

Frequently this was not what either partner had in mind when the decision to seek legal advice was made. "She came back from the lawyer's office full of crazy demands, and then announced that I couldn't talk to her directly, I had to talk to her attorney. Only I couldn't talk to him either, because now he represented her, so I'd have to get my own lawyer and then the *two attorneys* could talk!" one perplexed and exasperated father reported. "It's just a damn conspiracy to make more work for the lawyers!"

Although this is technically not true, in most cases the lawyer goes on the assumption that the problems between you may have to be settled by a judge, and that will require the presence of two opposing attorneys. It is not ethical for one attorney to represent both sides of a contested case; if he does so, he runs the risk of becoming involved in a conflict of interests, of denying you as a client the best representation, and inviting a malpractice suit at some later date. Malpractice actions are developing into as much of a concern for attorneys as they are for doctors, and the insurance premiums for lawyers have risen accordingly. Because of this, most attorneys are becoming very cautious in divorce cases, and many couples conclude they *each* have to have an attorney, whereupon they find themselves heading out of marriage and into divorce with a lot more animosity, rancor, and conflict than either of them had expected. Why should this come about, simply as a result of seeking legal help?

Part of the answer has to do with the already strained relationship between the partners, but part is also the result of the attorneys' attitudes. The divorce attorney, while hopefully well versed in the many details of family law, is still basically a legal warrior trained for battle, primed to be an adversary, and expected to view all others in the case as opponents to his client. This is the essential position of any attorney, and it goes back to the bedrock of all our legal concepts. It's well to examine this, not only so that you as a client will better understand your professional, but also to look for ways to improve the system.

The Attorney's Responsibility

There is a sentiment, dear to the heart of every jurist, which says, "Thank God we are a nation governed by laws, not by men." When I first encountered this concept, years ago, I was horrified at what I considered to be the inhumanity of it. Was there no place for compassion, for understanding, for recognition of relative circumstances; in short, the human emotions? And then the attorney I was working for pointed out that while there might not be much room for these aspects of human response, neither was there space for blind prejudice, individual antagonism, or the whim of a tyrannical mind which could warp power to some personal end. The law, in its purest form, is literal, direct, and impartial, simply because it is impersonal. And when looked at that way, the idea of holding all people equal under the law, to be universally responsible to the law rather than the emotional content of their own individual situations, seems remarkably fine. It may not be perfect, but in theory it's one of the best possible systems.

To translate this philosophy into actual practice we have developed a system in which both sides of the matter are presented by specialists trained in the knowledge and use of the law, who argue the relative *legal* merits of their client's position before an impartial third party, who then reaches a decision on the basis of those arguments. In that way, whatever judgments are rendered are based on law, either as it is written or as it has been interpreted over the past years of use in other cases. Neither emotions nor personal convictions are to be involved, regardless of whether the question is a matter of criminal justice or the settling of a civil dispute between two citizens.

Attorneys are trained in law school, and even more profoundly when they enter the courtrooms themselves, to argue, defend, and expound on the legal positions of their clients in opposition to whatever claims are being made against them. They are the adversaries, enemies, opponents and foes of whoever represents the other side of the picture, and are sworn to protect their client's interest at all costs. A lawyer cannot become personally and emotionally involved in a case and, above all else, he or she must not judge the client; that can be done only by the magistrate who listens to the legal arguments. Thus the attorney is expected to walk the fine line between knowing all that needs to be known about you in order to present the strongest arguments (and hide the weakest positions), yet trying not to form any moral or ethical conclusions on his own part. He needs to keep a degree of professional distance and aloofness between himself and the client on the one hand, while offering guidance, encouragement, and support on the other—a stance not always easy to maintain.

If the attorney has reservations about a client or that client's cause, he or she can do one of three things. He can refuse to take the case, although he may recommend another attorney. He can attempt to discourage the pursuance of the matter or even announce that it's too weak a case to be taken to court. Or he may take the case and put aside his own conscience in the matter by reminding himself that everyone deserves adequate representation in court, he himself must not play judge, and the fairness of the system will see that justice is done in the long run.

Given the system, this last is a reasonable philosophy to adopt. Attorneys are only human too, after all, and no one wants to carry around a moral dilemma for months, worrying it like a bone and finding himself constantly wondering if he did the "right" thing. By asserting that the rough-and-tumble of the courtroom battle, with each attorney scrapping fiercely for his own client, will see the emergence of some form of truth on which the judge can make a decision, the attorney relieves himself of any sense of guilt no matter which way the decision goes. As one lawyer put it, "I'm out there to get the most marbles I can for my client; let the judge worry about dispensing justice." Thus, presenting the client's case in the most vigorous legal fashion becomes the *only* criterion, so that when the hearing is over the attorney can walk away from it with some peace of mind, regardless of the result. Obviously this is not always possible, but it is what keeps courtroom lawyers sane. And it is one reason that most attorneys rely heavily on the impersonal, totally legalistic approach to domestic-relations cases.

More than one lawyer has told me about child custody cases

in which he's won the battle for his client, but felt that in the long run the children *lost*. "There was nothing else I could do, really," one fellow exclaimed. "It was an open-and-shut case on a technicality. The children had run away from the boarding school where their mother kept them, had traveled across the entire country to reach their father, and were old enough to be listened to by the court. But the judge sent them back to their mother— my client—because the father made a technical error when he filed for a change of custody. My sympathies were with the kids, but my professional loyalties had to lie with my client."

Here, then, you have a composite portrait of a good, solid, ethical attorney; an advocate who is committed to protect the client's rights even if he doesn't agree with the client personally; a professional who tries to keep up with the most current developments of the law, since they are the tools with which he argues for his client; and a staunch believer in the adversary system to provide the judge with enough information to render a wise and just decision. Whatever else he brings to his practice (a raging desire to "win" each case, a preference for out-of-court settlements, or sensitivity to the problems involved in domestic-relations work) is purely a question of personal orientation and makeup. His training is in the adversary arts, and his approach to family law will probably be the same as his approach to criminal cases; the same philosophy, technique, and practice are the basis for each. In all cases he is out to pick up your fallen standard and carry it into the arena for you. His first responsibility is to you, the client, and the fact that your ex-spouse and children may be adversely affected by his advice and decisions is only circumstantial. He is not, after all, representing them. The legal philosophy is simply "let their attorney protect their interests."

All of this is both reasonable and logical, provided that one sees divorce and child custody purely in terms of legal warfare and overlooks the emotional and psychological impact on the adults and children involved. Naturally, if you've just been served with all sorts of papers indicating that your ex is about to try to have your head presented on a silver platter, it's understandable if you're looking for the noisiest, most aggressive sword-rattler you can find. But if you are among the majority of couples who simply want to put an end to the hostilities as well as the marriage, you'd do well to stay away from the hired Goliath, as he'll be more likely to demolish everyone and everything in sight—including whatever savings the two of you may be hassling about.

Legal Alternatives

Everyone agrees that one of the biggest problems with the way we currently resolve custody questions lies in this use of the adversary system. Burton I. Monasch, Past President of the New York Chapter of the American Academy of Matrimonial Lawyers, has said:

> . . . the courts are the last place a person resolving a matrimonial dispute should be. . . . . Because of the adversary nature of the law, an atmosphere of heat and ill-will is immediately created, which is why I believe that the day a matrimonial problem gets into the hands of lawyers the individuals are in deep trouble.[2]

Yet there are frequently problems involved in the reorganization of a family which do require legal expertise; both the rights and responsibilities of all the people involved should be protected as well as defined, and lawyers are the logical professionals to do this. Monasch himself has therefore suggested the use of mediation as the most viable alternative to "springing into the adversary approach."

Mediation

The dictionary defines "mediation" as follows: "intercession or friendly intervention, usually by consent or invitation, for settling differences between persons, nations, etc." Thus a mediator is someone outside the dispute who doesn't take sides but endeavors to help a divorcing couple arrive at a suitable agreement about their differences. When such a person is an attorney, he or she is able to explain whatever legal considerations are involved, and can help draft the necessary settlement papers once the arrangement has been worked out. Mediation is generally handled with both partners present, and is specifically geared to finding a fair and equitable solution to the problems without having to resort to the adversary position.

The couple who go into mediation must agree not to ask the mediator to represent either one of them individually should the mediation fail, and to handle the court appearance *in pro per* (that is, appearing before the judge without an attorney), once the settlement has been arrived at and all the papers are drawn up. This last is not particularly difficult, provided that you have agreed to everything prior to coming before the bench, so that there is nothing to argue about and nothing for the judge to decide. You are simply requesting legal sanction for what you have already agreed to do.

A mediator takes a neutral position in the case, looking out for the welfare of the entire family, so to speak. If the mediator finds that he or she is no longer able to remain neutral, or that the difficulties can't be resolved without resort to the adversary system, he will withdraw from the case and/or recommend that each party seek separate legal counsel.

There are a good many problems involved in the use of mediation, and most of them befall the attorney. Because of the conflict-of-interest ethic, and the fear of a malpractice suit's being brought later, many lawyers refuse to consider handling divorces in this fashion; as long as they stay within the adversary system they don't run any undue risks. Some manage to adhere to the letter of the ethic while still performing the function of a mediator, however. One enterprising fellow explains the problem to the couple, then offers to act as their mediator with the provision that the legal papers actually show him as representing only one of them. "I tell them it's only a formality, and they can choose which one I'll officially represent by tossing a coin, if they wish. In fact, if they prefer to wait until all the matters have been settled and agreed to before deciding who will be my client, there's even less suspicion on their parts that I'll be playing favorites."

Ann Diamond, whose work as an attorney and professor of law is nationally known, has been using mediation in her private practice during the last several years. She points out that her clients are carefully screened, since she feels that mediation works best where husband and wife have a mutual respect, similar intellectual levels, and good communication. Although she feels strongly that the practice of dual representation in divorce cases will have to change in the future, she has hesitated to encourage younger, less experienced lawyers to rely on mediation. Partly this stems from the problem of conflict of interest, and partly it is because of judges' nervousness about accepting a mediated settlement. She herself has explained her approach to the judges who hear her clients *in pro per,* and because of her reputation and authority in the field, she has not had any trouble persuading the bench to accept such solutions. A less well-known lawyer might encounter problems, however, and until the practice becomes the established way of handling family reorganization, Diamond feels an understandable reticence about encouraging the use of this system for every family-court case.

All attorneys who act as mediators for a divorcing couple stress that either party is free to consult a separate attorney at any point during the mediation process. This is encouraged so that the fairness of the settlement can be verified, the clients' trust in the mediator be reaffirmed, and the conflict-of-interest problem be somewhat alleviated.

If you are looking for a professional who will handle your case in this fashion, be sure to have your homework done; make a list of already-agreed-to items, as much information about family finances as you can provide, and an outline of the areas you either have doubts about or simply can't agree on. Many mediators will suggest family counseling for one or all of the members of the family, and may ask that professionals in the field of child psychology be consulted before you settle the question of custody arrangements. And if you have a very complicated financial picture, with many questions concerning savings, investment funds, stocks, bonds, real estate holdings, pension plans, possible tax advantages, capital gains, and the like, a certified public accountant is often recommended. Again, this professional should be consulted by both partners, and his or her findings and recommendations turned over to the mediator (as well as to each of you). The more information that is readily and clearly available to the attorney, the more rapidly the matter will be settled, and the lower your legal bills will be.

When all the facts are assembled, and you have both been

apprised of the specific legal considerations involved in your case, the mediator makes suggestions and offers choices, provides legal advice, and helps you work out the details of your settlement, then draws up the papers to be presented at court. Unlike an arbitrator, however, he or she does not make judgments or binding legal decisions.

Arbitration

It has been said that arbitration is simply an informal court hearing, with an attorney taking the position of the judge, and to some degree this is true. Both parties agree beforehand that the decision of the arbitrator shall be legally binding, and to a large degree the arbitrator acts as a judge in listening to both sides, examining witnesses (particularly child psychologists and CPAs), and then rendering a decision. The advantages of arbitration have to do with the convenience of time and place; as with mediation, the conferences take place in an office, not in a courtroom, and hours can be arranged when everyone can conveniently be present. The public arena of courtroom fighting can be avoided, though it is often agreed that your individual attorneys may be present at the conferences, should you desire separate counsel. And the cost is usually considerably less than that of a Superior Court hearing. Obviously it is imperative that both parties trust, honor, and respect the person who is acting as arbitrator, and that you have all your homework carefully prepared.

The American Arbitration Association has developed a family-dispute service, which offers both mediation and arbitration, though the mediator is not necessarily an attorney. An AAA mediator does not give legal advice, but concentrates on helping you resolve those problems which you haven't found any solution to on your own, and then suggests that you take your final agreement to the family attorney for drafting in legal form. (AAA can also provide a family counselor if you are unsure whether dissolution is the route you really want to take.) There are American Arbitration Association offices in most major cities, or you can write to the association for further information at its headquarters in New York; the address is listed in Appendix A.

New Directions

There is much to be said for either of these new approaches to the question of settling custody disputes. They encourage everyone (including the professionals) to view the divorcing family as a unit which needs legal advice in order to accomplish its internal reorganization fairly. And mediation specifically works toward eliminating the adversary problem so common in custody actions. Certainly the idea of redefining the attorney's role in these proceedings is a step in the right direction.

Not only does the professional in family law need to be trained for something other than the adversary method where family law is concerned: he or she could help the client by working more closely with divorce and family therapists in many cases. A number of professionals, including Ms. Diamond, are convinced that all divorcing families can benefit from family counseling and guidance during the transition period, and that attorneys should be trained not only to recognize this, but also to work with family therapists. Too often what may be the most logical defensive legal maneuver, and therefore recommended by the lawyer, can shatter whatever tenuous rapport the family therapist has been able to set up. And what may be the best and most positive action for the whole family from a psychological point of view may expose one or all of the clients to unexpected legal hazards. If these professionals are willing to work together *for the welfare of the client family,* much of the chaos encountered in the typical divorce or custody case can be avoided. Some lawyers do make a practice of this, but at the moment it is the exception, not the rule, and while most professionals in both fields admit that there should be more contact between them on individual cases, it usually takes the clients' specific request to bring it about.

The Team Approach

Meyer Elkin, Past President of the Association of Family Conciliation Courts, points out that although both attorneys and counselors are involved in finding a lasting resolution of the divorcing family's problems, their methods and philosophies differ significantly. The lawyer is concerned with law and case history, and relies on the outside authority of the judge to tell the parents what to do, whereas the counselor encourages the couple to find a solution that is emotionally acceptable to the family and will be adhered to because of the individual's inner commitment. He goes on to state:

> . . . [T]here are differences between these professions . . . [which make] it difficult for either one alone to effectively function in the area of family law. The best of both professions are needed if the best interest of all members of the family system are to be served.[3]

Recognition of the value of such interprofessional cooperation has led to the development of the divorce-team concept. If the family in transition can meet with an attorney, a CPA, and a child psychologist or family counselor who all work together to help that family find its own solutions, it cannot only save time, energy, and money but also obviate a lot of heartache. Once you've done your homework, had the house appraised, tried to rearrange your budget, found out what you will or won't want to consider for custody, and know where the worst disagreements lie, you're in an excellent position to make use of such professional help on a team basis. And if the professionals view the entire process as a family matter, much of the traditional antagonism can be alleviated.

So far the team approach is more theoretical than actual; most of the groups I know of who are trying this method are very new and only just getting started. If there is nothing really like this available in your area, see if you can find individual professionals who will agree to work together for you as a team. Many people in these different fields have expressed interest in handling divorce in this fashion, but wonder how they can support themselves until it becomes an accepted practice. If you come to them with the request to establish such a team, however, they may be able to arrange it for you as a special case. Start with one or two professionals, such as a therapist and an attorney; it helps if you already know them and feel comfortable with them. Ask if they will work with professionals in the other fields, contact those people they recommend, and see if you can put together your own team. You would do well to ascertain what the charges will be in this sort of circumstance, however, before you commit yourselves to it. While those groups I know of are trying to make their services available on a sliding fee basis, you will need to determine for yourself how your own team will expect to be paid. Remember that the more homework you do, the less professional time and energy will have to be spent ferreting out the information.

Consultation

If you and your ex are in accord about getting divorced or changing your child custody, and have agreed on all the details (including finances), you may simply need information on how to make your agreement legal. This doesn't mean that you can't use the help of legal counsel: only that you don't need to hire him or her as a spokesman in a battle.

There is a big difference between retaining an attorney to pursue your divorce for you and buying an hour or two of his time and information. Since individual state laws differ, and local procedures vary from county to county, it's best to find out what's involved in the county where you're going to file. The two of you should go to this consultation together, ask all the questions you want, learn what the steps involved are, and then go away from the office and think it over.

When you call to make an appointment for such a consultation, be sure to explain what it is you want. Some attorneys refuse to see couples together, or won't agree to a conference unless they feel fairly sure you will hire them to continue the matter further. That is strictly a matter of personal attitude, and if you get turned down by the first couple of professionals you call, keep looking; sooner or later you'll locate someone willing to tell you about the necessary procedures.

If you and your spouse live in an area where it's possible to do your own divorce, kits and packets of information on the process should be available, along with books on how to handle it yourself. And if you're near a city with an active women's center, chances are it will be able to refer you to legal workshops, paralegal divorce clinics, and various other alternatives to the traditional adversary system.

You may find that you can write up your own settlement and create your own custody agreement; many people in the field of family law are using personal contracts more and more these days. Consumers' Group Legal Services in Berkeley, California, is involved in helping people to write their own divorce contracts, and examples of its custody paragraphs are reprinted in Appendix B. How much of a hand you want to have in making your custody arrangement legal depends on you; the tools are there if you wish to make use of them, and a growing number of attorneys will work with clients on this basis.

Once you've decided what sort of legal help you want, the next step is to locate the professional who can help you. The following chapter and checklist are designed specifically with that in mind.

13
Finding
an Attorney

Locating the Professional You Want

Most attorneys fall somewhere between the mediator and the hired legal gun. Except for those individuals who pride themselves on their courtroom reputations, they'll try to settle your disagreements out of court. Many take the position that if a divorce or custody matter has to go before a judge to be decided, the attorneys on the case have failed. Some believe that the more pressure they can put on the other party, the better results they will get, while others are definitely more involved in finding fair and amicable settlements without a lot of posturing. Much of an attorney's approach to a divorce case will have to do with who the other attorney is. If the other professional has a reputation for belligerence right up to the courthouse steps, it may be necessary for him or her to adopt the same stance. But if the other is noted for helping to create a climate for negotiation and the reconciliation of differences, an earlier settlement is likely to be arranged. All of these are important considerations when you are looking for a lawyer, as they will strongly affect not only how your case is handled, but how you feel about it afterward as well.

Because the client–attorney relationship is such a personal one, particularly where divorce or custody is concerned, there are as many different levels of understanding, communication, and expectations to it as there are people. One lawyer will put a good deal of stress on the public image, on "winning" each and every case, and on making the client feel secure and comfortable because of his or her outgoing, energetic attitude. Another will be more taciturn, and spend more time and energy looking for ways to settle your disagreements than in polishing up his courtroom manner. And a third, sometimes a younger and certainly more idealistic jurist, will work out of a storefront or through a legal service of some sort, and usually be willing and able to explore unusual solutions to your problems. Each approach has something to recommend it, depending on what the client's needs and desires are. But what is one person's best representative is another's disaster, so it's well worth your time and energy (and money) to find a professional you can work with. Among the people I interviewed who had done this (some of them after having become disillusioned with their original lawyers), it took meetings with up to four different professionals before they found one they were satisfied with. All of them stressed that the final results were certainly worth the effort involved. When asked what specific advice they would give someone else just going into a divorce, the answer was frequently "Find an attorney you can trust, and then stick with him!"

Once you have decided how much and what kind of legal help you want, the next step is to locate a professional who will provide it. Most county or state bar associations have a lawyer-referral service, and if you call and explain that you wish to talk with an attorney about divorce or child custody matters, the service can refer you to someone in your area and arrange a half-hour appointment for you at a limited fee. If you want a consultation as a couple, or are specifically looking for an arbitrator, be sure to specify that; in general such referral services don't screen the attorneys involved, but they may know who specializes in what.

The Legal Aid Society will help you if you meet its financial limitations (it has a sliding scale which depends upon the amount of income available to you). And if yours is a custody problem which involves another state, Legal Aid can usually arrange some form of communication with the same society in the other state.

If you have divorced friends, ask them for recommendations where attorneys are concerned. Even if they can't suggest whom you should interview, they may be able to tell you whom to avoid. It's usually not a good idea to go to an attorney simply because he or she drew up Aunt Tilly's will half a century ago and has been a friend of the family ever since. That may speak volumes for the staying power of the person, but it doesn't say how well versed he is in family law, and if you end up being dissatisfied and unhappy with the results, it may cause poor feelings in the family.

Be sure to talk to at least one past client of each professional you interview, either before you call for your appointment or as a result of the interview. If you don't have the name of such a reference, ask the lawyer for one. Since any divorce action is a matter of public record, there is no violation of confidence in giving out a client's name *as long as you don't discuss the specific case with him*. If the client feels like talking about it, however (and he or she often will), that's fine. Fifteen minutes with a past client may give you more insight into how that particular attorney works than several direct interviews with the professional will.

Family-Law Specialists

In the past, domestic relations cases were considered about on a par with bill collection and the defending of sex offenders: the lowest and most miserable of legal work. There were several reasons for this; both society and the law look upon divorce as a threat to the stability of the family, and at least give lip service to regrets that such measures are sometimes necessary. Thus you have many divorce lawyers who personally deplore the divorce rate all the while they're making their money from it. Then again, these are the cases in which emotions are highest; as one attorney pointed out, this is the area where someone is most likely to pull out a gun and shoot the opposition, the judge, or even the lawyer.

And for the attorney who has to listen to all the woes and anguish attached to ending a marriage, it can be a depressing and devastating way to spend one's days, particularly when you realize that the client will probably end up blaming you for everything that goes wrong in his life! No wonder few professionals wanted to specialize in the field.

That is gradually changing, however. Because divorce is so much with us, and the family laws of many states are changing so rapidly, more attorneys are attracted to the challenges of divorce and custody work. In the mid-1960s the American Academy of Matrimonial Lawyers was founded "to encourage the study, improve the practice, elevate the standards and advance the cause of matrimonial law, to the end that the welfare of the family and society be preserved." This group, which now includes several thousand members from across the country, holds both regional and national symposiums and conferences, publishes a list of Certified Fellows in each region, and provides family-law practitioners with an opportunity to exchange information and ideas in the field. (Its address will be found in Appendix A.)

Although it's logical to assume that such an individual will be more aware of the most recent changes and decisions in the law, it isn't absolutely essential to have a family law attorney. In several cases, a good general-practice lawyer turned out to be more helpful than the domestic-relations person had been. It all depends on what you're looking for, and how the two of you interact, because no matter how businesslike the relationship, your own personalities will get involved.

Attorneys' Fees

Different attorneys have different policies about charging for an initial interview. I've met some who don't charge for the first visit, during which you are getting to know each other, so to speak; you're asking about the lawyer's philosophies, and he or she is asking about your circumstances. Then there are those who charge their regular hourly rate right from the moment you walk through their inner-office door; with these people you would do well to have your list of questions all together, and remember to stick to the point. Still others will request a minimal payment for the first visit which then becomes part of the retainer if you decide to have them handle the case. It is well to establish what the financial arrangement for this first interview is going to be *at the time you make the appointment,* so that you know what to expect, just as it's very important to know exactly what the basic cost will be if you are considering hiring that attorney to represent you from now on. This too will vary from person to person, as well as from state to state.

In some cases the lawyer will quote you a flat fee if the divorce is to be uncontested and uncomplicated. (A word of caution, however: most phone calls, and any future visits, may constitute a complication, so be sure you understand exactly what is being covered by that set amount of money. Many clients have been stunned to discover that the final bill came to more than double what they expected because what they thought were *details* turned out to be *complications!*) Others will ask for a sizable retainer to be paid at the beginning, and then will add time and expenses as the case progresses.

Be sure you understand how these further expenses are accounted for, and at what rate the time will be charged. For instance, if the attorney has to schedule all morning for the court appearance, you may find yourself charged for four hours of work at $100 an hour, even though the actual hearing of your case took only ten minutes. This is not an unethical practice; frequently one waits for upward of three hours to be heard by the judge, so naturally the attorney has to plan all other work and appointments around that block of time on that day.

Knowing all these things in advance will help your blood pressure when it's time to get the bill. Beware of any professional who is vague about cost structure or fee schedule, or who shrugs off your questions with a pleasantry; if he or she can't communicate with you directly and clearly at the beginning, you're guaranteed to run into problems later on!

Interviewing an Attorney

When you go for the initial interview, remember that *you* are the one who is asking the questions, weighing the answers, and making the decision about whether or not to hire this lawyer. In order to come to any meaningful decision, you have to have some idea of his or her approach to divorce and custody, and you won't know that if you've spent the entire session explaining what your own circumstances are. That is not to say that you shouldn't tell him about your case; but it's easy to get so swept up in your own emotions that you end up knowing nothing more about the lawyer than the fact that he was an attentive and responsive listener. And if he's any kind of attorney at all, he'll be a good listener, so that doesn't tell you much.

Naturally, if you find the professional isn't willing to listen past the first couple of sentences, but is only intent on driving home his own preconceived notions as to what your family needs, you should cross him or her off your list right away. There are two basic types of lawyers: those who tell the client what to do, and then push him into doing it, and those who ask what the client wants and needs, and then suggest how to go about achieving that in legal terms. You want to find the latter, as the other will cost you heavily not only in money but also potential woe and grief in the long run. The checklist at the end of this chapter was developed with the help of several attorneys. Don't hesitate to take it with you on interviews and use it to evaluate each professional.

Individual Attitudes

The advisability of finding the right attorney at the beginning cannot be overemphasized. Time and again one hears of clients who, partway through what has become a long and nasty fight, have decided that a different lawyer would help get things cleared up faster, and therefore change horses in midstream. Not only is this doubly expensive, because the new professional has to check over everything that's gone before: it also muddies the water considerably, as each attorney brings his or her own prejudices and pet peeves into the case. And every lawyer has his own particular approach to divorce and/or child custody.

If he has been divorced himself, he may be more understanding and supportive, or it may have made him personally biased and more ardent in his pursuit of certain things, depending on his own experience. He'll probably be sure he knows what won't work for your family simply because it didn't work for his, and the chances are he'll be against the whole idea of shared custody right from the start. Most attorneys are so sure that it can't succeed, they never even mention it as a possibility to predivorce clients.

Many attorneys will accept the idea of splitting siblings between divorced parents better than they will the concept of shared time and responsibility. Probably this is due to the fact that the courts themselves have looked favorably on boys going to live with their fathers during the teen years. Attorneys are very much influenced by what they think the judge will or will not approve, and often make recommendations based on their knowledge of how a particular judge will look at the case. (This, of course, is one of the reasons for having an attorney; as the next chapter shows, the final decision in a custody battle ends up in the hands of one person, and that person may have any number of quirks, fantasies, or personal prejudices which make for a very biased decision. Having an attorney who knows the individual attitudes of the local judges may save you some unexpected surprises.)

If you and your ex have agreed about what you want your child custody arrangements to be but are still bickering over who gets the family pet/motorboat/TV set, by all means use your lawyers to settle the other problems—but remain firm in your agreement about the children. It is not uncommon for attorneys to try to talk parents out of joint custody, even if it has been successfully used during the initial separation. I know of a number of cases in which the parents had shared the children for periods of time ranging from several months to more than a year before deciding to dissolve the marriage, only to have their lawyers counsel them that sharing wasn't feasible, the judge wouldn't allow it, or that by doing so they were weakening their own bargaining position on money. (This last is using children as weapons and/or possessions, and is truly reprehensible, yet many attorneys and some parents slip into this type of thinking without considering what it does to the youngsters.) In many instances the clients ended up listening to the outsider instead of their own personal experience, and then polarized into the either/or attitude that leads to custody battles. So if you have been able to reach any kind of settlement about your children's welfare, hang on to it!

A particularly sensitive, though cautious, lawyer told me of one case in which the client kept coming back to the idea of joint custody over and over during the six months it took to iron out all the other settlement agreements. Each time he would discourage her, and each time she would discuss it with her opposite partner and come back to say that was what they wanted. Finally the professional agreed to write it up for them, although he had many doubts about the judge's reaction.

"That's one case that was extremely educational," he said later. "Most judges and attorneys are skeptical of shared custody because they feel there is too high a degree of uncertainty involved; yet by the time we actually had the hearing, the parents were absolutely certain about what they wanted, and had worked out all the details concerning amounts of time, school attendance, after-school care, weekend and holiday divisions, and financial responsibilities. The judge asked a lot of questions, then agreed to go along with it, once he was certain they knew what they were talking about. And really, that's the most important thing— knowing that the parents believe they can make it work on a realistic basis."

Controlling Your Professional

This brings up one of the most critical problems of divorce or custody cases. It's very easy, once you feel yourself to be in competent professional hands, to relax and assume that your attorney will take care of all your problems. That, after all, is what you are paying for. Unfortunately this is the very attitude which leads to the many misplaced expectations that plague the client–lawyer relationship. Instead of asking for legal counsel and recommendations, too many clients simply sit back and let the attorney make all the decisions. Whatever the lawyer suggests is immediately taken as gospel truth, and before long the attorney is left to run the entire show. When this happens, the client has renounced control of the case, and it sometimes leads to the professional's charging full steam ahead, doing what he has been trained to do best in the adversary role. That it may leave the family in tatters is unfortunate, but that's the way the system works.

I personally saw a very painful example of this unfold recently. One of the staunchest advocates of shared custody I have ever met was a man who was himself a noncustodial father. During the first year of separation he and his wife had shared the children on an almost equal-time schedule, and it seemed to work quite well. At the time of divorce, however, her attorney convinced her that it wasn't possible to make joint custody legal, so she asked for and got sole custody of the children. For the next three years the father talked of nothing but the unfairness of the either/or arrangement, its effects on children and fathers, and his desire to share more equally in the upbringing of the youngsters. He gave speeches on shared custody to any civic group that would listen, did interviews with newspapers, and became one of the most articulate spokespersons for divorce and custody reform. Gradually the tensions between himself and his ex lessened, and he decided that the time had come to negotiate a rearrangement of custody. So he hired an attorney with a reputation for custody work. Believing that now, at last, he had reason to hope for some kind of accord that would allow for sharing the youngsters, he called to tell me his good news. When I inquired as to exactly what he and his attorney were going to do, he said that they were asking for *full and sole custody* of the children! Appalled at this apparent change of attitude, I asked why on earth he was taking this approach when he had expounded on the benefits of sharing for so long. "My attorney says we have to do it to get her attention; sort of scare her into sharing" was the response. "And he charged me a three-thousand-dollar retainer just to take the case; he should know what he's doing!"

Naturally the mother feels betrayed, angry, and hurt. Her ex, who had seemed to be willing to be more friendly and cooperative, has suddenly initiated a legal battle, and she has been driven into a defensive position with her back against the wall and her own legal fees piling up. Regardless of the outcome of this new hearing, the cautious respect and trust that were beginning to develop between these two parents have now been shattered because of a very aggressive attorney and a client who isn't willing or able to control his professional. (It should be noted that no action can be taken without the client's permission, but a less warlike approach on the part of the lawyer might well have avoided the further deterioration of this couple's relationship.)

Too often the client forgets that he or she is the consumer, without whom the knowledge, experience, and professionalism of the lawyer would be useless. Attorneys are offering you a service, and you have the right to ask for their opinions, then decide for yourselves what you want them to do. If, for some reason, they *cannot* comply with your desires, they will tell you. If that happens, check out why: is it a question of personal philosophy, or a case of professional ethics? Do they have any further suggestions as to how to accomplish the end *you want?* And if not, what other ends do they themselves envision? What means do they suggest using, and how does that fit in with your own needs and desires for the family? Don't be afraid to ask this kind of question, to find out what's happening, to incorporate their information into your own plans and decisions. They should be treated as *consultants* to you, whose advice you can respect and rely on, but the final say on how things are handled is still your responsibility.

Client Responsibility

Assuming that you have now located an attorney you feel good about working with, there are a couple of things you must keep in mind about your end of the client–attorney relationship.

One of the most important of these is recognizing when *not* to call your lawyer. Divorcing clients have a tendency to reach for the phone every time some new thought, old memory, or present confusion comes to mind. If the client is a woman who has not been out on her own before, she may want to turn to her lawyer for advice on anything and everything that crops up. Often this is because she really doesn't know what to do about lots of things; if the roof develops a leak, should she have it repaired or replaced, and who pays the bill for it? Is it all right for her ex to borrow her station wagon to take the children camping on one of his weekend visits? And after he's come back from camping and she's discovered he took his new girlfriend along too, doesn't that constitute immoral behavior, mental cruelty to her, and grounds for throwing the bastard in jail?

Another reason for her barrage of phone calls may lie in the fact that she needs the reassurance of talking over everything with another adult in whom she has confidence. If she's been used to letting her husband run the family, she undoubtedly feels frightened and poorly equipped to make major decisions by herself. And sometimes she calls because she doesn't know what's important, legally, and what isn't. Even people well versed in the law have trouble paring down the information they want to give their attorneys, and the average layman is so awash in personal turmoil, he or she has no idea what the attorney really needs to know and what not.

Nor is it uncommon for a man to call and report each and every contact with his ex, to want to discuss whatever changes he thinks he perceives in either her or the children, and any bits of additional information, including clippings from out-of-state newspapers, that he feels might have some bearing on his case. The attorney has to listen to all these things, check out the details, and weigh the legal ramifications (if any), just to be able to reassure the client that everything is still okay. All of which is usually a large waste of time. It's one thing to ask your attorney how he thinks something should be handled, and quite another for you to try to run the case for him.

Many new divorce clients don't realize that the average lawyer looks at his or her watch the moment he picks up the phone and notes the time on his expense sheet. This is as much a part of the attorney's time and expenses as are office visits or calls to the other lawyer, and with attorneys' fees ranging up to $75 an hour and more, it doesn't take many ten-minute phone calls to add up to a surprising sum. Your lawyer is interested, and does care about your case, but his or her involvement isn't gratis, and if you're taking up professional time, you have to expect to pay the professional rate for it.

For most lawyers, the problem of how to be supportive of clients without adding to already unrealistic expectations is a very big one. Some are quite direct in their efforts to suggest that you'd do better to call someone from Parents Without Partners when you're feeling blue, let down, or confused by the whole thing. Others make an attempt at understanding the psychological problems their clients are confronting, and recommend individual or family divorce therapy. And some, unfortunately, foster the idea that they are the savior who can or will try to supply the tearful client's every need. It is somewhat reassuring to realize that most of the charges against attorneys that they have been taking advantage of the emotional and psychological vulnerabilities of their women clients in order to console them right into bed come from belligerent and furious ex-husbands, and have little or no proof to back them up. It does happen occasionally, though, and if you as a woman client find that your lawyer is pressing for more personal familiarity than your business relationship warrants, don't hesitate to say so. It may be all very flattering to have someone telling you what a delightful and desirable woman you are, particularly when you're so full of self-doubts and confusion, but it can quickly lead to much more trouble than it's worth. A firm refusal of the invitation to "finish this discussion over lunch" or "continue this with a drink" will usually establish the fact that you want to keep this a strictly professional relationship, at least until after the divorce is finished. And if his ardor has cooled noticeably by that time, you haven't lost anything; the man who only knows how to play Knight in Shining Armor tends to lose interest the moment the damsel is out of danger.

Another very important area of understanding between you and your attorney has to do with following instructions. When your lawyer tells you under no circumstances are you to use the joint credit card, call your ex's new flame to make mischief, or ignore the court's orders about visitation or support payments, for goodness' sake listen! While this may all sound like simple common sense at this point, it's amazing how many people do crazy things when caught up in the emotions of a divorce or custody case. Once you've established what you want from your professional and have agreed on a policy for achieving that end, it's up to you to follow through by obeying whatever advice he gives you. To the degree that he needs to be able to count on your behavior, your lawyer has a right to expect cooperation and support from you, and you're very foolish if you hire him and then don't provide that.

Most lawyers would prefer to resolve custody matters out of court, and if your professional tells you that what the other partner and his professional are offering is probably as good as or better than what you could hope for from a judge's decision, be willing to accept that he knows whereof he speaks. For all their willingness to champion your cause, most lawyers have a pretty shrewd idea of what is likely to be agreed to very early on in a case, and a good deal of their time and energy is spent trying to get the client to realize this. Unless you have a lot of money, and he is hell-bent on a court battle, your professional will probably counsel you to accept any reasonable compromise. Keep in mind that learning to make reasonable concessions between the two of you is one of the first steps in becoming coparents, and you have to begin somewhere.

It is terribly important to remember that this is *your* family, *your* future and theirs, and *your* divorce. You are the ones who will be living with it years hence, long after the attorneys have gone on to new cases, so it's up to you to establish with your lawyer what kind of outcome you want. Only by being sure that the two of you are working together in a partnership, with you setting the goals and standards and he or she providing the services and skills necessary to try to reach them, are you likely to feel satisfied about your relationship with your lawyer. There are many attorneys who work with their clients in this way, and once you find one with whom you feel comfortable, the two of you should be able to work together well.

ATTORNEY CHECKLIST

Copy this list onto ruled paper, leaving space on the left for as many columns as there are lawyers you wish to interview. (The entire list may be several pages long, but it is certainly worth the time and trouble to make it.) Take it with you to each attorney's office, and note the answers in the column under his or her name. When you are finished you'll have a record of what each professional told you, plus a means of comparing them.

1. How was contact made? (Name of client, referral service, or other source)

2. What is the cost of the initial visit?
3. Will s/he see you together in conference?
4. Will s/he act as a mediator?
5. Does s/he recommend arbitration?
6. What percentage of his or her cases is family law?
7. Is s/he a member of the American Academy of Matrimonial Lawyers?
8. How long has s/he practiced in this county?
9. Does s/he know the attitudes of different judges?
10. Does s/he recommend family counseling?
11. Whom does s/he suggest as a good divorce counselor (psychologist, marriage and family counselor, etc.)?
12. Does s/he recommend that you see a therapist together or separately?
13. Will s/he work with your family therapist to help reach a settlement?
    If not, why not?
14. Does s/he recommend using two attorneys?
15. Does s/he suggest a third attorney for the children?
    If so, who will pay for it?
16. How does s/he feel about joint legal custody?
17. How does s/he feel about joint physical custody?
18. Has s/he been divorced?
19. Does s/he have custody of own children?
    How did that get arranged?
20. What percentage of cases does s/he settle out of court?
21. What percentage go to trial?
    How many divorce or custody trials handled last year?
22. Fee arrangement:
    Amount of retainer
    Plus time and expenses?
    Per-hour rate
    Flat fee
    Estimate for this case
    What constitutes complications?
    How much does s/he expect the court to award in attorney's fees to either party?
    Will s/he send you a monthly statement?
    Other arrangements s/he suggests

23. How much child support does s/he estimate?
24. Spousal support (alimony) expected?
25. What are these figures based on?
    Can you see a copy of the local schedule used by judges?
26. What other professionals does s/he recommend you contact? (Fill in name and address if available.)
    Accountant or CPA
    Real estate appraiser
    Child psychologist
    Conciliation court
    Marriage and family counselor
    Custody-education, predivorce classes
    Other

REFERENCE: Write in reference's name and phone number

1. How well was client satisfied?
2. How close was cost estimate to final bill?
3. Did attorney keep client well informed?
4. What did client like least about attorney?
5. What did client like best about attorney?
6. Did the attorney help or hinder relationship with ex?
7. Any other comments?

14
Legal Outlook, Past and Present

What the Law Says

In the ancient Biblical story, King Solomon, noted for his wisdom and fairness as a judge, was called upon to make a child-custody decision between two women, each of whom claimed the infant as her own. In a moment of barbaric insight, he ordered the babe be split down the middle, with each woman to receive half. The false mother reacted with a shrug of her shoulders, but the real one screamed out, "Let her have him; at least he will continue to live!" And by this display of maternal concern Solomon proved to his own satisfaction which of the women was indeed the mother of the child, and awarded it to her.

Unfortunately, when the contest is between two equally involved blood parents, no such strategy can be called into play. Consequently, in order not to have to divide the child, we have resorted to the either/or system, although that generally ignores the psychological split such a decision creates in the youngster. And more than one parent, pushed to the end of his or her tether by this all-or-nothing system, has decided to fight it out on a win/lose basis rather than work out some way to keep the offspring intact emotionally. The results of this attitude show up in family court every day as contested custody matters. How we arrived at this system and where we may hope to see it change are certainly worth looking at, in order to get some perspective on the problem.

History of Divorce Laws

Divorce, in one form or another, has been available just about as long as marriage has been around. And though it was generally the prerogative of the man rather than the woman, some cultures recognized the woman's right to petition for a change of relationship. For instance, during the days of the Roman Empire a matron could sue for divorce, and had the right to expect the return of her dowry as well. For the most part, however, divorce was treated as the man's right and privilege, and whereas he could dispose of his partner for various reasons, the woman was expected to accept her lot in life without undo fuss, and certainly not instigate a divorce on her own.

With the coming of the Dark Ages, when the Church became the dominant and essential force in life, divorce was abolished. Marriage became a sacrament, and was seen as a sacred and holy institution; it was considered a religious matter rather than a secular one, and was handled entirely by the Church, which averred that there was no way for man to part what God had united.

It appears that the entire subject of marriage and divorce may have been more or less academic to the majority of people in those days. The serfs, slaves, and common folk went on their way with a great disregard for such formalities, living together or apart as the need or opportunity arose. It was only the nobles and aristocrats who, as purveyors of "right and proper conduct," kept the records, debated the laws, and sought official sanction for their marital activities.

As the merchant middle class developed, marriage became more important. One was married for life, often to a partner of one's *parents'* choosing. Marriages were usually based on social, financial, or political considerations, and as such were indeed contracts made for any number of reasons other than personal expectations of romance or emotional rapport. (Romeo and Juliet would never have ended so tragically if the personal desires of the prospective bride and groom had been considered of any consequence.) It is virtually impossible to compel people who do not wish to live together to do so over a long period of time, however, and the Church eventually recognized the need for legitimizing a separation between spouses, although neither was free to remarry unless the original marriage was declared null and void.

With the advent of the Reformation and its attendant stress on individual freedoms of worship and behavior, divorce began to be an option for the socially powerful and prominent. Henry VIII's falling out with the Pope over this issue in 1534 is probably the most famous of such cases, but even so divorce was not practical for the average family during the next several centuries. Although Henry's action in England had taken the problem out of the hands of the Church and made it a matter of civil law, it required an Act of Parliament to free the "unblemished" spouse from an offending partner. As this was both hideously expensive and terribly time-consuming, to say nothing of being public in the extreme, few people were willing or able to make use of it. In the early 1800s there were an average of *two* divorces per year in England! And Lord Ellenborough's divorce from Lady Jane Digby was such a public scandal that the gentleman was considered to have lost more by pursuing it than he gained in achieving his freedom.[1]

When settlers began to colonize the shores of America, they brought with them the legal attitudes and beliefs of the various countries they came from, and improved on them as they saw fit. Thus it was the Puritan colonies of New England which first made divorce legally possible in this country, believing as they did in the right of each person to determine his or her own life's needs. In the South, where the culture was based on the agrarian, expanded-family arrangement and the society was much more reminiscent of feudal aristocracy, there were no provisions for divorce at all. Husbands, wives, children, parents, grandparents, aunts, uncles, and cousins all lived within a loose-knit family, and if a couple found they were badly mismatched, they generally went their separate ways within the family structure. In South Carolina, for instance, divorce was forbidden, but the practice of concubinage was so prevalent that a law was drawn up to limit the amount of property a man could leave his concubine when he died.

In some areas, such as the state of Virginia, even the right to petition for divorce had to be approved by the legislature. The process was extremely complicated, and carried with it social condemnation and the stigma of public disgrace. Andrew Jackson's wife, Rachel, was under the impression she had been divorced in this manner when she married Jackson, and discovered only at a later time that while *permission* to divorce had been granted her first husband, the actual formalities had not been concluded until four years later in a Kentucky court. So shocking was her marital history in the eyes of his political opponents that both the fact she had been divorced and that she had, even unknowingly, been in a bigamous relationship with her second husband were used as heavy propaganda against Jackson during his first Presidential campaign. The message was very clear: although it might be miserable to continue to live together once the relationship turned sour, it was worse to do something about it legally.

While this background may seem tangential to the subject of child custody, it helps to explain why we have such a variety of laws and attitudes around the nation. Marriage, divorce, and family law are considered to be concerns of the state, not of the federal government, and each state built its legal system on that of the settlers' background. Thus you find the remnants of the Napoleonic Code in Louisiana, community-property states in the Southwest as a result of the Spanish influence, and English common law throughout the rest of the United States. As a result, the divorce statutes and attitudes have varied so widely that Nevada could establish a thriving industry based on its liberal residency laws and grounds for divorce, while New York maintained the position that adultery was the *only* reason for dissolving a marriage up until 1967. And just as the history of divorce law is a hodgepodge and patchwork of different philosophies, so is that of child custody.

Development of Child Custody Laws

The specific need for laws dealing with the children of divorce became evident only during the latter part of the nineteenth century. As long as divorce was limited to the rich and powerful it remained a fairly esoteric matter, but with the increasing pressure of Victorian family life and the deterioration of family support systems, more people began to perceive the right to dissolve a bad marriage as a necessary legal option, and more children were affected by their parents' separations.

Many scholars see the formation of the nuclear family as a result of the Industrial Revolution, since both came about at roughly the same time—the end of the eighteenth century. The mass migration from farm to city and the consolidating of families into small groups with more intensive interaction between the members coincided with the needs of factories for dedicated, hardworking, anonymous (and certainly not autonomous) workers. The support system of multigenerational families under one roof was done away with in this new order, and the modern nuclear family came into being.

It was shortly thereafter that philosophers, educators, clergymen, and the early social scientists all became enamored of that state known as "childhood." Prior to this point, children were considered of little or no importance, perhaps because so many of them were likely to die before reaching adulthood. For the first time parents began focusing specific attention on their youngsters, and while the coming of child-labor laws and the ending of indenture practices were still some time off, the society as a whole began to recognize children as people. This created further pressure on the family group, demanding that the parents (specifically the mothers) concentrate on giving their children an adequate background for more than mere survival. And the popularization of Freud's theories made mothers responsible for the emotional and psychological well-being of their offspring, as well as their education, recreation, and social adjustment—an attitude which has continued to this day and transforms many a suburban woman into a chauffeur, chaperone, and general servant to her children.

This idolization of childhood, coupled with the general Victorian romanticism of the late 1800s, turned the family into a sentimental sacred cow. Marriage was the expected lot of every normal adult, children were bundles of joy and blessings from heaven, and women were adored as being "pure spirits" who often had the "vapors" and other hysterical maladies, but were placed on public pedestals even as they were stripped of the right of self-determination and laced into corsets of whalebone and proper constraints. Family life, as dear Queen Victoria so often indicated, was the sacred duty and divine grace of a civilized society, and automatically brought forth the best of all possible human relationships.

Given this sort of definition and social status, what do you do with the marriages that fail to live up to the advertisement? How do you quietly dispose of the bones of those which don't work, aren't made in heaven, and cast doubts on all the glowing phrases? You create a way out, a means of dissolving the undesirable unions so as not to contaminate the whole barrel. And you have the beginning, about 1860, of the social phenomenon known as the rising divorce rate.[2]

At this point, when marriages began dissolving and there was no widespread family support system available to look after the offspring of separating parents, the courts were forced to study the question of what should happen to the children. Old English common law had given the father control of the youngsters no matter what, even upholding the right of a father to snatch an infant from its mother's breast and dash off into the blizzardy night with the screaming child.[3] During the Victorian era, however, motherhood had been so deified that it came to be treated as a divine right, and the conflict resulting from these two different attitudes led to court policies that were just as motley and conflicting as the legal approach to divorce, and just as uneven in their application. Thus we have the remnant of paternal right to child custody reflected in a 1926 *Indiana Law Journal* statement to the effect that the "father has a slight advantage over the mother,"[4] while a Wisconsin court had awarded custody to the mother in a different case in 1921 because "nothing can be an adequate substitute for mother love . . . the difference between fatherhood and motherood in this respect is fundamental."[5]

This last finding was more in keeping with the general attitude expressed by a U.S. Supreme Court decision in 1872 which announced:

> The constitution of the family organization, which is founded in the divine ordinance, as well as the nature of things, indicates the domestic sphere as that which properly belongs to the domain of womanhood . . . the paramount destiny and mission of women are to fulfill the noble and benign offices of wife and mother. This is the law of the Creator." [6]

It would seem that the highest court in the land was intent on locking all females into the matrimonial and maternal roles regardless of their capacities in other areas, and in so doing, left fathers out in the cold!

This conviction that mothers were naturally the better and more nurturing parent was reflected in many state statutes: the presumption that children of "tender years" should be awarded to the mother was often written into the civil codes dealing with divorce and child custody. However, like the "divine right of kings," woman's "paramount destiny and mission" to be wife and mother eventually began to be called into question, and by 1975 Utah was the only state left which carried a statute on its books specifically favoring child custody to the mother.

Present Status

As might be surmised from its history, and the fact that each state is responsible for its own laws on the subject, any attempt to talk about divorce or custody practices on a national basis would be rather like describing a constantly changing kaleidoscope. In Oregon there is only "no fault" divorce, while in neighboring Idaho grounds for the dissolution of marriage range all the way from adultery through cruelty, insanity, and bigamy. But the bigamist is not going to be sued for divorce in North Dakota—or at least, not on that charge—since that state does not recognize the problem as a ground for divorce! And child custody is an equally confusing situation, made worse because not all states recognize the custody awards of other states.

But besides noting that the situation is in a muddle, there is the encouraging fact that family law has virtually leaped into legal consciousness during the last ten years and is now being studied by a number of professionals with an eye to reducing these complications.

In an article for the *Journal of Divorce*, Harry Fain points out:

> Though we like to believe that law . . . rule[s] our conduct, the fact is that law is or must eventually be governed by our conduct . . . As divorces have increased and the number of children affected by separation or divorce has mounted to millions, law is being forced to recognize and accommodate to this situation.[7]

One such accommodation was the realization that the old practice of establishing blame in the divorce process only tended to push clients and attorneys further into the adversary situation, and aroused everyone's ire needlessly. Consequently, after a long and heated debate between specialists in the field, the California legislature finally passed the first "no fault" divorce law in 1969. Under the Family Law Act of 1970 (as it is officially called), either party can get a divorce simply by stating that there are "irreconcilable differences." No longer does one partner have to sue the other, there is neither plaintiff nor defendant, and the question of blame or past misbehavior is not considered. Forty-six other states have followed suit, and although most of them still retain the option of using other grounds for divorce if one wishes, it is now possible to accomplish dissolution of a marriage without all the public hostility formerly called into play.

Among the effects of "no fault" divorce, which are still being examined, there have been some interesting, as well as disturbing, reactions. For one thing, since the courts are no longer interested in why the divorce is desired, the emphasis has shifted from proving misconduct on the part of one of the adults to determining how to distribute the property involved. In some states the practice of punishing the "guilty" party has been removed entirely, so that property is now settled on a flat 50–50 division, without regard to who was the "injured" partner.

Hence many complicated financial questions, such as what

percentage of a man's pension should go to his ex-wife when he retires, are becoming the everyday concern of divorce attorneys. Since the laws and attitudes about this are both very complex and often quite different in different localities, it's worth your exploring the situation further with a legal counselor if you have any sizable financial holdings, or a marriage of long duration.

The second reaction has to do with custody battles. During the debate before the passage of the California Family Law Act, a number of experts warned that without a chance to vent their anger at each other in the divorce hearing, many embattled couples might turn to the custody suit as the next most logical arena for name-calling, because here the behavior of each parent is scrutinized closely. There has indeed been a notable increase in custody conflicts since the advent of "no fault" divorce, and Elizabeth O'Neill of the Conciliation Court in Alameda County has commented that they are "nastier and messier than ever before."

It's hard to say whether this increase is a direct result of the higher number of divorces being filed, the growing concern of fathers who wish to participate more fully in raising their children, or the specific desire to use the courts for a public brawl. The important fact is that more people are resorting to the courts to settle the question of how to restructure their families. This not only threatens to scar a large number of our children who end up being psychologically battered by their enraged parents and the callous approach of the adversary system, it also puts a tremendous burden on the judge.

When you cannot settle your disputes between yourselves and so must ask the court for some kind of judgment on the matter, you are relinquishing the right to decide your family's future yourselves. You're turning this over to an impartial, uninvolved, but clearly human third party, all the time praying that he or she will somehow have the insight, patience, and wisdom to find a good solution to the problems you've created. This is a chancy thing at best, and it puts the judge in the wretched position of having to play Solomon with the children's lives, a role few people feel qualified for or desirous of filling.

Judges

Almost all of today's custody statutes are based on the legal precedent set by Chief Justice Brewer of the Supreme Court of Kansas back in 1889, who wrote:

> . . . the parent['s] right to the custody of the child will depend mainly upon the question of whether such custody will promote the welfare and interest of such child . . . Above all things, [this is] the paramount consideration.[8]

This attitude, which gradually became known as the "best interest of the child" doctrine, has been the official guideline for judicial decisions during the twentieth century, and is still considered of utmost importance. Essentially it means that every case must be judged on its own merits; the gender, wealth or poverty, religious orientation, and specific life-styles of the parents must be examined in the context of the child's needs, and not judged in and of themselves. Thus what is in the best interest of any individual youngster is left open to question and to the discretion of the particular judge hearing the case.

This gives the judge an enormous amount of latitude in reaching his decision. Fain comments on this as follows:

> . . . one must always bear in mind that the exercise of discretion by a judge is far less a product of his learning than of his personality and his temperament, his background and his interests, his biases and prejudices, both conscious and unconscious.[9]

Thus the particular judge's attitude about children, about women who work as compared with those who stay home, about the sanctity of motherhood or the hiring of a housekeeper may all become factors in his decision. He may be swayed, subliminally but powerfully, by the loss of his own mother when he was little, or his feeling that every little boy should (or should not) have an electric train because he himself did (or did not) have one when he was growing up. All the factors of his own personal makeup come into play, and more than one attorney has pointed out that custody decisions are so dependent on the individual judge that almost identical cases end up with very different outcomes because they were heard by different judges, even in the same courthouse. And many is the judge who gets a reputation for being biased in one way or another; the judge who is sticking out a miserable marriage "for the children's sake" may inwardly take a very dim view of any parent who opts to end his or her marital discord, or the judge who is himself paying a high amount of alimony or child support may be extra hard on an unemployed father who is delinquent in his payments. This is not to say that judges are by and large *unfair,* only that they are very human.

Most judges dislike having to sit in family court. As one nationally renowned family-law specialist pointed out quite trenchantly, "Judges are simply attorneys with political affiliations. Their primary qualifications are that they knew someone with pull, and their training in family law may be little or none. Yet they are assigned to the family-law court when they first become judges simply because it's such a loathsome job, no one with seniority will take it."

In California, the municipal judges are assigned to hearing drunk-driving cases when they are new to the bench; the freshman Superior Court judges pay their dues by listening to the most sordid, miserable, and squalid of all legal matters, domestic-relations disputes. And if the case is going to be a prolonged, hard-fought battle that will last for a day or more, it's frequently assigned to whatever judge is free, not to a family court judge at all. In those cases His or Her Honor usually has about half an hour to become acquainted with the intricacies of the case before the hearing begins. To ask him or her to make decisions that will affect the entire shape of a child's future on such superficial information and emotionally charged testimony is expecting him to play God. It's no wonder that occasionally such a magistrate will throw up his hands in horror and ask the parents why, in heaven's name, they don't settle the matter between themselves.

Many judges will tell you that between 80 and 90 percent of their custody cases involve two fully competent and caring parents, neither one of whom is specifically "unfit," and having to make a choice between them may be all but impossible. Consequently, there are cases in which the judge announces that both parents are equally fit, but since he has to make a decision, he'll award the children to the mother because "it's customary to do so." Yet even with this means of letting himself off the hook, the difficulties of his position may well follow him home from the courtroom. One judge's wife mentioned in passing that it was not uncommon for her husband to wake in the middle of the night and pace about the house, worrying over a particularly difficult custody decision.

Nor are the problems involved limited just to an assessment of the battling parents. As Professor Robert Mnookin of Boalt Law School points out, judges are trained to reach decisions based on evidence of *past actions or facts*. To attempt to decide what will be most beneficial for the youngster *in the future* is quite something else again. It not only assumes an unusual amount of insight into the area of psychology: it also presupposes that the judge can foresee what the offspring will require in the years to come! [10]

Changing the System

As things presently stand, marriage, divorce, and custody disputes are governed by the same legal precepts as business and contract problems. This is certainly one way of looking at the subject, and accounts for why the divorce courts now busy themselves with determining to what extent the homemaker wife has been instrumental in helping her executive husband succeed, and therefore how much of his earnings were made possible by her behind-the-scenes (and unpaid-for) services. Yet the welfare of the children is a far cry from the question of community goodwill and earning capacity; you cannot measure a child's future in monetary terms alone, or his sadness and heartbreak by whether the case was "won" or "lost."

Many people in both the legal and psychological communities are aware of this problem, and are studying different ways to correct the deficiencies of the present system. Suggestions range all the way from improving the methods we now use to taking child custody completely out of the legal system.

One major point that concerned professionals bring up is the deplorable lack of training of most family-court judges. At present there is no requirement that judges who decide custody matters have any background in and understanding of psychology, child development, or the known effects of divorce on children of different ages. And since the vast majority of judges are white, upper-class, middle-aged, and male, a working knowledge of sociology, the economics of the single-parent family, and women in the work force would also give His Honor a more practical grasp of the problems confronting the families whose fate he must decide. It has been strongly suggested that classes or screening tests on all these subjects should be mandatory for family-court judges; certainly it would assure the public of better-informed (and perhaps wiser) magistrates.

Some people have been arguing for the need to do away not only with the adversary system but with the judge as well, where custody is concerned. They suggest that a panel of psychologists, teachers, clergy, or even friends of the family would be more sensitive to the needs of both child and parent than is a specialist who is versed only in law. Some have suggested that such a panel should be supplied by the court and made up of professionals who have been trained specifically for this job. And others argue that a panel chosen by the parents themselves would be more effective. As long as the parents agree to abide by the panel's decision there is no reason why this can't be done. Unfortunately, as many attorneys and judges are quick to point out, nothing else has the power to enforce a custody decision as fully as a court of law. So while an ad hoc panel could submit findings, reports, and suggestions, it wouldn't have the authority to make the parents comply with its final decision. (That, it seems to me, could be arranged if desired, just as arbitration with an attorney is arranged to be binding, but so far no one I've talked with seems to think that's a good idea.)

Then too, one hears strong statements about making joint legal and physical custody the standard expectation of divorce. Thus, unless one or the other parent is actually proved to be "unfit," the judge would have to order joint custody. In this way the parents themselves would be forced to work out a sharing arrangement between themselves. This too has some merit and several drawbacks.

On the positive side, when the cultural assumptions about divorce include the continued supportive parenting of the children, this method is the natural one for the courts to adopt. It provides that each parent's contact with the children will be assured, and reflects the attitude that both parents have an equal right to participate in raising the children. The visitation and custody cases that now come about because one parent feels he or she has been deprived of reasonable interaction with the youngsters will naturally be averted, since this will no longer be a major concern. As parents accept the responsibility for finding their own arrangements, the pressures on the judges will be considerably diminished, and the expectation that the children will be shared will provide the youngsters with a security not found in our present system.

On the other hand, those people who feel the need to denounce each other in public will be more likely to *automatically* attempt to find each other unfit. This is not to say that these people wouldn't do so anyway, but there is a fear that such a system would only add fuel to their fires.

Dr. Virginia Anne Church suggests that we use a system which makes shared custody mandatory during the initial stages of separation, while the parents attempt to work out (with private or court-facilitated counseling) a more permanent arrangement.[11] This enforced sharing would compel the adults to be cooperative since neither parent would be allowed to have sole control of the offspring. Eventually the most satisfactory arrangement would be made permanent. Under this system, if the award of custody had to be made solely to one parent, the judge's decision could be based on which adult had been the most cooperative during the sharing period. This makes excellent sense, as that parent would be less likely to generate problems for either the children or the other adult. And knowing that this was the major criterion of judgment would make all parents more cautious about creating unnecessary difficulties for each other.

Under our present system, if one parent demands sole custody while the other is requesting shared custody, the judge almost invariably renders a decision for sole custody to whichever parent he deems more responsive to the child, even though a shared arrangement may have been in operation for several months or years. Using Dr. Church's standard of cooperativeness, that parent who wishes to share would be the more logical one to receive the children, since he or she has already proved a willingness to be considerate of all concerned. Certainly the concept is worth exploring further.

The Family Court Concept

One of the most practical suggestions for improving our present legal system insofar as family matters are concerned calls for the establishment of a Family Court in each state. This concept has been discussed for a number of years, and various scholars have explored different aspects of it during the last decade.[12] The need to reconsider and possibly even restructure our legal handling of domestic relations is growing more pressing as divorce becomes more prevalent, and the Family Court concept would not only improve our present practices: it would also make use of already existing agencies.

A Family Court would be devoted exclusively to domestic-relations matters, and would provide a number of correlated services under one jurisdiction. Fully trained marriage and divorce counselors, such as are employed in our present Conciliation Courts, would be the first people to see a family seeking to reorganize, whether in an initial divorce action or because of custody and visitation changes. The investigative agency, which is now usually a branch of the Juvenile Probation Department, would evaluate the situation where the child is concerned, and both groups would attempt to work with the parents in order to facilitate the family's reaching its own decision about custody or visitation. The last person to have contact with the family would be a specially educated and screened judge whose appointment would be on a permanent basis—this replacing the rotating or temporary assignment system now used by most counties. Such a judge would be a well-qualified professional, not simply a freshman magistrate who couldn't get out of the assignment. The enforcement of court orders for visitation or child support, which at present is usually delegated to the local District Attorney's office, could be handled by a branch of the Family Court,[13] and for those parents who resent making out regular monthly support checks in their ex's name, arrangements could be made to have them pay that money directly to a Family Court agency which would then pass it on to the custodial parent. Thus all the legal aspects of divorce and child custody would be consolidated in one court, rather than spread throughout the county system, as is generally the case at present.

It is also logical to include various support services for the family itself in such facilities. For instance, a few courts already provide a supervised play area for children which can serve several different functions. In those situations where the judge feels it is necessary or advisable that he or she meet with the youngsters in a custody dispute, it gives the offspring a place to repair to while their parents' battle is being fought in the courtroom. As things currently stand, the children usually have to wait in the foyer or sit with a relative or baby-sitter on the steps of the courthouse, close enough to be available when the judge wishes to see them, yet out of range of their parents' brickbats when the case is being heard. Then too, such a playroom could be used as a neutral exchange point by warring parents at visiting times, and would provide the often harried visiting father with a safe and convenient place for interacting with his youngsters if, for some reason, he can't take them home with him. Postdivorce counseling for children as well as parents is often an excellent and much-needed service, and sessions for both adults and youngsters could be held concurrently at such a center.

Each of these things has been inaugurated in individual courts around the country, often with great success, and the idea of incorporating them all under the umbrella of a Family Court is seen as not only reasonable but also highly desirable. Dr. Robert Mnookin suggests that we should use the court primarily as a backup system to help and encourage divorcing couples to reach their own agreement, rather than relying on it to determine the outcome of their personal quarrels.[14] This ties in with Dr. Melvin Roman's contention that there should be a Conciliation Court in each court which deals with family law, staffed by people who are trained and knowledgeable not only about the psychological stages and problems of divorce and custody, but also about potential alternative arrangements.[15] While none of these proposals is as extreme as taking custody out of the hands of the court altogether, they would encourage the court to keep out of the decision-making process when a family is reorganizing. Thus only the most severe cases would require adjudication; in general the judge would simply formalize the agreement arrived at with the help of the Conciliation Court.

Conciliation Courts

In 1939 Los Angeles County established a court-connected marriage counseling agency and called it the Conciliation Court. Under the leadership of Meyer Elkin, the Conciliation Court broadened its scope to include divorce counseling and adjustment as well, and by the mid-1970s it had become an internationally recognized model for such programs. To date, twenty states have expanded their statutes to provide for the use of such services on an individual county basis, and there are approximately one hundred fifty Conciliation Courts throughout the country, mostly in urban areas. Australia, New Zealand, and Canada have now begun to set up Conciliation Courts patterned on those in the United States.

Conciliation Courts are supported by the county as part of the Superior Court, and are designed to provide immediate counseling and guidance to families going through divorce or custody changes. They are not limited to putting the family back together unless the family members *want* to reconcile, in which case the couple generally work out the terms of their new arrangement with the aid of a Conciliation Court counselor. Where divorce is unavoidable, the Conciliation Court staff concentrates on helping the individuals adjust to the dissolution of the marriage itself, and encourages them to find custody solutions which will do as little damage as possible. Those counties which provide these services do so at little or no cost, and view it as a crisis-intervention program, not as an ongoing therapeutic service, although there may be as many as six meetings available to the family which is trying to reach some sort of amicable accord about custody or visitation.

Where the service of a Conciliation Court is available, the

judges usually recommend it to all couples who have not reached an agreement prior to coming to court. In most cases this kind of counseling is voluntary, not mandatory, although if one partner indicates he or she is interested in such a service, the other is expected to attend at least the first session. Whenever possible, both the battling clients and their attorneys are sent to the Conciliation Court office *before* the court hearing, and in a vast majority of cases an agreement is worked out right there on the spot.[16] Once you have reached a settlement with the help of the Conciliation Court counselor and the approval of your attorneys, you can go back to the judge and stipulate what you've agreed to. Many potential court fights have been settled in this fashion, and the Conciliation Court system has proved its usefulness and value time and again over the years.

Occasionally such an agency also provides workshops and counseling for children, a service much needed and only just now being recognized as important.[17] Some states have similar services under different names; the Friends of the Court in Michigan provides comparable services in Wayne and Washentaw counties, for instance. You would do well to find out what kinds of domestic-relations programs are offered through your local court, and if there is nothing to help with divorce and custody matters, start asking why not. Begin with the local psychologists, attorneys, judges, and marriage and divorce counselors, and then present the subject to your county supervisors. (Chances are they will have the final say on the subject anyway, since it will probably be funded in part by the county.) Many states have provisions for such agencies, but it takes concerned professionals within the county to set up a program, and the more professionals you can get interested before you approach the supervisors, the better. For more information about starting a Conciliation Court in your area, contact the national headquarters of the Association of Family Conciliation Courts, whose address is listed in Appendix A.

Some or maybe most of these suggestions will probably be incorporated into our family-law system eventually. Divorce is too common an occurrence, and children too fragile a resource, to continue to handle the custody situation as crudely as we have in the past. With the changes and development of women's roles in society, and the growing awareness of fathers that they are important to their children (and their children are important to them), more and more people are seeking ways to share their parenting after divorce. The courts will have to recognize and support such changes in attitudes, and the attorneys will be forced to find some other approach to divorce and child-custody problems besides the adversary method.[18] As the public becomes more aware of what kinds of support systems are needed, the government will be called upon to initiate, upgrade, or renovate already existing agencies in the light of public demand. But until those changes come about, it's up to the individual parents to find ways of avoiding the hazards of our current practice.

15
Coping with the System

How the Courts Work

In ancient days a man could stand in the midst of the tribe and solemnly repeat, "I divorce thee, I divorce thee, I divorce thee," and thus put an end to an unwanted marriage. Today's process is a little more complex, but the results are basically the same: the public recording of changes in a contractual agreement. Just as a birth certificate is registered with the local government to verify the presence of a new child in the family, and a wedding is the social celebration of a state-sanctioned contract, a divorce is the legitimizing of a change of status in the eyes of the government as well as among your friends. Yet although it sounds simple and direct, the actual experience of working out the details, coupled with the austere and somewhat frightening prospect of court orders, depositions, and judicial decrees, can turn the whole thing into a nightmare of gargantuan proportions.

Suddenly you're confronted with a legal system which not only crystallizes your decision to change the status quo: it does so by employing language, techniques, and protocol that are totally foreign to the average person. The legal arena is a world of its own, full of specialized actions, unique demands, and all the pomp and power of government made manifest. Even with the help of an attorney, it's not surprising if you find yourself coping with sweating palms and throbbing temples. A young lawyer who has written an article about the effects of his own divorce comments:

> Although I had practiced law for over three years when my marriage broke up . . . I was in no way prepared for the shock of being a client in a divorce action. . . . My knowledge of court procedures and local practices did not give me solace during the pre-trial hearing . . . my respect for the judge did not assuage my criticism of his decision.[1]

To expose all the pain and fear and hope for your future to the scrutiny of a public hearing is bound to unnerve anyone, even an attorney. But although the emotional responses will probably all be there en masse when it's time for your case to be heard, understanding how it works may take some of the fear and mystery out of it. While individual details of family-court procedure vary from county to county, the basic concept behind them remains the same.

The courts of this country are generally open to the public for very good reason: to ensure that the administration of justice won't become a personal power source for the unscrupulous. Yet few people take advantage of this openness to acquaint themselves with the procedures in a courtroom. Like the emergency room of a hospital, it is a place to which one goes only under duress, having hoped or assumed that this sort of disaster happens only to other people. A day spent watching how our courts operate can be a fascinating experience, and one that I strongly recommend to anyone coming up for a divorce or custody hearing. Not only will you become a little more familiar with what happens, you'll also have a chance to see how the particular judge handles things.

The foyer of a metropolitan court presents a constant interplay of tensions, maneuvers, ploys, and miserable clients; messengers are running back and forth, attorneys are bustling in and out with bulging briefcases, witnesses are looking at their watches, and chain smokers are clustered by the ashtrays. The pressures that can build up in such a situation are tremendous, and if you have to wait for hours before your case is called, chances are you'll feel tattered and ragged by the time you approach the bench.

Your Day in Court

The functions of a family law court are twofold: to settle private disputes, and to look out for the welfare of the minors within its jurisdiction. The question of who will raise the children after divorce can fall into either or both of these categories, depending on whether you're fighting over it or not.

What happens when you actually confront the judge to end your marriage or change custody rests almost entirely on what you have agreed to prior to that time. Of the estimated 90 percent of divorce and custody cases that are settled out of court, a fair number are resolved in the foyer of the courtroom, where the stress and strain of waiting to do battle is likely to make the most stubborn of parties reevaluate their positions in order to find a solution between themselves. Yet no matter when or how you come to your settlement, if you can appear before the judge and stipulate that you are in agreement about the new arrangement and are only asking to have it made legal, everything will go much more smoothly. The judge, acting not as an adjudicator having to decide your private dispute but simply as the protector of minor children, will ask various questions about your arrangement and your finances, and possibly issue his or her orders right then. Most uncontested cases can be taken care of in as little as ten or twenty minutes, and you're free to leave without further ado.

Too often the client expects his day in court to include an opportunity to tell *the whole story* to the judge; to point out all the times when his ex has been unfair, treated him unjustly, or created unnecessary pain, tension, and strife. For many people this desire to spread the entire sordid mess out in public is the underlying motive behind the custody battle. As one judge remarked, "Half the time I know at least one of the parents literally expects me to shake my finger at the other, denouncing their activities and lecturing them about behaving better in the future. These people want me to play Big Daddy in their game of Tattle-tale, and are disappointed when they realize I won't do it."

The attorney, of course, knows this too, and recognizes that the judge neither wants to hear nor has the time to consider all the individual slights and cuts that have preceded the court appearance. Hence the lawyer tries to stick to those things which will have a direct bearing on the legal aspects of the case in order to avoid antagonizing the judge. The client, however, may not understand that the judge will get short-tempered and snappish if he has to wade through all kinds of petty squabbles, and therefore feels cheated and frustrated. This conviction that he was somehow slighted in his opportunity to "tell it to the judge" often leads such a client to claim, unfairly, that he was poorly represented.

Remember that by the time you reach the courtroom, the case is truly in the hands of your lawyer. He or she is a professional, an initiated member of this tribal council, who's now providing you with one of his most expensive skills, the ability to communicate with the judge. It is not so complex a matter that you can't handle it yourself if you are appearing *in pro per,* but if you've hired a professional to represent you, for goodness' sake sit back and let him do his stuff. As one judge told me, half of being a good lawyer is knowing the law; the other half is knowing what to expect from the judge who is hearing the case!

The hearing itself may consist mainly of verifying the paperwork already presented to the court, or it may take place in the judge's chambers with only the two attorneys in attendance. This method of handling things is often used if the children of the embattled couple are present in the courtroom, if both attorneys indicate they feel they can get their clients to agree to a settlement without testimony, or if either client appears to be so hotheaded as to be liable to cause a major disturbance during testimony. Your attorneys will come back to you, carrying messages of offers and counteroffers, and confer with you about what the next step should be. Nothing will be settled without your permission, but the arguing will take place out of earshot of either one of you.

In this situation you and your ex may be left sitting at opposite sides of the courtroom, glaring at each other, hating every moment of the uncertainty, and grimly wondering what is happening behind those closed doors. You'd do well to take along a book to read in the event the judge prefers to handle your case this way; an hour of counting the empty chairs in the jury box or the stars on the flag can drive you nuts!

The whole court appearance may end up being as dry and sterile as the reciting of a laundry list, and seem to have little or nothing to do with the actual trauma you're going through. Many clients complain of feeling displaced, as though they were watching a shadow play about someone else's life rather than experiencing something very real and vital that's connected specifically with them. And this sense of alienation sometimes triggers an onrush of conflicting emotions which have no outlet. The frustration level of a client can reach a point at which he or she leaves the courtroom shaking with rage, confusion, or sheer exhaustion. On one occasion the father involved, although having received a relatively favorable judgment, was nonetheless so unstrung by the whole experience that he continued to sit at the counsel's table, white and tense, for some time after the hearing was concluded. Taking in the situation, the judge called a recess, and in the ensuing milling about of people, the man's attorney turned to his client to encourage him to stand up, only to have the fellow round on him with clenched fists. The court bailiff, who had been moving smoothly but purposefully toward the bench, casually slid between the two, seeming to be there more or less accidentally, yet it was only his notably burly presence that kept the father from physically lashing out in blind fury at the person closest at hand.

Judges, attorneys, and bailiffs are all aware of the potential for emotional explosions when it comes to child custody hearings. Nowhere else do emotions run so high, accusations become so bitter, and tempers get so inflamed. Parents see their children as extensions of themselves. Each finds the threat of the other to be intolerable, and both can sincerely point to what they consider to be their own altruistic involvement. It doesn't much matter whether the dispute is over visitation rights or full custody: the potential for emotional chaos is always there. Consequently, court officials work to keep things as calm and dispassionate as possible. It's up to you, the client, to cooperate by keeping your own behavior under control. Any kind of outburst before, during, or after the hearing can only damage your case and may lead to further contention between you and your ex. So keep as cool as you can; afterward, when you're completely away from both your opposing partner and the courthouse, you can find a spot to let off some steam. Screaming in the shower with the water running full blast, or while you're driving by yourself on a little-used road, can be very helpful. So can beating a tennis racket on a bed, pounding your fist into an old pillow, or attacking a punching bag. All of these things use up the adrenaline you've produced during the courtroom scene, but won't hurt anyone else or yourself. You'd do well to find a safe outlet for your emotions before the court hearing, both because it will help you stay calmer during the actual confrontation, and because it's good to know what you can rely on when you need it later. Whatever works for you is fine, as long as it is not destructive in the final analysis.

Custody Investigations

Because of the complex factors involved in deciding what is in the best interest of the child, it is common for the courts to call in specialists who investigate the specific situation and report back to the judge with their findings. There are several different kinds of evaluations the judge may order, the first and most common being a report on the different homes of the contending parents. (This sort of investigation is not necessary if you have agreed to your custody arrangement between yourselves; it is used only when the court is forced to decide the issue.)

In the past these investigators were frequently members of the Juvenile Probation Department, social workers, or other employees of local-government agencies. Complaints about such investigations are legion; they sometimes take as long as a year, the reports are withheld from both attorneys and clients, and often there is an obvious bias in favor of mothers, simply because the investigators themselves assume that women are the more nurturing parents. Nor are the parents happy with the techniques used to collect information. Mothers find living with the expectation that some stranger is about to intrude into her life, talking with neighbors and relatives and nosing about in her private business, is a very unsettling experience. And fathers are sometimes given such short shrift that a few cursory questions make up the entire interview, and according to many men, the reports are grossly inaccurate and bear little resemblance to the actual situation.

Gradually it is becoming clear that such antiquated methods are inadequate; deciding the future of any child requires a great deal more than recording the gossipy comments of the mother's neighbor, or the marshaling of as many as five witnesses for each party, all of whom are assumed by the court to be biased and polarized to begin with. Some counties have set up special Domestic Relations Investigation units which are staffed by professionals with training in child development, psychology, and the related fields. Certainly, whether this service is offered by a new agency or made possible by the reorganization of an existing department, the idea of redirecting its energies is important.

In Santa Clara County, such a change came about in the mid-1970s when the new Supervisor took a long look at the traditional quagmire such agencies usually get stuck in and reorganized the entire procedure.

To begin with, any contested custody case is immediately referred to the Special Investigation Branch of Juvenile Probation, and the parents sent directly to that office as soon as the papers for a custody change are filed. In this first interview it is determined whether there is in fact a custody problem to be settled, since many custody actions are initiated because of anger and spite between the parents, not because there is any clearly discernible reason to change the arrangement for the good of the child. If it becomes obvious that this is the case, the parents meet with a trained professional who sits down with them and tries to work out some form of settlement right there on the spot. (Needless to say, although the court has been happy with this means of resolving the problem, some of the attorneys involved felt that the Probation Department head was overstepping his bounds—since he was often able to accomplish in one sitting what many hours of costly legal time had not brought about!)

Being able to screen out those cases which really do require active investigation from those which are of questionable validity lightens the load of the entire department and makes it possible to handle the other, more complex cases in a more professional manner.

Because this man took the position that his department's primary function was to represent the needs of the child, he shifted the emphasis from collecting negative information about the adults to examining what was happening within the family itself, and how it was affecting the children. Generally he interviewed the youngsters by themselves, and as he pointed out, this was often the first time anyone in a position of authority had taken the time to listen to what the offspring had to say. Often he talked with the family as a unit, observing the interaction between all the members and attempting to act as mediator as well.

If it seemed appropriate to recommend counseling for the family, he encouraged them all to see the same professional rather than each going to a different psychologist. This follows the concept of treating the family as a unit which is in the process of reorganization, rather than as separate individuals who are polarized against each other. Parents were encouraged not only to write out what they perceived the problems to be, but also to submit written reports about each noncustodial visit and the general progress or change in attitudes as the investigation went along. These reports, which often ran as long as ten to twenty pages per visit, were carefully read and compared, and occasionally he made a point of calling in the battling adults and pointing out the games they were playing through the children.

Throughout the entire investigation the parents were encouraged to explore different forms of custody arrangements that might be agreeable to both, at least on a temporary basis, and if the two adults and the children were willing to try some kind of sharing during the time they were waiting for their court hearing, the probation officer would help them draw up an agreement with the help of their attorneys.

If the matter was not resolved within the family itself, and the Probation Department had to present the judge with its recommendations in order to help him make a decision, not only was that report made available to the attorneys ten days prior to the hearing, rebuttals from either parent were permitted if either one felt it was unfair. Thus a parent who believed the report was specifically inaccurate could attach his or her own statement to it for the judge's further consideration. This is not a common practice, by any means. In some counties not even the attorneys have a chance to see what sort of evidence and recommendations are made by the investigators of the clients!

All of these things represent a departure from the long-established patterns of muckraking and personally biased evaluations which sometimes make such reports all but worthless, and certainly add to the hostilities. By attempting to look at the needs of the children first, and to encourage family participation in finding solutions to the problems in order to deescalate the hostilities, this department became one of the most progressive in the state of California. Although that professional has since been transferred to another branch of the Probation Department, he did much to make this investigative unit useful to both court and client.

Not all custody disputes require investigation, and it is up to the judge whether he or she feels it would help in deciding the case. But if His Honor feels that in the absence of an agreement between the parents, an objective report on the family will allow him to make a wiser decision, he has the authority to order it. How much weight such a report carries depends on the particular judge, the effectiveness of the department that is making the report, and how well the two of them work together. In some areas the judges rely heavily on the investigation's findings and recommendations, while in others they consider them a kind of formality and thus pay them little heed.

Special Reports

Occasionally a judge will feel that he needs a professional opinion on the psychological makeup of the parents and/or children involved in a custody case, and so requires that they be interviewed and examined by a local professional. In some cities specific custody clinics have been set up for this purpose, staffed by professionals and geared to determining which parent would be better for the child.

Generally such professionals concentrate simply on making

evaluations and recommendations, and don't try to work with the family on a therapeutic basis until after the case is out of court. Because of the question of confidentiality, there may be an ethical problem as to whether a psychologist or psychiatrist can be asked to testify about a client. Most professionals want to avoid overlapping the *investigative* aspect of their work and the *therapeutic* service. If you are going to such a professional, either as a client or because the judge has ordered an evaluation, be sure you understand exactly which function the professional is filling—investigator or personal counselor. If he or she has been ordered by the court to make a report based on your conversations, you should know that, and if he is acting as your individual therapist, you should be assured about the privacy of your communication. If you have any doubts on this subject, by all means ask the person. Any legitimate professional will explain to you what his or her position is.

Staff members of several clinics mentioned that they are recommending custody to the father in more and more cases. However, none of them supported or suggested any form of shared custody as a viable option for their clients. In part this may be because of the already polarized attitude of the adults, which often makes the idea of cooperative endeavor seem impossible. Certainly there appears to be a common belief among all these people that sharing, even under the best of circumstances, is somehow suspect and should not be encouraged.

In any event, if these professionals have been called in by the court, they will most likely render some form of judgment rather than offer you solutions. It is assumed that if you have gotten this far along in a battle over the youngsters, you're looking for righteous vindication, not a way of working out your problems between yourselves.

Enter the Third Attorney

Recognition of the fact that neither of the parents' attorneys represents the children has led to the introduction of a third lawyer in some cases. Based on the assumption that the youngsters' needs and rights must be both presented and defended before the judge, it makes sense from a legal point of view. If one is going to play the hide-and-seek adversary game (hide what is detrimental to your client's case, and seek to present only those things that will "win"), it stands to reason that the children whose future is being toyed with in this fashion would do well to have a participating pro on *their* side.

Since the presentation of *all* the facts, unvarnished and impartially displayed, is *not necessarily* what happens in a custody case, both attorneys and the judge may feel better knowing that someone is trying to protect the youngsters. Unfortunately, the advent of a third attorney can create as many problems as it resolves, and needs to be considered very carefully.

For instance, who is going to control that professional? How does he or she determine what the child's best interests are? Does that attorney argue for what the youngsters say they *want*, or what the attorney himself thinks is best, legally? What happens if there is more than one child involved; should each one have legal representation? Does the lawyer in such a position run the risk of a conflict-of-interest suit at a later time if he represents all the offspring at once? Who chooses him? And perhaps more important, who pays for this service? Does the child have a right to hire an attorney of his own, or must it be a court-appointed lawyer? Can a judge refuse to recognize a professional the youngster has chosen? Can the third attorney present independent witnesses, or even be a witness himself? As the *California Family Law Report* points out, these and a number of other questions have not yet been resolved, and certainly need to be clarified.[2]

Furthermore, many professionals have mentioned that the introduction of yet another adversary may well create additional problems within the family itself. Now there is a three-way battle going on, and instead of two sparring opponents, the whole thing has turned into a three-ring circus! So while the idea of having their own lawyer is meant to be beneficial to the youngsters in the courtroom, the question of how it affects their relationship with their parents, and what kind of psychological reactions are likely to come about because of it, should be closely considered.

At present there are twenty-three states which provide that either an attorney, a "guardian ad litem," or a friend of the court may be appointed to represent the interests of the minors in custody cases, if the judge feels it is necessary. In some states this person must be a lawyer, while in others he or she may be a teacher, counselor, or close adult friend of the children's. Wisconsin has been doing this for a number of years, and recently Michigan has made such representation mandatory. The concept of providing the youngsters with someone who is specifically designated to represent their interests is a good one; whether that someone should be a legal professional or not remains to be studied more fully.[3] In many cases where such an appointment is strictly up to the judge, the magistrate is reluctant to make use of it because of the added financial, emotional, and legal complications. Some judges mention that in cases concerning adoption, paternity suits, or juvenile delinquency it may be appropriate to provide separate counsel for the children, but they are extremely hesitant to order it in the average contested-custody situation.

Judges and Shared Custody

The court almost never suggests shared custody, though sometimes conciliation courts or juvenile investigation people will recommend it. If one parent continues to insist on sole custody, the judge will usually conclude that sharing won't work—certainly a reasonable reaction. Sharing does require a certain amount of cooperation, and as long as one parent is still caught in the win/lose trap, it is assumed that cooperation is not the thing uppermost in his or her mind. So don't expect the court to look favorably on the idea if you can't both agree to it.[4]

Even if you are able to agree to some form of sharing, you must be prepared to convince the judge that you know what you're talking about. Although the trend is away from interference between parents when they have reached an accord about custody, there are still some judges who refuse to accept joint physical custody as a legitimate solution. I've heard more than one weird tale about couples who, having worked out all the details, applied for joint legal and physical custody only to have the judge throw the whole thing out because he believed they were "making footballs" out of their children. In such cases it is common for the parents to agree to the sole custody the magistrate imposes, and then proceed to share the children regardless of what the paper says. Certainly it is unfortunate when the power of the bench is so overbearing it causes a judge to feel that he should impose his own beliefs on the petitioners *in spite of the fact that they are in agreement about sharing!* [5]

One couple who were denied a shared arrangement by the court, even though they had been using it for some time, appealed the decision during the time that is allotted for trying to get the judge to reconsider. They presented letters from professionals (teachers, child-care workers, and a psychologist) all upholding the fact that this arrangement had worked well for the family in the past. One of the professionals stated the case beautifully when she asked His Honor to "recognize and validate the cooperation and consideration these parents have been willing to show in order to arrive at their request for shared custody." Although the parents appeared *in pro per,* the judge was so impressed with their determination and practical approach to the problem that he reversed his original decision and permitted them joint legal and physical custody.

Some judges who are not generally in favor of shared custody will nonetheless grant it if you present a united front. If you've worked out the questions of who is where for how long, have arranged for satisfactory child care if you both work, and are determined that this is what you really want to do, the judge is much more likely to accept your solution. He or she will probably be highly suspicious of arrangements that are vague, ill defined, and based on some sort of idealized notion of utopian futures; so if having your own arrangement officially sanctioned is important to you, do your homework, and be prepared to defend your position if necessary.

Not *all* judges are hostile to the idea of sharing. In Alameda County there is a judge who not only granted the petitioning couple the right to share their children, he also took the time to compliment these parents on their efforts to continue to provide their offspring with a supportive and well-balanced family. "I know this was a hard decision for you to make, and maybe you're feeling a bit doubtful and confused about it. But if more couples were willing to put their children's needs first, we'd see far fewer children devastated by divorce. Certainly I want to congratulate you on this matter." Needless to say, when those parents left the courthouse a tremendous burden of worry, fear, and uncertainty had been lifted from them.

This judge has had an extensive background in working with children. "I'm very careful about shared custody," he said, "and have to feel very sure that the parents know what they are asking for. But in my considered opinion, if the parents are capable of working out their differences and the details of their arrangement before they come to court, I'm supportive of their desires."

To Fight or Not to Fight

It has been said that there are no victimless divorces, and while that may or may not hold true any longer, there are certainly no victimless custody battles. If you simply cannot bring yourselves to compromise in a reasonable fashion, and are self-righteously demanding personal vindication in court, please recognize that (a) you may not receive it, (b) you have to abide by the magistrate's decision, whether you like it or not, and (c) the children may forgive you both as they get older, but they will never forget it. It is their entire future that you are dealing with, and *only* if they themselves are adamant about not wanting to have further contact with their other parent should you delude yourself into believing that such a battle is being waged for their good. (If there has been a history of physical abuse, of continuing drunkenness or drug addiction, or some other form of behavior which is truly hazardous to the youngster's well-being, then court intervention may be necessary. But that is a far cry from the average custody dispute which is predicated on the bruised egos of the adults and a desire to "win" the children in order to punish an ex-partner.)

So before you decide to carry your conflict to the public arena, take a long look at why you want to do battle. Do you really wish to leave the family future up to a possibly biased, hostile, or antagonistic judge? Is it truly a matter of the children's welfare, or more honestly a case of unresolved conflict between the two adults? How do the youngsters feel about such a fight? If you have to have a donnybrook, can you confine it to money and possessions, and leave the children out of it? (Judges much prefer to spend their time working out financial division with their little pocket calculators rather than dealing with the psychological problems inherent in custody cases.) What do you envision the future to be if you are "awarded" sole custody, or if you "lose" and are relegated to the "visiting parent" status? You aren't dealing with the "wouldn't it be nice if . . ." questions anymore, but rather the "how do we live with it from now on . . ." realities. It's time to really stop and consider, IS IT WORTH IT?

16
All Those Concerned Others

Finding, or Creating, Support Systems

Divorce has been called "the greatest consciousness-raising process of the twentieth century." [1] We have been through two World Wars, social and political upheavals, the Great Depression, and the disaster of Vietnam, yet nothing has affected so many people so deeply, or forced them to reevaluate old standards and traditional concepts as much as the ending of their marriages. It causes a major confrontation between social expectations and your individual reality that can result in a positive time of new growth, or a negative warping and the development of bitterness and despair. How you handle it will probably depend not only on your own inner resources but also on the type of support you have available to you during that time.

In the past a person going through a major transition could turn to the elders of the family, a member of the clergy, or the "wise man" of the village for help and guidance. It was part of the function of such counselors to provide insight and advice to the person in crisis, and they drew on their own knowledge of life and living in order to help the seeker. In our modern mobile society, however, chances are your elders live a good distance away (and quite possibly wouldn't understand your problems anyway), you may or may not be affiliated with a specific church, and you probably haven't lived in a small enough community long enough to learn who is "wise" and who isn't. So coping with a situation as difficult as divorce can be a lonely and isolating process.

Fortunately, a number of support systems are being developed specifically for helping families like yours manage the reorganization of their life patterns. Marriage and family counselors, psychologists, and psychiatrists work specifically with people in transition; churches and community agencies often provide workshops for single parents; and many institutions such as conciliation courts, major universities, and adult school programs offer information or education on divorce and custody matters. And there are a number of nonprofessional, but certainly helpful, organizations such as Parents Without Partners and Equal Rights for Fathers which have come into being because people with similar problems banded together to support each other. It is not necessary for you to flounder around all by yourself, feeling scared, hurt, depressed, and very much confused by it all, when there is so much help available.

Most of the organizations presented here are national in scope, and have branches or chapters all over the country. If you are having trouble locating such a group in your own area, write to the national headquarters and inquire as to where the nearest chapter is located; addresses for these headquarters are listed in Appendix A. Naturally, information about adult-education classes and workshops sponsored by local groups will best be found through your library, women's center, church or synagogue, or college campus.

Who's Out There

When I first divorced, in 1958, there was nothing available to help the newly single parent cope with all the problems that suddenly appear. In these past two decades the divorce rate has more than doubled, and now there are numerous classes, workshops, clinics, and conferences for divorcing parents. By far the most common are those that deal with how to be a single parent; you'll probably find night-school adult-education classes listed under such titles as "Single Woman, Head of Household." These are sponsored by local school districts, by community colleges, and sometimes by such groups as the YWCA. They are geared to helping the mother who has never been on her own before (at least, not with a bunch of kids in tow), and they cover everything from credit and financial information to handling household repairs, expanding your social life, and generally assuming control of your situation. For the woman who never expected to be a single mother, and perhaps doesn't even know how to open a checking account, this sort of information is essential. Not only can you learn how to file your income-tax return, there is the added solidarity of discovering you're not the only one in this mess, a reassuring factor that is very important for most divorced parents, whether they have custody of the offspring or not.

On the more therapeutic level, there are many Family Service Agencies which provide ongoing workshops for divorced parents, where the problems can be shared and explored with others in the same circumstance. Sometimes these are designed with the different stages of divorce in mind. For instance, the Mid-Peninsula Family Service Agency in Palo Alto, California, has organized a total of six different weekly groups for families in transition: Divorce Adjustment, for people who are currently going through the process; Children and Divorce, which is designed for youngsters and provides them with a chance to work with games, films, and various other activities that they share with other children whose parents are divorced or divorcing; Single Parent workshops and Non-Custodial Parent groups, which concentrate on adjusting to the new arrangements; Moving On Out, for those who have come to terms with their divorce; and a group called Stepparenting, which is offered to help new spouses become part of a "blended" family. While not every agency across the country can provide such a complete program, more and more seem to be aware of the usefulness of such workshops, and if you make your desires known to your local family-therapy agency, chances are you can bring about the initiation of a similar program.

The same applies to the YWCA, which bases its classes and workshops on the local needs of each chapter. Some "Y"s have extensive programs on this subject, while others do not. Write, call, or go in person to your nearest "Y" and describe the sort of group you would be most interested in attending; better yet, get several other divorced parents to go with you. All such organizations are trying to meet the needs of the people in the community, so speaking up about what you consider an important support group may well get one started.

Jewish Family Service agencies, many hospitals, and a number of universities offer therapeutic assistance to families with children in divorce, either on an ongoing basis or by occasional daylong workshops. Some of these programs are designed to help the family through the entire process of reorganization, right from the beginning, and so can be very useful while you're actually adjusting to the separation itself.

Support Groups

There are also a number of groups which offer help and support *after* the divorce, and probably the best-known of these is Parents Without Partners. PWP is primarily a social group, in that it isn't organized around the idea of therapy, but it does provide a great deal of support and reassurance for the newly separated parent. Nor is it limited to custodial parents; I know many divorced, noncustodial fathers and mothers who are active members in their local PWP chapter. Because each chapter is administered on a local level, there is a broad range of effectiveness, depending on the interest, time, energy, and ingenuity of the people involved. If you're willing to get involved, you can help make yours an active, exciting kind of group.

Not only does PWP offer lectures and sometimes sponsor workshops: it also provides a much-needed service in organizing family activities which are geared to youngsters of various age groups. One of the problems encountered by so many single parents is the lack of things to do with other families; the single parent is still considered an anomaly in many suburban communities, and so his or her family may not be included in local activities. Also, sometimes there is an understandable strain on a child whose only friends have both parents living at home; such youngsters may feel shy or embarrassed about visiting their friends' homes, for instance. To be able to play with other children who also have divorced parents can be comforting for such children. And because all the parents are single (for whatever reason; it doesn't matter whether it's death, desertion, divorce, or the decision to have or adopt a child by yourself), the adults share a great many problems and amusements.

I have known many people who began to see their PWP friends as an extended family; it's good to know you can call and talk to another parent with a similar problem if you're feeling blue, depressed, overwhelmed, or generally frazzled by your situation. And it's not uncommon for PWP members to help one another with child care if a single parent has to go to the hospital, for instance, or some other unexpected problem comes up. If you can't find such a group in your own area, write to the headquarters of PWP and find out how to go about starting one.

A new kind of support group which has much more recently arrived on the scene is for the divorced father. Growing out of the indignation noncustodial fathers felt as a result of being unfairly treated by the courts, these organizations began as local groups, and so have different names in different cities. Yet whether they are called Equal Rights for Fathers, Fathers for Equal Justice, Male Parents for Equal Rights, or United Fathers Coalition for Fair Divorce and Alimony Laws, the purpose is the same: to educate the public about the inequities fathers face in the courts, and provide moral support, information, and as much political clout as they can muster for the divorcing father. Their aims and objectives are certainly reasonable; unfortunately, this is not always true of their public utterances. Like the early militant feminists who spent a great deal of time attacking men, these men often undermine their own best interests by the stridency of their presentations. (It's worth noting that the divorce and custody courts are probably the only public areas where a man in this culture does not have the automatic advantage of controlling power. And it's not unnatural that some men react with the same kind of vengeful rhetoric that women who feel they are powerless express; one has only to compare their complaints to recognize that they spring from a similar source.)

There are an estimated eighty divorced fathers' organizations in thirty states and Canada, and many of them are now sponsoring legislation in their states which would make more equitable custody and visitation rights mandatory. These groups also provide a valuable personal service to divorcing fathers by informing them of their rights, sharing information about attorneys, and offering a forum in which to let off a little steam. It is reasonable to assume that when their hostility level diminishes a bit, they will become even more active and successful participants in establishing some of the much-needed custody reforms.

Another group which came into being because of the common needs and problems of the parents involved is Children's Rights, Inc. (CRI, pronounced "cry"). Founded in 1975, it now has seventy chapters in thirty-one states, and offers both information and support to parents going through the trauma of having lost their youngsters because the opposing partner has snatched them and vanished into anonymity in the world "out there."

It is estimated that there are as many as 100,000 children snatched each year, an appalling number when one considers the trials and terrors such youngsters go through in that process. Statistics are hard to come by, since there are no real records kept on such complaints. Government agencies, whether local police, county sheriffs, state police, or the FBI, are loath to get involved in what they consistently term "domestic squabbles," and little or no official help is offered to parents with this problem. The U.S. Passport Office in Washington, D.C., does make an effort to help parents who think their offspring may be taken out of the country. Although it assumes no legal responsibility, the Passport Office suggests that you write a letter stating that you do *not* give permission for your child to leave the United States, and include statistics on the child involved and your former spouse, as well as a copy of your custody order and both your home and business phone numbers.

The Lindbergh Law specifically excludes parental kidnapping from its jurisdiction, probably because at the time it was passed there were so few cases of snatching. With divorce now affecting an estimated one out of five children, and more fathers becoming so frustrated by the present custody situation, child snatching has become a major problem. Not, of course, that this is a crime which is limited to men; some mothers, even with lawful custody, will take the children and decamp. CRI has been attempting to get Congress to look more closely at the problem with the hope of making child snatching a federal offense, no matter which parent does it, so it is possible children will be protected from this kind of abuse in the near future.

Some individual states have hearkened to the problem, however—in part because of pressure from such groups as CRI and Equal Rights for Fathers. Arizona and California now have laws which make it a felony to snatch your child. In Arizona the charge is lowered to a misdemeanor if the youngster is returned unharmed, and in California the law applies to either parent, regardless of who is the legal custodian. Thus the sole-custody parent who picks up and moves without informing the other parent where the child will be faces not only felony charges but also notable fines. These laws have not been on the books long enough to indicate how successful they will be, but in Arizona, two hired snatchers have been charged under the new law.

CRI has headquarters in Washington, D.C. If you are one of the parents confronted with the heartache and terror of such a situation, by all means contact the organization and see where the closest chapter is; being able to express your pain and grief with other parents in the same position can be quite helpful, and many chapters have a "Lend an Ear" service specifically to help relieve the emotional chaos that comes of losing a child in this manner.

Religious Groups

Not unexpectedly, most churches have been slow to recognize the needs of divorcing families. There are several reasons for this, not the least of which is that most religions have held the family to be a sacred unit, bound together by God, and not to be split by anything other than death. Thus the rising divorce rate is seen as a threat to the stability of civilization, religious observation, and ethical living, all of which are pretty heavy trips to lay on the already hurting and confused parishioner who is seeking to end a bad marriage. When divorce is decried from both pulpit and pew, the person going through that trauma is unlikely to find much solace for his or her pain within the church. Then too, many still-married people find the presence of a divorcing person a threat to their own marriage, particularly if it is being held together by willpower and a lot of denial about how bad it really is. And the stigma of sinfulness and guilt may still be attached to the idea of dissolving a union that was "made in heaven." These attitudes can combine to cause the members of a congregation to avoid the person whose marriage is ending, even though they may express sympathy, compassion, or even understanding for the problem. And if the minister, priest, or rabbi feels uncertain about counseling the divorcing parent, there may not be much help available on that level either.

Largely because of ambivalence on the part of the clergy as well as the layman, most churches tended to ignore the plight of the member going through a family reorganization. They frequently provided social activities for those who were already single, and some even sponsored workshops for divorced parents, but they didn't provide help and support during the actual time of crisis.

That has been changing since the mid '70s, however, as more religious organizations realize that sweeping divorce under the rug is simply avoiding a difficult area where they could, in fact, offer a great deal of assistance. Many ministers, rabbis and even a few Catholic priests have begun to address the problem directly, and are looking for ways to create more support systems within the church framework.

The results of an interdenominational survey of ministers and their divorced parishioners [2] disclosed that the clergy often had little understanding of the problems divorcing couples are confronted with, and had a number of misconceptions about divorced parents' concerns as well. Among other things, the clergy assumed that feelings of guilt and failure were the most difficult aspects of divorce adjustment, whereas the people in transition reported financial burdens and worry about their children's welfare were their prime considerations. This sort of discrepancy led Garner Odell to initiate The Divorce Ministry, an educational program designed to help both ministers and lay members understand the problems of divorce, and be more supportive of the divorcing family.

The Ministry's classes and workshops are frequently presented to a cluster of churches in a given area, thereby making it possible for Odell to travel to different towns and share his information with a number of churches at one time. Although he works primarily in California, the Presbyterian Counseling Center offers the same kind of program out of Seattle, Washington, and there are similar services in different parts of the country, sponsored by different churches.

It's also promising to note that there has been a marked increase in the number of ministers who are now going back to school and getting advanced degrees in Marriage and Family Counseling. Since this is part of their function within their flocks, it's only logical that they should make use of such educational programs to develop their own skills.

Another interesting expansion of an already available support system is the Quakers' use of a Clearness Committee when divorce or custody problems arise. It has long been the practice in Quaker congregations for individuals or couples who are making major decisions to ask for a committee made up of several members of the community to listen to their feelings, problems, and tentative decisions. This sort of system was used during the Vietnam war, for instance, if a young man wanted to apply for Conscientious Objector status in the draft. And it has frequently been used by engaged couples *before* getting married as a way to explore and better understand what they each expect their forthcoming marriage to entail.

Each person has the right to pick one of the committee members, and both partners have to agree to the final composition of the committee; three or four people is the usual number. In special cases, the committee members may be appointed by the minister and council. The couple meet with the committee and each talk about what they are planning to do, why they want to do it, how they think it will work, what they expect it to involve, and so on. Then the committee meets with each partner separately to discuss the matter in greater depth. There may or may not be further meetings with the couple together again, depending upon the situation. Usually the meetings take place over a three-month period, at the end of which the committee can either recommend the marriage because both people seem well prepared for the venture, or suggest that perhaps the couple need to take more

time to investigate certain areas because they seem to have dif-
fering assumptions about those specific things. In the last five
years, the use of a Clearness Committee for divorcing couples
has been greatly encouraged, as need for help during the crisis of
actually restructuring the family has become more and more evident. No judgments or decisions are rendered by the committee,
which sees its purpose as helping the couple get their own feelings
and ideas organized and communicate more successfully with
each other. Certainly it is a reasonable system which has a great
deal to recommend it, as it provides not only support and understanding during the time of difficulty but also some much-needed
help in clarifying what the parents want and expect from their
custody arrangements.

Even the Catholic Church, long an ardent foe of divorce, has
begun to recognize the need for helping the divorced members
within its ranks. The North American Conference of Separated
and Divorced Catholics (NACSDC) has been in existence since
1971, when Father James Young founded a group for divorced
Catholics in Cambridge, Massachusetts. Father Young has been
outspoken about what he sees as the Church's lack of compassion
and sympathy for "those whose marriages have broken down."
In a recent interview he commented:

> The Church of Jesus Christ should beat its breast and do penance,
> because it has been so hurtful, so rejecting, and so harmful to those
> who don't measure up to the Gospel's ideal. We must remember that
> the Church . . . is not a gathering of the perfect, but a gathering of
> the troubled and struggling." [3]

Father Young has prepared a series of ten cassette tapes titled
Catholics: Divorce and Remarriage which are available by mail
order from N.C.R. Cassettes, whose address is included in Appendix A.

The NACSDC sponsors a national convention each year, and
members from the estimated six hundred chapters all over the
United States and Canada are encouraged to attend. And in
1977 Pope Paul VI revoked the automatic excommunication
of American Catholics who had divorced and remarried. While
this hardly constitutes condoning the process of reorganizing

one's family, it is a shift in the official position which was grate-fully received by the eight million divorced Catholics of this country.

Divorce has been available to the Jewish community for sev-eral thousand years, and although originally considered a right of the man rather than the woman, the law gradually changed enough to allow wives to initiate a change in status. It should be pointed out, however, that while the laws were fairly lenient about what constituted justifiable reasons for divorce, the social reaction was much stricter, and divorce did not become a major factor in Jewish life until quite recently. The means for ending an incompatible relationship had been there all along, but few people took advantage of it, and the rising divorce rate among Jews is now viewed as an epidemic by some rabbis. The formalities in-volved depend largely on whether one is Orthodox, Conserva-tive, or Reform, but they generally have little to do with helping the couple through the transition process. Like many of their Christian counterparts, a number of temples offer workshops, singles groups, and social activities for unmarried people, which are useful *after* the transition has been made, but there is little being done to provide support during the crisis time of decision and separation. (I am speaking of programs sponsored by the organization as a whole; many fine individual ministers and rabbis offer help and guidance within their own congregations.) This is certainly an area where all religious groups could develop much-needed programs, and it is to be hoped that such support systems will begin to take shape in the near future.

Hail and Farewell

One aspect of the divorce process which has come to the fore of late in the thinking of both psychologists and the clergy is the need for some sense of closure, of completion and ending, not only of the marriage but also of the divorce process as well. Although divorce is one of the most traumatic experiences there are, we have done little to acknowledge it in any more than a legal fashion. Many people complain that they feel dissociated from the actual event of becoming unmarried, whether they appeared in court or not. Here you are, declaring the ending of an entire life-style by submitting various papers to a government official, and if nothing is contested, the whole process may be dispensed with in ten minutes' time. There is rarely any sense of resolution and certainly nothing cathartic about having your future shuffled around in a stack of papers on some judge's desk. It's no wonder so many people experience an enormous letdown and numbness following such procedures.

Divorce is a major change in life direction, a passage from one phase to another, and should be recognized and validated as such. This need has long been understood but rarely acted upon. In the last several years, however, different members of the clergy have been developing Divorce Ceremonies, and the use of these rituals is being advocated by both therapists and ministers. Rabbi Earl Grollman points out, "We have ceremonies for birth, puberty, marriage, death, but nothing for divorce." He has written a specific ceremony for divorce, which he considers to be "a humanistic service rather than a religious service," and it can be found in his book *Living Through Your Divorce*.[4] The Alternate Rituals Project of the United Methodist Church has produced a book entitled *Ritual in a New Day*[5] which includes a divorce ceremony in which the children participate along with their parents. And the Reverend Henry Close has written a fine service which is reprinted in Appendix D.

It is not uncommon for couples to write their own ceremony, or to ask a close friend to do so for them, usually incorporating a reading from Ecclesiastes which begins "To everything there is a season, and a time for every matter under Heaven." If this idea appeals to you, discuss it with your opposing partner and see if you can agree on some form of saying "hail and farewell" which will help both of you ritualize the end of the old partnership and the beginning of the new, coparenting relationship.

If your ex isn't willing to participate in such a ceremony, you might consider creating one of your own. Anyone who has suffered a broken heart and thereafter carried a torch until it burned his fingers knows the frustration, hurt, and exhaustion that can come from being unable to let go of the past in order to muster the energy to live now and plan for the future. One woman I met finally devised a symbolic funeral for her marriage, sitting quietly in a country setting and holding a small service "for the future that would never be; the person I had thought my lover was, but who in fact is as gone from my life as if physically dead." She reported that the solemnity, the grief and tears, and the profound sense of release she experienced afterward took the whole thing out of the macabre and helped her to let go of two years of pain and anger. While this does not have the same sense of "agreeing to disagree" that most divorce services include, it is still a very valid way of concluding the mourning process. (Remember, it is the ending of the old relationship you are commemorating, not the burying of the actual person!)

Other Ideas

The need to say a profound personal farewell to one's marriage is only part of the last phase of the divorce process. There is also the need, and desire, to reach out to a new life. While many of the support groups already mentioned can help with this to some degree, there are things which you yourself can develop on your own.

I ran across a Divorce Center which struck me as an excellent idea, well worth passing on. It started as a combination social and therapeutic gathering of kindred souls, brought together by a marriage and family counselor who was himself divorced, but it went on to become part of the community. Its members developed a library which included books on all aspects of divorce, single parenting, children, remarriage, and anything else that was pertinent to the needs of the group. And they established a "referral file" which contained everything from attorneys to restaurants, where the name, address, and general information about the person or business was written on an 8×5 card by someone who had made use of the service offered. Baby-sitters, day-care centers, pediatricians, child psychologists, real estate agents, roofers and repairmen, reliable (and unreliable) mechanics, singles organizations, social clubs, and the like all found their way into this index, along with pertinent comments from consumers. Information about night-school classes, lectures, workshops, conferences, concerts, and other events were posted on a bulletin board, and the old basement which became the headquarters for this group was transformed into a warm and comfortable center of activity. During the holiday periods, a time that is generally highly stressful for noncustodial divorced parents, those family members without families got together and created their own festivities. On more than one occasion several noncustodial parents arranged to hold "alternate" holidays at the center, when they could bring their children and celebrate a second Thanksgiving, for instance. And all this came about because of the energy of one man in starting it, and the members' willingness to develop a support system which met their needs. This is very much a "do it yourself" kind of thing which doesn't depend on an outside agency or organization, and there's no reason why you can't set up such a center of your own, if you wish.

Groups for Children

Most of the support systems already mentioned are geared specifically to the adult, although some work with the family as a whole. There is a very strong need, however, for the development of similar systems for the children of divorce, such as self-help peer groups. Of the several programs I've heard of, one is sponsored by a local Family Service Agency and two have been established through counseling departments at schools. Parental permission was required before a child could participate, and each group was organized by age: one for children from the third through sixth grades; another for junior high students; and the third composed entirely of high school teen-agers. For many of these children, the discovery that they were not the only ones with divorced parents and that a number of the difficulties they were experiencing were also problems their friends coped with came as both a shock and a relief. Being able to discuss their own feelings and express their angers, fears, frustrations, and confusions with others who had had similar experiences was very important to these youngsters. Naturally, the teen-agers were the most vocal and active of these groups, and each of the students interviewed mentioned the importance of being able to talk with others confronting the same situations. One said:

We're not a cry-baby group—but it does help to share your experiences with someone who understands. Friends whose parents aren't divorced may want to help but all they can do is say that's too bad.[6]

So far, groups of this kind are the exception rather than the rule; in some cases they are pilot programs being conducted on an experimental basis.[7] Certainly this sort of program, through either the schools, the local "Y"'s, or family-service agencies, would meet a need which has too long been ignored. Although we talk a good deal about the problems of divorce and its effect on children, our social systems do very little to protect their interests or meet their needs. Just as it is time for parents to start working out their own custody arrangements with the offspring's needs and desires in mind, so too it's time to develop better support systems for those children. As with the forming of a local Divorce Center, the establishment of self-help peer groups for kids can best be brought about by the concerned parents themselves. Talk to your school's counseling staff, your local family-service agency, or the leader at the "Y." Although the adult adviser should *not* be a parent of any of the youngsters involved, your support and interest can do much to bring about the formation of such a group, and your children will reap the benefits. Remember, any support system, whether funded by the government or created by the voluntary commitment of its members, still boils down to being a people-caring-about-other-people situation. Therefore it's up to us as individuals to participate in creating such systems to meet our own needs and those of our children.

17
Aftermath:
In Any Case

Things to Consider as a Single Parent

Regardless of your gender or the details of your custody arrangement, the success or failure of your divorce depends largely upon your own attitudes. Unfortunately, many social scientists, writers, and even legal professionals have taken the position that the status of the divorced parent is both temporary and disastrous. It has been assumed that the single-parent family is "abnormal," "deviant," or "disintegrated," and that parents in this circumstance will hasten to correct the situation as soon as possible by finding new mates and remarrying. That the man who is paying a goodly part of his salary for the support and care of his children and the mother who is coping with holding a job, running a home, and raising the youngsters by herself may not be in any emotional, mental, or financial condition to "reenter the marriage market" is simply overlooked.

The results of these assumptions have been twofold. Many divorced parents view being single again as a transitional state, a kind of unfortunate hiatus between spouses, and a difficult time to be gotten through as rapidly as possible. Thus they tend to rush into ill-advised next marriages, wherein they repeat all the same mistakes that caused the problems in their earlier partnerships. Or failing that, they develop the conviction that somehow they have become "losers" in the overall pattern of life, and embrace their single state with a kind of bitter resignation. Neither one of these responses is going to promote any kind of healthy personal growth, however, and when there are children involved such reactions can be downright devastating for everyone. Consequently, it's a good idea to take another look at your circumstances and see if they are really as bad as you may have believed.

There are a number of potential advantages to be found in the single-parent situation which are not readily available to the traditional nuclear family. These go far beyond the cessation of conflict between warring partners, or the chance to replace your old spouse with someone new. For the most part they are possible no matter what sort of custody arrangement you choose to follow, and while some of them require a certain degree of cooperation between the ex-partners, many are simply the result of necessary changes in philosophy once the traditional family roles are no longer applicable. The reorganization of your family structure provides you with an excellent chance to reassess your concepts of parenting, and being a single parent often creates opportunities for both you and your offspring that are generally lacking in the typical married family. A single-parent family need not be bad per se.

Parental Expectations

Marriage and family life are considered to be fundamental to the health and well-being of this society; the law states that marriage is the right of every citizen, and procreation the natural objective of marriage. Yet for all that, we have precious little background, education, or support in the parental role. As Dr. Thomas Gordon points out in his book *P.E.T.: Parent Effectiveness Training,* "parents are blamed, but not trained"; [1] they are expected to put

all their energies into rearing healthy, well-adjusted, self-confi-
dent youngsters, and whatever problems arise in the child's later
life as an adult are brought home and laid directly on the doorstep
of the parent. The modern parent not only takes on the responsibility of providing material necessities for the youngsters: he or
she must also meet the psychological and emotional needs as
well—a sizable undertaking in anyone's book!

Too often this leads to unnatural and unrealistic expectations
on the part of the adults. Having taken up the sacred mantle of
parenthood, they feel compelled to meet standards that are all
but impossible; they must be always considerate, always loving
toward their children, always mature and stable and tolerant,
self-sacrificing, impeccably fair, and for the most part all-know-
ing, wise, and generous. In an effort to make the youngster feel
"secure," they present a united front on as many subjects as
possible, shield him or her from the realities of adult concerns,
and try to maintain total power and control in the family in order
to keep things running smoothly. As Gordon shows, such standards are almost never met and, if they were, would deny the
child the opportunity to know, interact with, and learn from real,
honest, and human parents. (No wonder the American family is
"in trouble," as so many sociologists put it.)

In order to cope with all these expectations, the typical nuclear family has been organized along much the same lines as a
corporation. The two adults, having designated themselves President of the Company and Chairperson of the Board, get together
behind closed doors and lay out policy guidelines for the entire
family in high-level administrative meetings. They take care of
whatever business is required at the particular moment (whether
or not to grant Johnny an increase in allowance, what time Susan
has to be home from a date), then hand down memos to the
children, who dutifully (or grudgingly) acknowledge these new
directives, but haven't the slightest idea of how they were arrived
at, or why. Decisions are reached, measures adopted, and policies initiated with the troops' having little or nothing to do with
the process. The result, of course, is children who are cut off
from any real contact with the dynamics of running a family, who
have little sense of direct input where major issues are concerned,
and who are basically kept in a powerless and dependent posi-

tion, all under the guise of protecting them from the confusions of adult considerations. And while they may certainly feel protected, they don't learn much about what it is to be an adult, except on the most superficial levels.

Parental Functions

If the primary purpose of parenting is to help children grow into healthy, confident, independent adults, capable of living comfortably within their social structure and able to realize their best potential, keeping them powerless, ignorant, and dependent seems a poor way of accomplishing these ends. Yet our traditional concept of family organization and parental function does just that. Dr. Helen Mendes suggests that American parents too often see themselves as "supplier/providers" rather than "contributor/coordinators," [2] and while these terms may be somewhat cumbersome, the ideas behind them are very important, especially for the single parent.

The parent who assumes the role of supplier/provider takes on the entire responsibility of meeting all the children's needs personally. He or she decides what is wanted, locates a source for it, procures it for the offspring, and presents it to them as a completed whole. If the child desires something the adult feels is unsuitable, or not within the family budget, he tends to simply veto the request without much explanation. He may feel bad about not being able to provide it, but in order to keep the progeny from feeling "insecure," he isn't going to admit to any financial pinch; besides, what good is a supplier who can't produce?

This attitude about parenting goes hand in hand with the corporate family structure, and while not all traditional families fall into this trap, it is a natural extension of the traditional expectations of parenthood. Unfortunately, this sort of parent becomes a filter through which everything from the outside world must pass, creates a heavy dependency on the part of the children, and limits the potential of progeny and parents alike.

The contributor/coordinator, on the other hand, acts as a kind of adult consultant, encouraging the child to make use of the available resources to meet the present need. This parent helps the youngster decide what is actually needed or wanted, suggests sources of supply, aids in the coordination of efforts to attain it, and encourages the offspring to make use of their own energies to fulfill their desires. This approach provides parent and child with an opportunity to work together cooperatively, and in so doing broadens the horizons of both.

While there is nothing that says married parents can't be contributor/coordinators, the sheer problem of logistics makes it all but impossible for the single parent to be a supplier/provider. If you're going to have any sanity in your life, you have to shift over to the principle of being a coordinating parent; otherwise you'll exhaust yourself and deny your children much that would be beneficial for them. The single parents who feel they must be the central source of supply for everything their youngsters do find themselves run to a frazzle, depressed, or guilty about what they are unable to provide, and frequently resort to a kind of blind authoritarianism. The coordinating parent helps the child open his own doors and enrich his own life, however, and by being willing to allow the youngster greater contact with the world, creates a family sense that is supportive but not confining.

These different attitudes show up in many aspects of family interaction. For instance, if your youngster wants to go fishing, but has to wait until you can find the time and energy to take him, it may be weeks or months before your schedule makes the excursion possible. But if you will encourage him to call his *other parent*, or contact grandparents, aunts, uncles, cousins, or peer-group friends to see who else might be interested in such a project, one of them may be able to provide the transportation and companionship you can't. And rather than dashing about trying to locate poles, bait, and other paraphernalia yourself, help the child make a list of what is required and then use the phone to track down the necessary items on his own. You might have to do the actual hauling and fetching, particularly if your offspring is young, but his having taken a hand in making it all happen will add both to his enjoyment of the outing and to his sense of self-reliance and personal capability. That you aren't along won't diminish your importance in his eyes, while your support and guidance will have reinforced his sense of family cooperation. And the fact that you didn't stand in the way of his sharing extra and special time with his other parent won't go unnoticed, either.

Not all single parents are able to adapt to the role of coordinating parent, but for your own sake and that of the youngsters it's worth thinking about, and seeing what you can do to make this philosophy part of your concept of parenting.

From Corporate to Single Parent

The transition from married to single parent generally involves not only a reassessment of parental roles: it frequently includes a change in personal relationships between children and parent. Once the typical corporate family structure is done away with, all kinds of new possibilities develop. To begin with, you don't have the advantage of dual authority; when the kids ask about something, you can't hedge by telling them to speak to their other parent about it. Nor do you have anyone to take up the slack; if you're tired and out of sorts, they're stuck with a parent who is tired and out of sorts. And there isn't any partner to help perpetuate the myth that parental wisdom, decisions, and authority are somehow sacred and beyond question. (In many households the adults take turns running along and crying, "Oh, look at the Emperor's new clothes!" in order to uphold the role-playing. The single parent doesn't have this automatic backup service, and you're as open and vulnerable to your children's scrutiny as the Emperor's conceit was.) If you attempt to fall back on the unilateral power of your parenthood for every situation that arises, chances are it will have a minimal effect; you'll take on the appearance of a dictator or martinet instead of an adult guide and teacher, and the kids will probably poke holes in your boat faster than you can bail.

Yet this very inability to make use of the traditional pattern of child raising opens the doors for a much more realistic and healthy relationship with your youngsters. The single parent is nothing if not a real person! Whether you're just now going through the process of adjusting to your single-parent status or have been at it for some time, you're still the immediate adult your children focus on. If you're worried about money, hopeful about a new job, considering the pros and cons of moving, happy with your freedom, or feeling sad and lonely, your kids will spot it. They may not know the exact cause of your feelings, but chances are they'll want to know what it's all about, and you should tell them, provided it doesn't relate directly to the divorce and their other parent. (As mentioned before, this is one area where it's taboo to involve the children on any but the most general level, especially if you are feeling negative and bitter, as it's almost impossible to keep any kind of perspective about what you're saying. The best you can do is explain that you're exasperated or hurt, that it has nothing to do with your love for them, and that you don't want them to get caught in the middle of it.)

Your offspring will feel better knowing that you share your feelings with them. Not only will they be more likely to open up and tell you about their own emotions and responses, they'll also feel more secure; most anxieties and many fears are based on *not knowing* what is going on, and therefore conjuring up all sorts of frightening notions. So feel free to discuss all kinds of things with your children, answer their questions, ask their opinions, and explain your own philosophy regardless of whether the subject is large or small. Don't be afraid to share yourself with them; as Dr. Gordon says, children want to have real parents to relate to, not God-like images to be governed by. And youngsters who see their parents coping with the numerous emotions of living will be better able to cope with their own humanity when they grow up.

Children as People

Many divorced parents have noted that they got to know their offspring better after their marital partnership ended; divorced fathers frequently spend more time with their children than they did when the family was all together under one roof, and single mothers naturally relate more directly with the youngsters when there's no other adult around. This is a logical development when you stop to look at it. Whereas the adults of the traditional family rely on each other for help and companionship in their daily activities, this isn't possible in the single-parent home. Although it's good to know you can turn to your ex when major decisions must be made, on the everyday basis it's the children you look to for conversation, cooperation, and the sense of family companionship. It's the kids you chat with in the evening, talk to while running errands, or coordinate with to get housework done. Whether it's exploring potential vacation plans around the dinner table or discussing Scouts, kite flying, or school problems over a cup of cocoa before bed, they'll be more likely to share their casual thoughts with you than they would if your attention were being divided between them and your partner. This leads to more exchanges of viewpoints, humor, trivial observations, and personal confidences than the traditional parent will probably ever encounter.

Your children are each unique in a thousand subtle ways, and you have an excellent opportunity to discover who they are without being distracted by the presence of another adult. By all means take advantage of this to relate to your youngsters as specific, individual people. And if possible, try to make time to be with each one of them alone; it will do wonders for all of you.

It has often been noted that siblings, when met separately, are quite different than when seen in each other's company. When they are together, the outgoing, talkative child may well slip into a pattern of dominating the time and attention of the adult, while the shier, more reticent one looks on, never venturing to compete with the more communicative brother or sister. There may be rivalry between them that leads to tensions and strains you aren't aware of, and you may be so used to dealing with the brood as a whole that you've never had the time to get to know each of them independently of the others. In this area, however, the divorced family has a very specific advantage over the corporate family.

Quite often the traditional family assumes that the entire unit not only lives together but also plays together. Hence family outings, excursions, vacations, or even extended trips are arranged for the entire group. The scenery changes, but the interplay of family relationships stays exactly the same as it is at home. The fact that these special occasions could well be used to give both child and parent a chance to relate on a more personal and individual basis is generally overlooked, or if considered at all, is rejected for fear that dividing the children might lead to resentment and hassles about who goes with whom, and thus create more trouble than it's worth.

The divorced family, however, has the opportunity to arrange visits and vacations in such a way that each child can be with one parent alone for more extended periods of time. It's possible to plan the various combinations of parent–child visits to allow everyone an equal amount of time, while opening the doors for a much more intimate relationship between offspring and parent. My ex and I had two youngsters, so it was fairly easy to split the summer vacations. If Chris went to stay with his dad first, he had the chance to interact with him without Tasha's continuous presence during the first two weeks of the summer. Tasha stayed with me, we ran around doing the flea-market and museum things she so loved, and after two weeks she went north to join her father and brother. At the end of the summer Chris came back two weeks before Tasha did, giving her time with her father while Chris and I went fishing, miniature-golfing, or whatever else he particularly enjoyed. No one felt cheated, everyone benefited from being separate for a while, and the system worked very well.

The same periodic "special attention" times can be arranged during midweek visits. Every child from a divorced family whom I talked with remembered some particular time when, for one reason or another, the noncustodial parent took him by himself for dinner and a movie, or an evening at the skating rink, while the others stayed home. Usually this was because the siblings were sick, preoccupied with schoolwork, or in some other way unable to come too; rarely was it because of intentional planning. Yet it was invariably a high point where the child was concerned, and often remembered in the most glowing terms. Provided that such special attention is spread out equally, and each youngster gets an opportunity to have his or her own personal time with the noncustodial parent, there is no cause for jealousy or resentment.

If you are planning such division of visits, talk it over with the siblings; they will probably prefer to spend Christmas, birthdays, and other special family occasions together rather than separated, and you should never plan a once-in-a-lifetime event at a time that would exclude any of your kids. But with a little organization, this system can be put to excellent use and is well worth considering.

Visitation in General

The importance of regular visitation between the noncustodial parent and the children can't be stressed too strongly, as it is a vital factor in how well the youngsters will adjust to their new situation. In the Wallerstein and Kelly study[3] the only children who were at all satisfied with their new living arrangements were those who had extensive and frequent contact with their noncustodial parent, often as much as several times a week. Those who saw the other parent only on alternate weekends complained sadly that it was just not enough. (It should be noted that this study looked only at typical custody arrangements, and there were no sharing parents among the families involved.)

Parents sometimes find that having too flexible a schedule leads to an invasion of privacy and the sense of never knowing when you have your children to yourself. For instance, if the visiting pattern is left completely up in the air there is a strong chance of arguments' arising when both parents make plans for the offspring at the same time. Therefore it would be wise to work out a basic schedule which includes not only weekends but also several evenings during the time in between. By all means, consult with the youngsters during the planning stage; there may be times which are more or less convenient for them, and they will appreciate having some say in how the timetable is put together. (As with everything else in the one-parent family, the children should not be allowed to control the decision-making, but knowing that their needs and desires are considered in the process of reaching an agreement will help them feel more secure.)

After you have arrived at a basic schedule, don't feel that you have to adhere to it rigidly. There should be enough flexibility on both your parts to allow extra times or even an occasional rearrangement if something special comes up. Some parents establish a policy of "right of first refusal" when it comes to baby-sitting. This is particularly helpful for the divorced father who often complains that the baby-sitter sees more of his offspring than he does! If you have regular plans for night-school classes, for example, having your ex spend the evening with the youngsters can be valuable for everyone concerned. But if your outings are of a social nature, you might do well to consider letting the offspring go stay overnight with their other parent instead of having him come to them. The divorced man who spends an evening in the family home while his ex goes out on a date may well begin to experience jealousy, anger, and frustration while he waits for her homecoming. Nor do most dating mothers feel comfortable about the possibility of a scene when they get home. Much of this depends largely on the relationship between you and your ex; but there's no point in tempting fate, and it's awkward if you want to invite your date in for a cup of coffee. In the long run you'd be wiser to simply pack up the blanket and Teddy bear and let the youngsters sleep over at their father's home.

Many couples work out occasional longer-term baby-sitting in the family home when the custodial parent goes away on business, for instance, or for a short vacation. This has several advantages as well as a couple of hazards, but it's certainly worth thinking about. The adult who is traveling can go about his or her business without worrying about the children or the cost of a professional baby-sitter, while the visiting parent has a chance to interact with the children on their own turf, and be part of their normal everyday activities in the comfort of familiar surroundings. For some people this arrangement is absolutely unthinkable, as the presence of your ex in your own nest, even though you aren't there, can be very unsettling. Yet what is an impossibility for one couple may be only a matter of logistics for another. I know of one case in which the mother agreed to have her ex "live in" for a month once he promised to sleep on the couch and not in her bed.

Remember that your children's time with their other parent is extremely important to them; visits that are ruined by parental bickering, downgrading, or outright fighting leave everyone in a bad temper and create needless nightmares for the youngsters involved. Nor should you use the children to carry messages back and forth, no matter how innocuous their content. Children come to dread having to deliver such communications for fear of the visiting parent's reaction, and an otherwise enjoyable time may be spoiled. If you have anything to say to each other, do it on your own time, whether it's about a lost sock or the support check.

It's also tremendously important not to use your offspring to spy on the other parent. It's one thing to inquire whether the children had a good time, and what they did, but it's quite another to put them through a Spanish Inquisition about what sort of food they ate, whether he got any phone calls, and how he does (or doesn't) keep house. Children caught in this position either become manipulative and competent at saying exactly the sort of thing that will drive you up a wall, or retreat into sullen silence and resent your intrusion into that part of their lives. So let them tell you what they want to, but don't pry, ask them leading questions, or fly into a fit of rage because your ex bought a new color TV; they have enough problems balancing between the two of you without your adding to it by creating scenes when they come home.

The Eye of the Beholder

It has been said that beauty is in the eye of the beholder—an observation that certainly is borne out by the diversity of popular arts and styles over the generations. By the same token, divorce, child custody, and visitation arrangements can be adjudged only through the eye of the experiencer. You can make it a disaster for yourself and your children, a self-pitying parody of lifelong anguish guaranteed to drive away friends, relatives, and even youngsters. Or you can salvage as much dignity and self-knowledge as possible, and set about reorganizing your family in a way that will do the least damage to all the members. It is even possible to arrive at the point where the ending of a bad marriage and the development of a new family arrangement is beneficial for everyone. Certainly this last is what every caring parent espouses; the problems come in agreeing on what is beneficial to whom, and why. One of the most important criteria, however, should be how it affects the children: what will they perceive from your separation or custody rearrangement, how will they interpret their new life patterns, and what will their personal experiences be?

Remember, children learn by experience. Words are only the symbols of ideas, whereas experience is the fact of being, and children are more deeply affected by what they experience than by what they hear. When the words are one thing and the experience is another, they will remember the experience long after they have forgotten the reasons offered. For instance, no matter how much you tell them that both parents still love them, if they are denied access to one of their adults, they certainly won't *experience* the feeling of being loved by both. And how can a child believe that parental anger is not more important than their own love and need for each parent if that anger keeps their love from being shared and their needs from being met? What sort of reassurance can you give your offspring that you do indeed love and respect them if you can't say anything nice about the person from whom they got half their genes? And can you possibly expect a child to understand the value of cooperation if his or her parents won't demonstrate the use of it, even for something as important as their youngster's well-being?

How your progeny will be affected by your divorce and custody arrangements (or battles) will depend largely on how you answer these questions, and what you are willing to do about it both individually and together. When parents are unwilling to develop an equilibrium of dissent, the unresolved angers, spite, hurt, and hostility can go on for years. The carrying over of your own personal vendettas, wounded egos, and ancient grudges will only scatter misery throughout your offspring's childhood, and deny them both the expression and the fulfillment of their desires for two loving, supportive, and understanding parents.

It has been pointed out that although we are a pro-natal society (that is, everyone is expected to marry and have children), we are *not* a child-oriented culture. And nowhere is this more evident than in the divorce and child-custody situation. As long as our common practices continue to divide the parents into warring camps, perpetuate a state of dissatisfaction and imbalance, and deny the youngsters' need and right to two loving and caring parents, there isn't much likelihood of things' changing. Only when we begin to recognize divorce as a reorganization which allows the adults their separate futures and *still maintains a family support system for the children* will we be able to save our offspring from this kind of needless heartache and sadness.

Fortunately, you, as individual parents, are in the best position of all to help effect this change. I hope you have gained from this book enough information and insight to feel confident about working through the stages of your divorce, developing a new relationship as coparents, and finding the best custody arrangement to meet the needs of your specific family. Divorced parents, and to some extent their children, are frequently likened to pioneers; there is very little social precedent to help us get through the transition process, and not much more established support for the single-parent family once it is reorganized. In that sense, living as a divorced family is pretty much a do-it-yourself project. Don't hesitate to ask your own questions, develop your own ideas, and try your own system, whether it's one of the various arrangements talked about in this book or a totally new concept that fits your particular needs better. In a very real way your family is the *only* group of experts there is on the subject. If you are willing to communicate, discuss, and negotiate your differences, chances are you'll be able to reach a reasonable agreement; thousands of other couples have.

And if you get stuck, or seem to have come to an impasse, there's one last question by which you both should always be guided: what do you want for your children in the long run? Will the ending of your marriage bequeath them a legacy of loss and sorrow and conflicted feelings? Will they experience guilt or shame or unnecessary poverty because the adults were more interested in getting even with each other than in looking after their youngsters' needs? Or will they grow up knowing they can depend on each of you to help them through the difficult times of maturing? Will they find that their space and time patterns have been rearranged, but the security and comfort of having two caring parents has been maintained? With any luck and some strong help from you, your children will also be able to say, "Thank goodness my parents loved me enough to let me love both of them." It's up to you—both.

Appendix A

HELPFUL ORGANIZATIONS

VETERANS
   ADMINISTRATION
   CENTRAL OFFICE
810 Vermont Avenue, N.W.
Washington, D.C. 20420

FAMILY SERVICE
   ASSOCIATIONS OF
   AMERICA
(This includes many agencies,
   among them the Jewish
   Family Service)
44 East 23rd Street
New York, N.Y. 10010

ASSOCIATION OF FAMILY
   CONCILIATION COURTS
10015 S.W. Terwilliger Boulevard
Portland, Ore. 97219

PARENTS WITHOUT
   PARTNERS
7910 Woodmont Avenue
Washington, D.C. 20014
PWP publishes a monthly
   magazine called *The Single
   Parent,* and also offers a
   bibliography of children's
   books about divorce.

CHILDREN'S RIGHTS, INC.
   (CRI)

3443 17th Street, N.W.
Washington, D.C. 20010

U.S. PASSPORT OFFICE
Legal Division
1425 K Street, N.W.
Washington, D.C. 20415

AMERICAN ARBITRATION
   ASSOCIATION
140 West 51st Street
New York, N.Y. 10020

AMERICAN ACADEMY OF
   MATRIMONIAL
   LAWYERS
Suite 8504
John Hancock Center
175 East Delaware Place
Chicago, Ill. 60611

DIVORCE MINISTRY
Garner Odell
1131 Mestres Drive
Pebble Beach, Calif. 93953

PRESBYTERIAN
   COUNSELING SERVICE
1013 Eighth Avenue
Seattle, Wash. 98104

MINISTRY TO DIVORCED
   CATHOLICS
Father Holden
300 Broadway
Newark, N.J. 07104
The *Newsletter for Divorced
   Catholics* is available from
   this address also.

NORTH AMERICAN
   CONFERENCE OF
   SEPARATED AND
   DIVORCED CATHOLICS

5 Park St.
Boston, Mass. 02108

N.C.R. CASSETTES
115 East Armour Boulevard
Post Office Box 281
Kansas City, Mo. 64141
The tapes entitled *Catholics:
   Divorce and Remarriage* can
   be ordered from this
   company.

Appendix B

SAMPLE CUSTODY PARAGRAPHS

Consumers Legal Services in Berkeley, California, is a low-cost legal service headed by attorneys and staffed in part by paralegals. Attorney Harriet Lee has noted that more than 50 percent of the new clients coming to use the Divorce Assistance Service have already decided that they want to have some form of shared (joint) custody, and to that end the Service has drawn up several sample paragraphs to choose from. You and your attorney may wish to modify them in some way, or write new ones, but these will give you some idea of what to include in your agreement.

1. *Child custody:* The parties agree that both are fit and proper persons to have custody of their minor child, and in the best interests of their child, agree that they shall have joint legal custody of their child, and acknowledge that at the present time their child is physically residing with (wife/husband). It is further acknowledged that the physical residence of their child may be changed in full or in part at any time by mutual agreement of the parties.

2. *Child custody:* The parties agree that both are fit and proper persons to have custody of their minor child, and in the best interests of their child, agree that they shall have joint legal and physical custody of their child.

Any or all of the following paragraphs can be added to your contract under either paragraph 1 or 2 above:

3. The parties realize that the welfare of the child of their marriage is of paramount importance and for that reason both parties are reluctant to restrict visitation rights to any rigid schedule. It is therefore agreed that their child may visit the noncustodial parent at any time the parties themselves agree on.

4. All decisions pertaining to education, health, summer activities, and welfare of their child shall be decided by the parties after adequate consultation has occurred between them. Neither party shall do anything which may estrange their child from the other parent and hamper the natural and continuing relationship between the child and either parent.

5. At all times each party hereto agrees to foster love and respect between their child and the other parent. Each agrees to consult the other and to confer together on matters affecting the education and welfare of their child, taking into account the best interests of their child and so far as possible, the desires of their child.

6. It is agreed that the parent with whom the child resides will have day-to-day jurisdiction of the child; however, all decisions of a substantive nature will be made by consensus if time and circumstances reasonably permit.

Appendix C

GUIDELINES FOR DIVORCED PARENTS

1. *Your youngsters need the security of knowing that they have two loving and considerate parents.* Whether they have two equal families in a shared situation or one primary home and lots of contact with the other parent, they need to feel loved, accepted, secure, appreciated, understood, and validated as worthwhile people in their own right, even though their parents no longer live together. Any situation that forces them to take sides, make loyalty decisions, or become pawns in a power game between warring adults is going to be detrimental to them.

2. *The children's right to love each parent must be honored.* It's imperative that you recognize and respect your youngsters' feelings about their other parent, and allow them to feel comfortable about loving both of you. To do anything else is not only unreasonable and incredibly selfish: it attempts to deny one of the strongest of human emotions and desires. Attitudes that downgrade the other parent, scorn his or her worth, and make the youngsters feel guilty, resentful, or conflicted about the love they feel for their progenitor only add to the pain and confusion they already feel. As one 6-year-old told her mother, "I won't say bad things about your daddy if you quit saying bad things about mine!"

3. *Your opposing partner's right to be an active parent must be validated.* It's vitally important that you understand and accept this, and support the youngsters in their efforts to maintain contact and reassure themselves of each parent's love and commitment. Whether this means cooperating in making visits easier for the noncustodial parent, going out of your way to be flexible in your demands and expectations, or being willing to explore some form of shared custody, your primary consideration should be to allow the children and their other parent a chance to interact in a normal, natural, and comfortable manner. If your attitudes make this impossible, you're likely to find that the difficulties between you and your ex will increase, and the children will be the losers in the long run.

4. *Stop and consider what your children are feeling and experiencing.* Everyone's emotions run high during a family reorganization, but

your kids won't have the same outlook on the problems that you do. What to you may be good riddance to a rubbish heap of broken dreams and promises may leave them feeling abandoned, deserted, guilty, unlovable, or tainted by the same brush with which you tar and feather your ex. Their emotions are just as complex and subtle as your own, although they may lack the sophistication to be able to explain them in adult terms. Every caring and concerned parent has to be willing to disengage from his or her personal feelings long enough to provide emotional support and reassurance to the youngsters when the children are under stress; this is a major part of the parental function, and you owe it to your children regardless of whether you are married, single, separated, or divorced.

5. *Remember that it is healthier for your children to have two divorced coparents than to have an "intact" family which is constantly filled with stress and hostility.* Divorce can be an honest and constructive solution to the problems created by "irreconcilable differences" in a marriage that has deteriorated, but it is up to you to complete your divorce stages so as to reach your equilibrium of dissent. If you continue your grudges and battle with your ex for months or years at a time, your children may see you as the constantly angry and hostile authority in their lives, and be frightened of expressing their own feelings for fear of bringing your wrath down on themselves. Or if you appear to be the poor martyred victim, complaining pitifully about each day's existence, they may not be willing to share their own pain with you lest it add to your already too heavy burden and make things worse. Therefore, for both your sake and theirs, you would do well to work through your divorce and put your energies toward building a constructive future for all of you.

Appendix D

PRINCIPLES OF DIVORCE

Beloved friends, we are gathered here today with sadness, to bear witness to the painful side of our human existence, to the part of life that is associated with death. We bear witness today to the death of a marriage; and to the death of the dreams, the hopes, the expectations that brought this relationship into being. Somehow in the mystery of human failure these aspirations were not fulfilled. In spite of noble purposes, of good intentions, of sincere effort, this marriage has died, and the process of grieving has begun. And we here today stand with you in your grieving, to affirm our ties with you, our support in this anxious time of transition of God's rebuilding, and to affirm very clearly your place in the community of God's people. Marriage is a difficult venture, and there can never be guarantees of its success. It is to your credit that you tried.

You have been as two trees that were transplanted so close together that their branches became intertwined, and their trunks grew together and became engrafted into one another. And as the rain fell on the soil, and the sun shone on their leaves and the wind blew in their branches, they would be sometimes competing and sometimes sharing; sometimes pushing against each other and sometimes supporting each other; sometimes fighting and sometimes loving. But as the trees grew, they inevitably influenced each other—permanently. And when the time came that the trees were separated, torn apart, there were painful wounds where the trunks had grown together; and roots were torn and branches were broken. And as both trees are transplanted again, they face the struggle of putting down new roots to sustain them and growing new branches with which to reach out to their world.

(A CHARGE TO THE COUPLE)

As you _____(man)_____ and _____(woman)_____ have committed yourselves to this separation and transplanting, you will experience a confusing array of feelings of relief and of regret, of hope and of fear, of frustration and perhaps most of all, of uncertainty. But the step has been taken, and it is important now to follow this new course and to find fulfillment in a new way of life.

As you commit yourselves to the process of creatively unmarrying, I offer you the following tasks:

I invite you to *forgive* each other. At this point, you will have many resentments about what your spouse was and was not, or has done and not done. Perhaps you have even told yourself that if only he or she had been different, everything would have worked out beautifully. But you cannot resent without clinging to the past, and so it is important to forgive.

I invite you to forgive *yourselves*. Each of you will experience guilt for what you have been and not been, for what you have done or not done, for time and energy wasted in futile activity and inactivity. But this is now behind you, and you can forgive yourselves.

I invite you to *grieve*. There is much that has died and is still dying, and you will both experience a deep sense of loss. What you wanted to be, and what you wanted each other to be and the relationship to be are all dreams that were unfulfilled, that have died. And your task is to face these deaths, to finish the work of grieving, and to go on to what lies ahead.

I invite you to *learn*. What you expected from yourselves and from each other and from marriage you did not find. Perhaps much of what you expected is not available anywhere. The ways you presented yourselves or asked for each other were not adequately effective. And it is important to learn anew what you can realistically expect from life, and how to achieve it.

I invite you to *find yourselves* again. Your identities have been closely intertwined with each other, and you have each given up some sense of yourself as individuals. To find yourselves again, you must separate from each other without the guilt and bitterness that clings to the past, and without the naive optimism that clings to an illusion.

I invite you to *love* again. There have undoubtedly been times when you have each felt very unloving and unlovable, and perhaps have despaired of ever again risking intimacy and love. But as human beings there is a hunger within you to reach out to other people, to touch and be touched. And I charge you this day to awaken and nourish this hunger to love and to be loved.

This ceremony, written by the Reverend Henry Close of Coral Gables, Florida, will appear in his own book *The Mystery of Intimacy* and is reproduced here with the gracious permission of the author. All rights are reserved by Reverend Close.

Appendix E

DIVORCE CHECKLIST

	Yes	No
1. Does your state require "grounds" for divorce?	_____	_____
2. Can you file for "no fault" divorce if you wish?	_____	_____
3. Are you willing to work out your own property and custody arrangement out of court?	_____	_____
4. Have you and your spouse agreed to some form of settlement already?	_____	_____
What don't you agree on?		
Child custody	_____	_____
Child support	_____	_____
Visitation	_____	_____
Division of property	_____	_____
Division of debts	_____	_____
Alimony (or spousal support)	_____	_____
Length of time to be paid		
_____		
_____		
5. Does your county have guidelines for support payments?	_____	_____
Have you seen a copy of it?	_____	_____
6. Do you have copies of your financial records for the last year?	_____	_____
7. Have you worked out a budget?	_____	_____
Do the two of you agree to it?	_____	_____
8. Have you talked with a real estate appraiser, CPA, tax consultant, or other financial expert about the value of your assets?	_____	_____

9. Are you interested in doing your own divorce?

    Is that allowed in your area?   _____ _____

    Are there kits, books, a clinic, or a divorce counselor you can go to for help?   _____ _____

10. Are you interested in a legal consultation for *both* of you together?   _____ _____

11. Would you consider mediation in some form?   _____ _____

12. Would you agree to arbitration?   _____ _____

13. Is there a minister, rabbi, or family counselor you can ask for help with your dissolution?   _____ _____

14. Is there a divorce team available in your area?

15. Is there a conciliation court in your county?   _____ _____

16. In the case of disputed custody, who investigates and reports back to the court?

    Juvenile probation officer

    Special investigator (psychologist)   _____ _____

    Private clinic   _____ _____

    Individual therapists   _____ _____

    Others   _____ _____

  Do you know what their reputation is among the parents who have used these services, or been investigated by them?   _____ _____

17. Is there postdivorce counseling available in your area?   _____ _____

18. Are there custody classes available?   _____ _____

19. How much do you think your overall expenses for this legal action will be for *each* of you?

    $_____

    $_____

    On what do you base that estimate?

20. Is there any way to lower those expenses?   _____ _____

21. Would you each agree to put the money you could save into a special account for the children?   _____ _____

Notes

CHAPTER 1

1. "No-fault divorce" is the term commonly used to indicate that neither party is considered the plaintiff or defendant in the legal action to dissolve the marriage. Some states have done away with all other grounds for divorce, so that declaring there are irreconcilable differences, or that the marriage is simply no longer functioning, is all that is required. The majority of states still allow for specific charges to be made, however, if one of the parties feels specifically aggrieved.

2. There are no accurate or reliable statistics on the subject of custody, most states not having bothered to compile such information as how many divorces include contested custody, how many are settled out of court, or even how often custody is awarded to the father, either by agreement or as a result of a legal battle. The rising interest in this subject has caused some states to begin collecting these data, but at the moment researchers have to rely on estimates from judges, attorneys, and other writers, or projections made from census figures. These figures generally agree, but one wonders if that's just because no one really knows, and so uses the commonly heard percentages over and over. Throughout the book these common figures are used unless there is more precise information, in which case the source will be referenced in the notes.

3. Lamb, Michael, "Father-Infant and Mother-Infant Interaction in the First Year of Life." *Child Development,* March, 1977, Vol. 48 (1), pp. 167–181.

4. Both the Wallerstein and Kelly studies and the Hetherington, Cox, and Cox research have been written up for professional journals and are noted in the Professional Bibliography. For the layman the projects have been summarized in popular magazines, and they are well worth looking up: Hetherington, E. Mavis; Cox, Martha; and Cox, Roger, "Divorced Fathers." *Psychology Today,* April, 1977. Streshinsky, Shirley, "How Divorce Really Affects Children: A Major Report." *Redbook* Magazine, September, 1976.

CHAPTER 2

1. Dr. Melvin Roman noted this sociological change during a discussion with the California Women's Bar Association, San Francisco, Calif., February, 1976.

2. Levine, James A., *Who Will Raise the Children? New Options for Fathers (and Mothers)*. Philadelphia and New York, Lippincott, 1976.

3. Rorris, James P., "Separation Agreements—Support for the Spouse and Minor Children." *Minnesota Family Law, Minnesota Practice Manual 50;* Minneapolis, University of Minnesota, 1971, p. 75.

CHAPTER 3

1. No real statistics are available on the size of the gay population in the United States. At present the most widely accepted figure is approximately 5 percent, and that includes both men and women of all ages. By comparison, approximately one out of six, or almost 18 percent, of the school-aged children in the 1960s spent some time with a single parent, and that percentage has been continually increasing until today's estimate places two out of five (or 40 percent) of the children born in the '70s in a single-parent home during their youth. If there were a direct and unavoidable correlation between single mothers and homosexual sons, we would already be experiencing an increase in homosexuality far beyond the wildest fears of even the most strident anti-gay agitator.

2. Hetherington, Mavis, "Girls Without Fathers." *Psychology Today,* June, 1973, p. 47.

CHAPTER 4

1. Tanner, Ogden, *Stress*. New York, Time-Life Books, 1976.
Thomas Holmes and Richard Rahe's Social Readjustment Rating Scale indicates that divorce and marital separation are the second and third most stressful events that can befall an individual.

2. Bernard, Jessie, *The Future of Marriage*. New York, World Publishing, 1972.
This is an extremely erudite work on both the past and present status of connubial relationships, which offers a number of thought-provoking points for the interested reader.

3. Hetherington, E. Mavis; Cox, Martha; and Cox, Roger, "Divorced Fathers." *The Family Coordinator,* October, 1976, p. 417.

4. Roman, Melvin, address to the California Women's Bar Association, San Francisco, Calif., February, 1976.

5. Weitzman, Leonore, "Legal Regulation of Marriage: Tradition and Change." *California Law Review,* Vol. 62:2, 1974.

Although published in a professional journal, this article is certainly of interest to the layman as well. It explores many of our legal assumptions, and questions a number of our social expectations of marriage; the economics of the subject is just one portion of the article.

CHAPTER 5

1. The Wallerstein and Kelly studies of children and divorce noted that the children with the greatest and most consistent visitation with the noncustodial father were the best able to handle the separation. See Note 4 of Chapter 1.

2. See Goldstein, J.; Freud, A.; and Solnit, A., *Beyond the Best Interests of the Child.* New York, The Free Press, 1973.

CHAPTER 6

1. Dale, Stan, in personal conversation, November, 1976.

2. It is interesting to note that in Sweden fathers are allowed to take "paternity" leave after the birth of a child, in order to stay home with the infant during the first months. Their jobs are held for them, there is no loss of seniority, and they receive 90 percent of the prebirth salary during their stay at home.

3. The terms "seeker" and "assenter" were coined by Dr. Helen Mendes in her article "Single Fatherhood." *Social Work,* July, 1976, p. 308.

4. Hirshey, Gerri, "When Mommy Leaves Home." *Family Circle,* August 23, 1977, p. 70.

5. The early writings about shared custody were by the people who were doing it, not by professionals who were studying the subject. See Baum, C., "The Best of Both Parents." *The New York Times Magazine,* October 31, 1976, p. 44; Fager, C., "Coparenting: Sharing the Children of Divorce." *The San Francisco Bay Guardian,* February 3, 1977, p. 7; Holly, M., "Joint Custody, The New Haven Plan." *Ms.,* September, 1976, p. 70.

CHAPTER 7

1. Gettleman, S., and Markowitz, J., *The Courage to Divorce*. New York, Simon and Schuster, 1974.

2. Hetherington, E. Mavis; Cox, Martha; and Cox, Roger, "The Aftermath of Divorce." *Marriage and Divorce Today*, September 26, 1977.

Kelly, J., and Wallerstein, J., "The Effects of Parental Divorce: Experiences of the Child in Early Latency." *American Journal of Orthopsychiatry*, Vol. 46, 1976, p. 20.

3. Elkin, Meyer, "Postdivorce Counseling in a Conciliation Court." *Journal of Divorce*, Vol. 1 (1), Fall, 1977, p. 55.

4. Kressel, K., and Deutsch, M., "Divorce Therapy: An In-depth Survey of Therapists' Views." *Family Process*, December, 1977.

5. Doyle, Jacqueline Larcombe, "Couples in Crisis." Panel discussion, May 16, 1978, Tiburon, Calif., sponsored by The Family Mediation Center.

6. Kressel, K., and Deutsch, M., "Divorce Therapy: An In-depth Survey of Therapists' Views." *Family Process*, December, 1977.

7. *Ibid*.

CHAPTER 9

1. These figures, based on a 99.6-hour workweek which includes such jobs as nursemaid, housekeeper, cook, dishwasher, laundress, dietitian, food buyer, chauffeur, and maintenance person, were the results of a survey compiled in 1970 by Chase Manhattan Bank in New York. Considering the change in the cost of living since then (including the increase in the minimum wage), the actual present-day price of hiring people to fill the different jobs expected of a wife and mother is probably much, much higher. Leghorn, Lisa, and Warrior, Betsy, "What's a Wife Worth?" Pamphlet published by New England Free Press, Somerville, Mass.

2. Eisler, Riane Tennenhaus, *Dissolution: No-Fault Divorce, Marriage and the Future of Women*. New York, McGraw-Hill, 1977.

Ms. Eisler offers a trenchant and well-documented appraisal of the current divorce situation as it affects women, and includes a good deal of information about the economics of divorce and child support.

CHAPTER 10

1. Kellog, M. A., "Joint Custody." *Newsweek,* January 24, 1977.
2. Gardner, Richard A., *The Boys and Girls Book About Divorce.* New York, Bantam Books, 1970.
3. King, Barbara, "Children of Divorce: How to Help Them When the Split Comes." *Town & Country,* October, 1976, p. 135.
4. Gettleman, S., and Markowitz, J., *The Courage to Divorce.* New York, Simon and Schuster, 1974.
5. Ricci, Isolina, "Dispelling the Stereotype of the 'Broken Home.' " *Conciliation Courts Review,* Vol. 12, No. 2, January, 1976, p. 7.

CHAPTER 11

1. Committee on Professional Ethics of the State Bar, Formal Opinion No. 1976 37 as reprinted in *California Family Law Report,* 1977, 1126.
2. Peterson, Iver, "Child Snatching: The Extralegal Custody Battle after Divorce." *The New York Times,* October 17, 1977.

CHAPTER 12

1. Unfortunately, there are some attorneys who have such a brutal and callous attitude about divorce cases, they are admittedly out to *destroy* their client's opposing partner. One such lawyer has been quoted as boasting, "All I leave them with is a bar of soap and a toothbrush." Such professionals do irreparable damage to the family involved, and make the possibility of future rapport and understanding all but impossible. These are the people who have given family law such a bad name, and it is unfortunate that the many fine attorneys who are willing and able to help resolve domestic disputes without intentionally shattering either parent have to overcome the bad reputation created by a few. Bob Berlin, himself an attorney *and* a licensed marriage counselor in Georgia, addresses the problem of attorneys' attitudes in *Marriage and Divorce Today,* April 10, 1978.
2. Monasch, Burton I., in *Marriage and Divorce Today,* December 19, 1977.
3. Elkin, Meyer, "Marriage, Family and Divorce Counseling in the Courts: A Position Paper." Unpublished.

CHAPTER 14

1. Lord Ellenborough, who was a great many years older than his beautiful and headstrong wife, sought a divorce after she left him to join her lover, whose child she was obviously carrying. Although there was no doubt about her infidelity, the question of why she had needed to seek a lover was made such an issue, the good lord was almost denied his divorce!

2. O'Neill, William L., *Divorce in the Progressive Era*. New York, New Viewpoints, a Division of Franklin Watts, Inc., 1973.

The first chapter of this book offers one of the most thoughtful and thought-provoking studies of the history and development of family structure, and the evolution of divorce as a social necessity brought about because of the stresses created within the modern family.

3. King vs. DeManneville, 5 East 221, 102 Eng. Rep. 1054 (K.B. 1804); in Ploscowe, Morris, and Freed, Doris Jonas, *Family Law: Cases and Materials*. Boston, Little, Brown, 1963, p. 469.

4. Brown, Robert C., "The Custody of Children." *Indiana Law Journal* 2 (1926–27), p. 326.

5. Jenkins v. Jenkins, 173 Wis. 592,181 N.W. 826, 827, 1921; cited in State Ex Rel Watts v. Watts, 350 N.Y.S. 2nd 285, p. 289.

6. Bradwell v. Illinois, 83 U.S. 130, 141 (1872).

7. Fain, Harry M., "Family Law—Whither Now?" *Journal of Divorce*, Vol. 1 (1), Fall 1977, p. 31.

8. Chapsky v. Wood, 26 Kan. 650, 40 Am. Rep. 321 (1881).

9. Fain, *loc. cit.*

10. Mnookin, Robert, "Child-Custody Adjudication: Judicial Functions in the Face of Indeterminacy." *Law and Contemporary Problems*, Vol. 39, 1976, pp. 226–293.

11. Church, Virginia Anne, in personal interview, August, 1977.

12. When Herma Kay wrote a proposal for a family court in 1968, she noted that the concept of such a specialized institution was certainly not new. Most of the ideas I present have been gleaned from various sources, including Ms. Kay's article, Gordon Shipman's essay, and personal conversations with Meyer Elkin, Robert Mnookin, and Conciliation Court members Warren Weiss, Nathalie Hawley, and Jay Folberg.

Kay, Herma, "A Family Court: The California Proposal." *California Law Review*, 1968, p. 1230.

Shipman, Gordon, "In My Opinion: The Role of Counseling in the Reform of Marriage and Divorce Procedures." *The Family Coordinator*, October, 1977, p. 395.

13. The Child Support Enforcement Program requires Congress, the federal government, and state governments to cooperate in locating runaway parents who are not supporting their children as ordered by the courts. In 1976 it was ruled that Social Security numbers could be used to trace such parents, and if the state cannot find them, the Federal Parent Locator System will help do so. From mid-1975 through 1977, $1.6 *billion* in delinquent child support was recovered, and in those cases where the family had been on Aid to Families with Dependent Children, the collected money was repaid to the AFDC. Runaway fathers are a major problem in this society, unfortunately, and it is not necessarily a question of their inability to meet the responsibility of supporting their youngsters; according to Louis B. Hays, Deputy Director of the HEW program, some cases involve fathers who are earning as much as $60,000 a year! *Marriage and Divorce Today,* April 17, 1978, p. 3.

14. Mnookin, Robert, in personal interview, October, 1977.

15. Roman, Melvin, and Haddad, William, *The Disposable Parent: The Case for Joint Custody.* New York, Holt, Rinehart and Winston, 1978.

16. Weiss, Warren, and Collada, Henry, "Conciliation Counseling: The Court's Effective Mechanism for Resolving Visitation and Custody Disputes." *The Family Coordinator,* October, 1977, p. 444. Mr. Weiss estimates that 90 percent of the cases processed through his department result in the conclusion of an amicable agreement before the case is heard by the judge. Most of the couples *have not* been able to find a suitable arrangement through their attorneys, and so are facing a court battle at the time they are sent to the Conciliation Court. Weiss stresses that although he talks with the parents privately, no final agreements are made without the attorneys present. He has outlined the practices of his department in the above-referenced article.

17. The Conciliation Court of Minneapolis has developed an excellent program on the divorce experience. Offered during three evenings, it includes a session specifically for the children. The youngsters are divided by age, are allowed to act out pretend divorces in a real courtroom, and are encouraged to ask questions, express their own feelings, and in general relieve their fears about the strange and somewhat frightening experience their family is going through. Hawaii has a similar program, and Nathalie Hawley of Napa County in California is organizing daylong workshops for children which include many of the Minneapolis techniques.

18. Attorney Ann Diamond has noted that between 30 and 40 percent of the marriage dissolutions filed in Marin County, California, are *in pro per;* that is, neither party is represented in court by an attorney. Since

Marin has one of the highest incomes per capita in the nation, this trend is certainly not based on lack of money for legal fees. She suggests that many couples decide to do their divorce themselves rather than risk having whatever tenuous rapport they have managed to achieve destroyed by the automatic adversary situation created by the legal system. If this becomes a nationwide phenomenon, the legal profession will have to find new ways to approach the handling of divorce and custody matters or risk losing a large market for their services. Ann Diamond, Meridian Associates Conference, Palo Alto, California, February, 1978.

CHAPTER 15

1. Fishkin, Jerome, "A Lawyer Gets Divorced." *The Single Parent Magazine,* April, 1977, p. 8.

2. Editor's Report: "Separate Counsel for Children: Essential or Futile?" *California Family Law Report,* 1977, 1173.

3. The problems involved in this question are examined by Wallace J. Mlyniec in the article "The Child Advocate in Private Custody Disputes: A Role in Search of a Standard." *Journal of Family Law,* 16: 1–17, November, 1977.

4. There have been several cases in which judges have written well and lucidly in favor of shared custody, and certainly they are worth researching; I suggest you start with the New York case Perroti v. Perroti as listed in *Reports of Selected Cases Decided in Courts of the State of New York,* Vol. 78, Miscellaneous Reports, 2nd Series. Albany, Williams Press, Inc., 1975, p. 131.

5. One California judge says that he sees joint legal and physical custody as being a viable solution, but hesitates to order it because the statute governing child custody states that the child shall go to *either* parent and so his hands are tied. An effort is presently being made to reword the statute to read "either or both parents", which would alleviate the problem. At present a number of states, including Iowa, North Carolina, Oregon, Maine and Michigan have already made such changes.

CHAPTER 16

1. Ricci, Isolina, in personal interview, January, 1978.

2. Odell, Garner, "A Study of Divorce Among Church Members in San Francisco Presbytery, United Presbyterian Church in the United

States of America, with Implications for Divorce Ministry." Unpublished dissertation, San Francisco Theological Seminary, 1975.

3. Young, James, in *Marriage and Divorce Today*, November 7, 1977.

4. Grollman, Earl, *Living Through Your Divorce*. Boston, Beacon Press, 1978.

5. *Ritual in a New Day: An Invitation*, Hoyt Hickman. Nashville, Tenn., Abingdon Press, 1976.

6. "Divorced Kids: A Self-Help Peer Group." *Marriage and Divorce Today*, January 23, 1978, p. 1.

7. Cantor, Dorothy, "School-based Groups for Children of Divorce." *Journal of Divorce*, Vol. 1 (2), Winter, 1977, p. 183.

CHAPTER 17

1. Gordon, Thomas, *P.E.T.: Parent Effectiveness Training*. New York, Peter H. Wyden, Inc., 1970.

2. Dr. Helen Mendes, in personal conversation, April, 1977.

3. Kelly, Joan B., and Wallerstein, Judith S., "The Effects of Parental Divorce: Experiences of the Child in Early Latency." *American Journal of Orthopsychiatry*, Vol. 46, 1976, p. 20.

See also Note 4 of Chapter 1.

Suggested Reading

The bookstores are full of volumes on divorce, children, the reforming of your own life, and just about anything else one can think of which might be helpful to the family in transition. The books mentioned here are by no means the only good ones on the subjects, but they have been recommended consistently by divorced parents as being useful, encouraging, or informative, and I pass them on to you on that basis. Don't let the fact that a title may appear under the Men's section keep you from reading it just because you're a woman, however, and remember that every man would do well to understand the woman's side of divorce as well.

Divorce: Men

Creative Divorce, Mel Krantzler. New York, M. Evans & Co., Inc., 1973. Available in paperback.

A tremendously popular work, this book provides both useful information and encouragement for the newly divorced.

Part Time Father, Edith Atkin and Estelle Rubin. New York, Vanguard Press, 1976. Available in paperback.

Lots of advice and examples from the files of two psychologists. Written specially for divorced fathers.

Divorce: Women

World of the Formerly Married, Morton Hunt. New York, McGraw-Hill, 1966. Available in paperback.

One of the first books on the subject, it is both lively and useful as a general introduction to divorced life.

Creative Survival for Single Mothers, Persia Woolley. Millbrea, Calif., Celestial Arts, 1975. Softcover.

An informal discussion of the single-mother experience, approached from a positive point of view.

How to Father, Fitzhugh Dodson. Los Angeles, Nash Publishing, 1974. Available in paperback.

Somewhat heavy going in the text, this book offers a series of very useful appendices for fathers of all ages.

Women in Transition: A Feminist Handbook on Separation and Divorce. New York, Scribner, 1975. Soft-cover.

A thoroughly useful book that looks at all aspects of the problem and provides many excellent suggestions and addresses.

DIVORCING PARENTS

The Courage to Divorce, Gettleman and Markowitz. New York, Ballantine Books, 1974. Available in paperback.

An extremely thoughtful, well-researched look at our social biases against divorce, with an eye to helping mismatched mates feel less guilty about dissolving their poor relationships.

Who Will Raise the Children? New Options for Fathers (and Mothers), James A. Levine. Philadelphia and New York, Lippincott, 1976. Available in paperback.

An excellent book about present social changes in the relationship between fathers and children. Although the book is not specifically about divorce, the author does devote a full chapter to fathers and custody.

Co-Parenting: Sharing Your Child Equally, Miriam Galper. Philadelphia, Running Press, 1978. Soft-cover.

First-person accounts of shared custody by parents who are using it, with special stress on how and why it works for them; this is a good book for parents who are interested in sharing.

The Disposable Parent: The Case for Joint Custody, Roman and Haddad. New York, Holt, Rinehart and Winston, 1978.

A thoughtful, well-researched work which looks at the professional, political, and economic bias against shared custody, and makes a strong argument for reassessing both our custody practices and our family law system.

Father Power, Biller and Meredith. New York, McKay, 1974. Available in paperback.

This classic work on the importance of fathers should be essential reading for all parents, and certainly for those who are in the process of divorce.

The Parents Book About Divorce, Richard A. Gardner. New York, Doubleday, 1977. Available in paperback (Bantam).

This timely and well-written book is the companion to *The Boys and Girls Book About Divorce,* and although directed to the adults, it deals with many of the problems divorcing parents encounter with (or generate for) their children. A strong resource book for parents in any phase of reorganizing their family structure.

CHILDREN OF DIVORCE

Talking About Divorce: A Dialogue Between Parent and Child, Earl A. Grollman. Boston, Beacon Press, 1975. Soft-cover.

Written and illustrated for the young child, this book is not only an excellent tool for communication between parent and child: it also contains valuable pointers for the adults.

Children's Book About Divorce, Richard A. Gardner. New York, Jason Aronson, Inc., 1970. Available in paperback.

This marvelous book is written directly to children, but is extremely valuable for parents as well. Any divorced parent with a child in third grade or up should have a copy of this book in the house.

How to Get It Together When Your Parents Are Coming Apart, Richards and Willis. New York, David McKay, 1976. Available in paperback.

An honest and reassuring book that should be available to every teenager whose parents are divorced or divorcing. Although written specifically for the youngsters, it will give parents pause for thought as well.

GENERAL BOOKS WITH A WEALTH OF IDEAS

The Intimate Enemy: How to Fight Fair in Love and Marriage, Bach and Wyden. New York, Morrow, 1969. Available in paperback.

A deservedly popular book which deals with fighting fairly and gaining constructive results; even if your opposing partner doesn't read it, it will be useful for you.

The Angry Book, Theodore I. Rubin. New York, Macmillan, 1969. Available in paperback.

An examination of anger in its healthy state, as compared with the various perversions of it that lead to such emotions as spite, bitterness, and rage.

I'm Okay, You're Okay, Thomas A. Harris. New York, Harper & Row, 1967. Available in paperback.

A long-standing classic in the field of self-awareness and personal growth, this book is as readable (and applicable) today as it was when originally published. An excellent introduction to Transactional Analysis.

Own Your Own Life, Richard G. Abell. New York, David McKay, 1976. Available in paperback.

This popular book offers a combination of personal experience and information about both Transactional Analysis and Gestalt Therapy. Its best features are the chapters on change, and the exercises therein.

P.E.T.: Parent Effectiveness Training, Thomas Gordon. New York, Peter H. Wyden, Inc., 1970. Available in paperback.

An exceptionally readable, practical, and useful book on parenting, this work is highly recommended for all parents, divorcing or otherwise.

What Color Is Your Parachute? A Practical Manual for Job Hunters and Career Changers, Richard Nelson Bolles. Berkeley, Calif., Ten Speed Press, 1972. Soft-cover.

This delightful book takes a new look at the problems of building or changing careers, and should prove useful to anyone changing life directions.

SPECIAL BOOKS FOR (AND FROM) THE HEART

How to Survive the Loss of a Love: 58 Things to Do When There Is Nothing to Be Done, Colgrove, Bloomfield, and McWilliams. Simon and Schuster, 1976. Available in paperback.

Unique in both its presentation and its content, this little gem promises to become a classic. It is caring, tender, understanding, *and* helpful for anyone touched by the loss of a dream.

The Art of Loving, Eric Fromm. New York, Harper & Row, 1956. Available in paperback.

This is one of the all-time great books on the subject of loving. A combination of psychology and philosophy, it is well worth reading and rereading at different times in your life.

Professional Bibliography

Bohannon, P., ed., *Divorce and After*. New York, Anchor Books, 1971.

Brandwein, R. A.; Brown, C. A.; and Fox, E. M., "Women and Children Last: The Situation of Divorced Mothers and Their Families." *Journal of Marriage and the Family*, 1974, Vol. 36, p. 498.

Cantor, Dorothy, "School-based Groups for Children of Divorce." *Journal of Divorce*, Winter, 1977, Vol. I (2), p. 183.

Despert, J. L., *Children of Divorce*. New York, Doubleday, 1953.

Folberg, J., and Graham, M., "Joint Custody of Children Following Divorce," *University of California-Davis Law Review*, 1979, Vol. 12.

Gardner, R. A., *Psychotherapy with Children of Divorce*. New York, Jason Aronson, Inc., 1976.

Gettleman, S., and Markowitz, J., *The Courage to Divorce*. New York, Simon and Schuster, 1974.

Goldstein, J.; Freud, A.; and Solnit, A., *Beyond the Best Interests of the Child*. New York, The Free Press, 1973.

Herzog, E., and Sudia, C. E., "Children in Fatherless Families," in B. Caldwell and H. Ricciuti, eds., *Review of Child Development Research*, Vol. 3. Chicago, University of Chicago Press, 1973.

Hetherington, E. M.; Cox, M.; and Cox, R., "Divorced Fathers." *The Family Coordinator*, 1976, Vol. 25, p. 417.

Kay, Herma, "A Family Court: The California Proposal." *California Law Review*, 1968, p. 1230.

Kelly, J., and Wallerstein, J., "The Effects of Parental Divorce: Experiences of the Child in Early Latency." *American Journal of Orthopsychiatry*, 1976, Vol. 46, p. 20.

Mnookin, Robert, "Child Custody Adjudication: Judicial Functions in the Face of Indeterminacy." *Law and Contemporary Problems*, Summer, 1975.

Wallerstein, J., and Kelly, J., "The Effects of Parental Divorce: The Adolescent Experience," in E. J. Anthony and C. Koupernik, eds., *The Child and His Family: Children at Psychiatric Risk*, Vol. 3. New York, John Wiley & Sons, 1974.

Weiss, R. S., "The Emotional Impact of Marital Separation." *The Journal of Social Issues*, 1976, Vol. 32, p. 135.

Weitzman, L., "Legal Regulation of Marriage: Tradition and Change."
   California Law Review, Vol. 62:2, 1974.

PERIODICALS DEVOTED TO FAMILY LAW AND TO
MARRIAGE AND FAMILY THERAPY

California Family Law Report, 706 Sansome Street, San Francisco,
   Calif. 94111.
Conciliation Courts Review, Association of Family Conciliation Courts,
   Room 241, 111 North Hill Street, Los Angeles, Calif. 90012.
Family Advocate, American Bar Association, 1155 East 60th Street,
   Chicago, Ill. 60637.
The Family Coordinator, 1219 University Avenue, S.E., Minneapolis,
   Minn. 55414.
Family Law Quarterly, American Bar Association.
The Family Law Reporter, Bureau of National Affairs, 1231 25th Street,
   N.W., Washington, D.C. 20037.
Family Process, 149 East 78th Street, New York, N.Y. 10021.
Journal of Divorce, Hawthorn Press, 149 Fifth Avenue, New York, N.Y.
   10010.
Journal of Family Law, University of Louisville, Louisville, Ky. 40208.
Marriage and Divorce Today, 2315 Broadway, New York, N.Y. 10024.
   (This biweekly newsletter is an excellent resource.)
Marriage and Family Review. Hawthorn Press, 149 Fifth Avenue, New
   York, N.Y. 10010. (A bimonthly review of the major journals in the
   field; very handy.)

Index